Being There

Being There

THE FIELDWORK ENCOUNTER
AND THE MAKING OF TRUTH

Edited by
John Borneman
Abdellah Hammoudi

UNIVERSITY OF CALIFORNIA PRESS
Berkeley   Los Angeles   London

University of California Press, one of the most distinguished university presses in the United States, enriches lives around the world by advancing scholarship in the humanities, social sciences, and natural sciences. Its activities are supported by the UC Press Foundation and by philanthropic contributions from individuals and institutions. For more information, visit www.ucpress.edu.

University of California Press
Berkeley and Los Angeles, California

University of California Press, Ltd.
London, England

Library of Congress Cataloging-in-Publication Data

Being there : the fieldwork encounter and the making of truth / [edited by] John Borneman and Abdellah Hammoudi.
    p.   cm.
Includes bibliographical references and index.
ISBN 978-0-520-25775-7 (cloth : alk. paper)
ISBN 978-0-520-25776-4 (pbk. : alk. paper)
    1. Ethnology—Fieldwork.   I. Borneman, John.
II. Hammoudi, Abdellah.
  GN346.B443 2009
  305.8'00723—dc22   2008025401

Manufactured in the United States of America

18 17 16 15 14 13 12 11 10 09
10 9 8 7 6 5 4 3 2 1

This book is printed on Natures Book, which contains 50% post-consumer waste and meets the minimum requirements of ANSI/NISO Z39.48-1992 (R 1997) *(Permanence of Paper)*.

Contents

Acknowledgments

This project began as a panel organized by Abdellah Hammoudi and John Borneman at the 2006 Annual Meeting of the American Anthropological Association in San Jose, California. One of our initial contributors, Christophe Robert, could not participate in this volume, and we subsequently added two other original essays, by Eugene Raikhel and Stefan Senders. In conversations with our contributors (and following a suggestion, enthusiastically received, from Mona Zaki), the initial title of the panel, "Fieldwork Experience and Subjectivity: Theory, Discovery, and Anthropological Insights," metamorphosed into *Being There: The Fieldwork Encounter and the Making of Truth*. We prepared this book as members of the anthropology department at Princeton, and we thank all our colleagues for intensive intellectual stimulation around the issues of this book. We also thank Carol Zanca, Mo Lin Yee, and Gabriella Drinovan, who, though charged only with helping us in our teaching, have assisted us greatly in assembling research material and making this collaboration possible. We are very grateful to Jonathan Spencer and Stephania Pandolfo for their critical readings and suggestions for improving the text, and to all of the contributors for key comments. We also wish to acknowledge the support of former University of California Press director James Clark and of the current executive editor, Naomi Schneider, whose wise guidance has brought this book to fruition.

ONE

The Fieldwork Encounter, Experience, and the Making of Truth

AN INTRODUCTION

John Borneman and Abdellah Hammoudi

CRISIS AND THE CRITICAL MOMENT

American anthropology opened up a Pandora's box the moment it specified culture as its object, simultaneously setting itself at a distance from the natural sciences and defining itself in contradistinction to both American cognitivism and French structuralism. By the 1980s, the discipline was engaged in a soul-searching movement to critically assess its object, its principal method, and the most current form of the write-up of research results. In 1986, two books appeared seeking to provide a focus for this wide-ranging debate: *Writing Culture: The Poetics and Politics of Ethnography,* edited by James Clifford and George E. Marcus, and *Anthropology as Cultural Critique: An Experimental Moment in the Human Sciences,* by George E. Marcus and Michael M. J. Fischer. Both attempted to take the pulse of the discipline—to assess culture, fieldwork experience, and the classic anthropological monograph.

In part, this stocktaking was a consequence of the attack launched by Edward Said on "Orientalism" in his famous book of that name published in 1978. Said examined the rhetoric of Western scholarship in colonial or neocolonial settings and radically questioned its authority and claim to grasp the objective truth of non-Western societies. In a similar move, Marcus and Fischer (1986: vii, 8) wrote that the limitations of the ethnographic form and its failure "to describe social reality" had brought anthropology into a political and epistemological "crisis of representation." Clifford (1986: 12, 26) argued for "hybrid textual activity": a shift in "dominant metaphors for ethnography . . . away from the observing eye and toward expressive speech (and gesture)." Both volumes urged anthropologists to engage in experimental writing that was more partial, historical, and self-critical of its truth claims and authority than ethnographic accounts of the past had been.

This diagnosis drew its strength from the identification of what were said to be three denials running through the practice of anthropology: that ethnography is a literary genre which denies itself as such; that reliance on observation leads to a denial of the role of the ethnographer in shaping the object/subject studied; and that ethnographers tend to deny the constructed character of their objects and of the knowledge they produce, from the initial period of fieldwork through to the writing of their essays and books. These denials, according to the many subsequent exponents of this diagnosis, were buttressed by the colonial and postcolonial relations of domination, which turned colonized peoples into objects of the ethnographer's "gaze."[1] Ethnographers, primarily members of Euro-American societies engaged in the pursuit of science, were accused of fixing other people in totalizing cultures and representing them as radically distinct from their Western selves in time and space.

The sense of crisis among anthropologists was much stronger in the United States than in Europe, although one might have thought, given the European origin of colonial projects, that the legacy of colonialism there would have been more burdensome. Despite the critique lodged by Said on representation, and by Johannes Fabian (1983) on the use of the visual in fieldwork, the practice of "participant observation" in field-work, as elaborated by Malinowski and Boas, remained in favor in many quarters—especially outside the United States, where anthropologists also turned to the study of difference and domination in their own soci-eties.[2] European scholars had generally kept a distance from the Ameri-can penchant for a clichéd casting of the whole of anthropological research conducted between the two world wars as being just about kin-ship and ritual in "primitive societies." Major research on themes and topics such as power, politics, violence, resource use, production, and consumption, to cite only a few examples, has a long, uninterrupted his-tory, exhibiting continuity as the same objects were reelaborated in light of changes brought about by processes of decolonization.

We ask, in this volume, about the current status of this epistemologi-cal crisis in the wake of these critiques. Specifically, on what basis can ethnographic work and experience claim to authorize socially significant and accurate accounts? For while the "writing culture debate," as it has come to be called, has cast doubt on the authority of the ethnographer, it at the same time has deferred addressing the relative truth-value of the ethnographic account itself, resulting in a quiet renunciation of any rig-orous notion of the validity or comparability of fieldwork discoveries. What then remains, in particular of the ethnographic record, and more generally of the anthropological enterprise?[3]

This debate, though quite narrowly oriented toward a review of the representational strategies used in ethnographic texts and the authority derived from such strategies, has nonetheless broadly influenced how research projects in the discipline are formulated, and it has subse-quently shaped public understanding of what anthropology does. At the same time, the focus on representation and authority has often, espe-cially in graduate education, supplanted the art of reading ethnogra-phies for what knowledge they reveal about the people and places studied, and it has nourished a metadiscourse suspicious of the ability of any ethnography to offer an adequate, much less a "true," account of the encounters on which fieldwork is based. While the general call to be reflexive, also a central tenet in this critique, has had a salutary effect on the discipline, it has been displaced by a reflexivity exercised on and about *ethnography-surrogates*—more often than not limited to representations of the past or present rather than addressing the practice of contemporary ethnography.

In the past two decades, anthropologists have indeed embraced the call for experimentation. Sufficient time has passed, we think, that an appraisal of the result of this move is now possible. It was only logical that the critique swept away many of the assumptions about the objects of ethnography: their primitiveness, isolation, ahistoricity, statism, resistance to modernity. Acknowledgment of change, temporality, movement, wide-ranging circulations of people, things, and meanings, and transnationalism led researchers to question the relevance of all interpretations and explanatory theories based solely on cultural frames and on information gathered through fieldwork experience alone. "Culture" itself has since been rethought and not infrequently abandoned as a central concept. Now anticipated and imagined futures are often privileged over action informed either by past experience or by patterns of interdependent traits and local factors. And there is full agreement that we all, Western and non-Western alike, are contemporaries living in an era that resists simple classification.

In response to the diagnosis of an anthropological "crisis," one experiment proposed to do away with "traditional" fieldwork altogether in favor of an approach that Marcus (1986) summarized rather obscurely as "putting things together," a formula he correlates with the concept of culture as cultural critique. Putting things together relied heavily on vignettes, travelogues, media images, texts, and literature of the most diverse origins and types. Clifford (1986) proposed replacing prolonged acquaintance with places and people with travel and moments of "hanging out." Another alternative, suggested by Arjun Appadurai (1990), was to follow the global flows of finance, ethnicity, media images, ideas, and technologies, thereby focusing on the transnational constitution of social imaginaries.

Today there is a bewildering assortment of approaches within the discipline, including anthropoesis, dialogism, genealogies of modernity, history, world system, transnationalism, auto-ethnography, the staging of multiple voices, science studies, simple activism, and critiques of knowledge through the study of constructed subjectivities. Dialogism purported to avoid power and domination, and performance became a key word in framing how fictionalization was at work in every description and interpretation. Proposals proliferated for reconfiguring cultural analysis, for blurring genres, for recapturing anthropology, or for rethinking, rethinking, rethinking. . . . Today the crisis seems to have receded; but for all the novelty of issues opened for inquiry and approaches tried out, we find ourselves in the presence of new orthodoxies that leave some of the most crucial epistemological conundrums in anthropology unexamined.

By any standard, contemporary anthropological work is uneven and, despite the multiplicity of approaches and sites studied, makes repetitive theoretical claims. Things are constructed; things are plural; things are unstable; things have histories; most things are in-between. Many anthropologists now see the world as being in constant motion and as consisting of fragments with no wholes, "assemblages" with no criteria of inclusion into descriptive or analytical units other than the choice between alternative narrative theories or the subjective interests of the writer. Along these lines, the insistence that all translations are partial, all truths relational and perspectival—sound ideas and assumptions with which we agree—often becomes an excuse for offering superficial translations that prefer surface over depth.

Understanding the problems entailed in the translation of meanings is central to the anthropological project, but it goes far beyond the ethnographer's linguistic skills in translating utterances or texts from one language into another. Obviously, anthropologists translate—or at least they used to—their interlocutors' key words and of course, wherever found, also texts; such translations get at deeper levels of meaning as anthropologists become more thoroughly acquainted with the languages and ways of life of their interlocutors. But for those engaged in the debate surrounding the culture concept (with some notable exceptions, such as Dennis Tedlock and Paul Friedrich), insistence on the multiplication of the languages of the translator and of the translated went hand in hand with an abandonment of deep translation. Instead, the focus has been on representations, as researchers draw from theories and paradigms of writing or from genealogical investigation. The "representations" school tends to neglect the fact that the construction of reality has always already been undertaken by the people themselves in their own languages before the intervention of the ethnographer as translator.

This prior reality, of both the ethnographer and those he or she studies, is what haunts the interactions of Stefan Senders (chapter 7) with German repatriates from Russia. When translation entails speaking in a mother tongue that one must first acquire as an adult, the translation of words and concepts and texts is relatively simple compared to the emotional difficulty of translating accumulated experience into effective responses to legal and bureaucratic narrative demands. To obtain access to prior and present realities and to reach an understanding, Senders must first submit to and acknowledge a mutual castration in language. Translation costs.

In the name of experiment, then, it is not necessary to accept three common correlates: that ethnography is primarily a "style of writing," that anthropology is primarily about the translation of other linguistic concepts and cultural worlds into the languages of the anthropological profession, or that anthropological accounts cannot be read for the truth-value of their depictions. On the last point, we contend that the relation of power to our depictions of reality is highly ambiguous, largely because of the ambiguities of power itself. For example, if relations with our interlocutors were truly ones of domination, in any unambiguous and nonreciprocal sense of the term, then we might expect most of our depictions to take the form of essentialist projections. But how many ethnographers in the field in fact have such simple relations, unsullied by difficult transferential and countertransferential investments? If the ethnographer invests in a long-term relationship with others, and over time manages to bridge some of the cultural differences and achieve a level of trust, then the relations between power and the depictions of reality are likely to be highly nuanced and contradictory, as every essay in this volume demonstrates.

Sally Falk Moore's narrative (chapter 6) of the riddles and contradictions of her own long-term fieldwork experience in Africa, affected by uneasy and changing balances in relationships both official and unofficial, speaks most directly to the issue of power and representation.

But the conclusions we might draw from her account apply more to the ambiguity and unpredictability of these relationships, and their uncertain relation to forms of knowledge and power, than to the macro-narratives of neocolonial domination or theories of the ethnographic gaze. Along similar lines, Leo Coleman (chapter 5) analyzes a respite he took in the context of his first extended fieldwork in India in terms not of the predictability of power but of the different emotional investments made and asked for by Christian, Hindu, and secular actors. Likewise, Eugene Raikhel (chapter 8) takes up encounters in two clinical settings of alcohol treatment in Russia that are anything but linear narratives about biomedical authority; one demands of him that he be a scientist, the other, a patient in recovery.

In short, when the theory of Orientalism is made into a dogma, followers run the risk of depicting interaction either as determined by power and domination or, alternatively, as taking place in the absence of power and domination.[4] Neither depiction does justice to the ethnographic enterprise.

Although debates about culture and power have had considerable impact in shaping new approaches to fieldwork, some anthropologists have continued to employ functionalist, structuralist, and interpretive approaches. The opening of new topics of inquiry does not mean that "old" ones have been abandoned. At best, the old approaches develop in new directions, as is evidenced by nearly a century of work on political economy, inspired by Marx; on value, inspired by Simmel; on collectivities, inspired by Durkheim; on rationalization, inspired by Weber; and on psychic processes, inspired by Freud. In any case, at the same time that approaches have diversified, the notion of evidence itself has enlarged, as well as the sorts of arguments or propositions advanced and deemed acceptable by the varied constituencies of the profession.

Being There assesses the effects of these critiques on the practices of anthropology, but not by engaging in another discursive analysis of the discipline, or by offering prescriptions about what should be done. We instead attempt to demonstrate what, in fact and in writing, anthropology does or can do in and through experience-based fieldwork. Authors in this volume query the nature of encounters, experience, experiments, reflexivity, truth, subjectivity, objectification, projection, transference, risk, and affect with primary but not exclusive reference to Morocco, Saudi Arabia, Syria, Tanzania, the Canadian Arctic, India, Germany, and Russia. With a focus on what happens in fieldwork encounters, each of the eight essays attempts to bring ethnographic practice and reflexive writing together so as to produce knowledge that can acknowledge its relationality and still aim for truth.

SUBVERSION OF EXPERIENCE AND THE CIRCULATION OF ETHNOGRAPHIC EFFECTS

Within anthropology, recent theoretical discussions of fieldwork have largely undermined belief in the necessity of experiential encounters and consequently have limited researchers' ethnographic curiosity. In "writing culture," knowledge from encounters is replaced with the use of what we are calling surrogate ethnography, puppeteering, and textualism, discussed below. Our purpose here is not to document the widespread resort to these new practices but merely to draw attention to their popularity, to how they work, and especially to what they are replacing. We therefore focus, in this introduction, on two key representatives of the textualist turn within anthropology: Talal Asad and Nicholas Dirks. While criticizing the effects of this turn to texts and discursive genealogies on fieldwork practices, we nonetheless wish, at the outset, to acknowledge the significance of such work.

Talal Asad, for example, decries the importance given to the "shift from armchair theorizing to intensive fieldwork," which resulted in "the pseudoscientific notion of fieldwork." He thus prefers to locate the rise of modern anthropology in Marcel Mauss—who brilliantly read and theorized ethnographic accounts—rather than in the ethnographic work, on which Mauss's writings are based, of "Boas, Rivers, and Malinowski" (2003: 17). But collapsing the practices of ethnography and the ingenious interpretive skills of Mauss into the term "modern anthropology" elides the significance of ethnographic work altogether. Would anthropological theorization have been possible without prior encounter-based fieldwork? Asad's proposal for anthropology to be "the comparison of embedded concepts (representations) between societies differently located in time or space" (17) could just as well serve as a program for true armchair disciplines such as modern philology or comparative literature—divorced from the risk-laden practices of engagement with others in the exchange of knowledge in fieldwork. These disciplines and this proposal, of course, have their merits. But Mauss himself, after all, appreciated the empirical possibilities of ethnography and strongly encouraged his students to do fieldwork. He even assembled the thirty lectures he delivered every year under the title "Instructions in descriptive ethnography, intended for travelers, administrators, and missionaries" into a "manuel d'ethnographie."[5] Why should modern anthropologists reject their own tradition of ethnographic fieldwork in favor of mimicking textual analysts?

To be sure, many other factors conjoin to make practices of fieldwork seem quaint and out of touch with a "postmodern" reality. The advent of the Internet alone, with the rapid rise in its widespread use, has furthered a concern for the virtual over the immediate and face-to-face and has encouraged the practice of "surfacing," which substitutes thin for thick description. Much the same can be said about approaches that rely on other media such as television. In many instances, downloading from the Internet and watching television together have substituted for (rather than being incorporated into) Malinowski-inspired notions of fieldwork as co-residence in a place over a sustained period of time.

Particularly unfortunate is the way in which this lack of interest in experiential encounters has influenced the use and understanding of theory. For example, media artifacts are often used to demonstrate how producers dominate their audience, especially the poorest of them, and at the same time such analyses assert the inscription of all viewers, including American anthropologists, in networks of cosmopolitanism. These networks themselves are then glossed as yet other aspects of transformation and globalization, an explanation that is then equated with theory making.

Perhaps even more important for ethnography is that glossing cosmopolitanism seems to obviate the necessity to describe how it plays out in the daily concerns and concrete actions of people: that is, in their subsistence activities, family structure, marriages, relations with parents, siblings, and neighbors, interaction with bureaucracies, communication with the dead, practices of religion—all domains of ethnographic inquiry that have become somewhat marginal over the past several decades. Chat room participants or characters on the screen never share conversations, fights, arguments, or affection with each other or with anthropologists in the ordinary sense of these terms. It is precisely intensive, intimate, reflexive engagement with the quotidian that provides Parvis Ghassem-Fachandi (chapter 4) with access to the meaning of a visceral experience of disgust with an image of meat in India. After having witnessed the 2002 anti-Muslim pogrom in Gujarat, he reaches a deeper understanding of forms of complicity in this violence only through face-to-face interaction and mutual investments in individuals. On that basis, he finds that culinary practices, linked to religious affiliation and caste, have become integrated into aspirations of social class that align with a politicized Hindu nationalism.

Rather than explore what possibilities unfold in fieldwork encounters in the present, two of the dominant approaches have relied instead either on deconstructive procedures inspired by the work of Jacques Derrida, which emphasize the instability of binaries and the nondirectional "dissemination" of meanings, or on genealogies of "knowledge/power" inspired by the work of Michel Foucault, which track historical concepts or categories back to colonial times (and only rarely to the precolonial). These approaches to reading have been especially productive in the fields of history and literary studies. But as utilized within anthropology, such procedures and genealogies have frequently had the effect of limiting curiosity. The practices of participant observation are reduced to visualization, or a predatory dominating "gaze," as fieldwork is denounced as "fetish," a "metaphysics of presence," a "power-laden construction." Fieldwork settings therefore become suspect, cast as arenas of overdetermined, perverse relations.

Despite assertions that the site of the field encounter is, at base, unethical, and not a fertile space for the production of knowledge, the turn to historical and genealogical work still aims to produce an ethnographic effect through the use of *surrogate ethnography,* a practice that Abdellah Hammoudi (chapter 2) analyzes with reference to depictions of ritual.

Proto-ethnographic texts from colonial archives and diverse "native" texts supplant the ethnographer's embedded and negotiated, experience-based knowledge of a place, a people, a culture. Or the ethnographer is situated in fieldwork only at the beginning of a narrative, whose author-ity is thereafter derived solely from the reading of archival texts. Ethno-graphic authority is exchanged, in these accounts, for expertise in understanding textual patterns and "arrangements" or "assemblages": anthropologists read written accounts of events, which they redact into sequences and situate in discourses. Another popular form of authority is *puppeteering:* the act of arranging and manipulating texts and staging contests between theorists (usually drawn from a small number of philosophers canonized within an imaginary monument to High The-ory), or between a theorist and her fieldwork interlocutors, to buttress the puppeteer's claims to know.[6]

Writing based on these premises sets up fieldwork as equivalent, if not inferior, to historical-archival reading or to purely discursive analysis of the written by the West on the Rest and on itself, as if these substitutes could not only replace fieldwork experience but also escape its ethical dilemmas. One of these dilemmas is how to prevent the Rest from becom-ing invisible except as peoples engaged in battles constructed by the dis-courses of the West. Such a focus on the West as source of discourse and domination turns much anthropological writing into a one-track critique of modernity within modernity. When such writing makes an appeal to the agency of the Rest, it is frequently to a textual agency of what peo-ple—usually elites who claim to represent the group—say or write above themselves. Insofar as the Rest is concerned, anthropology as cultural cri-tique becomes rather muted, if not engaged in apologetic discourses. The result is often single-edged critiques that avoid critical encounters with the other; concepts are almost always asked to interrogate the West, its constituted and seemingly complete knowledges, alone.[7]

Ironically, the anthropological embrace of *textualism* is a position that historians have since abandoned—what Pierre Nora calls the "cult of the document . . . a religion of preservation and archivalization" (1996: 8). For example, Nicholas Dirks, an influential proponent of textualism who has quite productively inflected historical accounts with an "ethnographic sensibility," wrote in an essay on the textualization of India: "For all of anthropology's emphasis on its originary encounters, ethnographic presents/presence, and fieldwork, anthropological knowledge has always been dependent on texts. The textual field that is the pretext for fieldwork has been erased[,] . . . but the erasure has further fetishized the anthropological field in relation not only to an earlier disinterest in ethnographic writing but also to a systematic inattention to ethnographic reading." He then scolds anthropologists for their resistance to footnotes, which "conceals a lack of serious concern for the reading behind (before and after) the writing of culture" (Dirks 2000: 153).

Not satisfied with denigrating the cultural encounter as mere fieldwork fetish, Dirks also proposes a focus on the written, and on reading the written, rather than on the process of writing. A putatively non-fetishized, redemptive form of anthropology—the reading and writing of textualized history, with footnotes—replaces the fieldwork encounter and the process of making the other and the possibilities of communication with the other present in writing. No longer haunted by the metaphysics of presence and the fetish of fieldwork, work of this sort testifies to a "superstitious respect and veneration for the trace, [which]," writes Nora, "negates the sacred but retains its aura" (1996: 9).

"Traces" in the text retain the aura of the sacred—when properly collated into a historical narrative that foregrounds the relation of action to power in its textual qualities—while negating any possibility of experience that might if not approximate the sacred, then at least unsettle the authority of textual codifications of the past. As Hammoudi (chapter 2) demonstrates in a critique of constructions of Muslim religious experience drawn solely from literary sources, such texts are set up as either prior or equivalent to action, and only rarely evaluated in light of the concrete actions and experiences of the protagonists written about.[8]

It is revealing to dwell on Dirk's use of "fetish," "erasure," and "presents/presence," because his deployment of such concepts epitomizes the invocation of High Theory to support a radical shift from fieldwork encounter to textualism. *Fetish* takes its meaning as a contrast to what Dirks might call "reality." But fetishized fieldwork in relation to which reality? Dirks complains about a "disinterest in ethnographic writing." Presumably, reality is the reading of "ethnographic writing," in contradistinction to the fetishized activity of anthropologists who do fieldwork. Hence, rather than viewing reading and fieldwork as being in a mutually supplementary relationship—alternating in turn, with neither activity reducible to the other—reading is seen as epistemologically superior to or, more radically, as encompassing fieldwork experience.

So what about the "erasure" of the textual field as a pretext for fieldwork? For one thing, the wealth of texts written by anthropologists has hardly been erased in the discipline. On the contrary, pre-fieldwork graduate study in anthropology in the United States consists largely if not entirely of acquiring textual knowledge, of debates about evidence, representation, history, argument, theory. This American training contrasts with a northern European tradition of fieldwork "expeditions," large and small, in which groups of scholars work together intensely in one place over a period of time.

From Dirks's perspective, the "textual field" might be understood in terms of "structuration," or that which structures the field of inquiry, to use the rather heavy but useful Bourdieuian concept. But here is the problem: There is no way to draw a clear line between the structure of the textual field and the actual vagaries of fieldwork.

At issue, ultimately, is both a fear of the field situation and a desire to incarcerate the anthropological endeavor in what we might call "textoscapes." Perhaps only a library habitus could inspire a theory that posits a relation of parallelism between the experiences of reading and of fieldwork. Relatively speaking, these two experiences are quite dissimilar: the former a highly structured field within a larger tradition, the latter a highly unstructured field reliant on serendipitous encounters. In fact, this discrepancy itself, between the textual field and the fieldwork setting, tends to generate for the researcher more felicitous and infelicitous surprises than does textual analytics alone. The gap between reading and fieldwork activity might well account for much of the innovation within anthropology as a field, explaining why paradigms change, or why earlier views codified in texts are repudiated. Moreover, experiences of power relations between cohorts, or rivalries between colleagues and schools, might well be more integral—the central pre-text to fieldwork—to the choice and popularity of topics within anthropology than is the practice of reading.

Finally, why the discomfort with the notion of "ethnographic presents/presence"? The phrase refers, at least obliquely, to Derrida's critique of what he calls the "metaphysics of presence," a concept that John Borneman (chapter 9) queries in his interactions with the ubiquitous secret police in Syria. It is certainly true that an encounter and an exchange, verbal and nonverbal—Being There, in short—guarantee nothing. And indeed, discrepancies between what is said and what is meant, in interaction, in writing, in reading, can play out ad infinitum; ambivalence, contradictory meanings, tensions cling to every word and utterance. Such is the predicament of discourses that every meaning implies a deferral. It is also certainly true, however, that the more one shares time and speaks with people, the better acquainted one becomes with the texture of other life, making it more probable there will be a closer fit between the order of words and the order of things.

In her attempt to understand what may move young people to suicide among the Inuit in Canada, Lisa Stevenson (chapter 3) demonstrates precisely how Being There—intimate acquaintances and mutual investments in one place over time—makes possible an alternative and deeper understanding of the words used for life and death. To be sure, within anthropology, except for some reference to witnessing, the notion of Being There has lost its tragic register. Its relation to visuality changed forever with the 1971 publication of Jerzy Kosinski's novel by that name. In the 1979 film made from the book, Chance (played by the incomparable Peter Sellers), when asked what kind of sex he liked, replied: "I like to watch." Yet anthropologists need not reduce themselves to the comedic and performative senses of Being There, to being the voyeur or tourist who watches and then, depending on textual skills and mastery, cynically decodes what is seen. Co-presence is also a source of knowledge that makes possible a transformation of what we know, specifically of the anthropologist's own self-understandings. Misunderstandings, tricks, double meanings, opaque metaphors, and self-interested distortions are always present in communication, but what is important is that the engaged ethnographer learns something of the "grammar" that guides the actions of his interlocutors.

In light of the above, it is important to understand the attitude toward texts displayed by Clifford Geertz, the American Ur-Vater of much of this cultural rethinking. He was perhaps the most prominent anthropologist of his generation who drew inspiration and language from philosophy and literary criticism, as he practiced a style of writing that mixed genres. In his well-known essay elaborating Ricoeur's idea of modeling social action as a text, Geertz (1973) never assumed that social action actually was a text. Reading the text was merely analogous to interpreting social action from fieldwork experience, and he equated neither of these two comparable modes of study with fieldwork. Geertz directed his primary attention to many objects that are not texts (such as political action and markets in Morocco, rituals and agricultural practices in Java) and that he, in his interpretation, did not reduce to or make dependent on textual qualities. Unlike the textualisms derived from Derrida or Foucault, Geertz's use of the text was merely heuristic. He did not retreat from fieldwork encounters to pure library work or to an exclusive reliance on vignettes, pictures, media materials, and rhetoric.

In criticizing textualism, we do not dispute that many of its forms are indispensable, particularly for understanding the history of ideas—including anthropological ideas. Without such documentation and reading, we could hardly acquaint ourselves with our predecessors or with the work of our colleagues, or decipher texts produced by interlocutors in our fieldsites. To ignore written accounts would thin our notion of tradition and severely limit our ability to understand in what traditions we work. Nor do we dispute the anthropological insights generated from an appreciation of philosophy. But an appreciation of texts within ethnographic research is not the same as the textualism that is the necessary province of literary studies, history, and philosophy. No doubt the study of literary output, with a recognition of the authority of textual constructions, adds a good deal of information about prevalent concepts and their institutional settings, but it does not tell us much about the pertinence of all this to human action. For instance, it says little about the reception of these texts, about the processes of making decisions or taking risks, and about how humans understand concepts—and if and how they follow through on those concepts in their own networks of action.

Ultimately, an exclusive reliance on texts relegates to the background the study of political action, the social structures and consequences of power, and it restricts the ethnographic to the study of producers and readers of texts, who most often are members of local and international elites. However creatively we might interpret documents, a textualist approach is often duplicative of literary studies and, in its insistence on power as the core substance of all experience, overlaps with political science. By insisting on it, we ignore what anthropology can bring to literary scholars and to political scientists, what other scholars cannot produce or intuit from the study of documents: the diverse forms of social action and interaction, interlocution in experience.

These considerations lead us to conclude that it is perhaps a crisis of identification among ethnographers that motivates them to prefer philosophical reflection on the practices of textual reading, deconstruction, genealogy of concepts, and discourse analysis to the fieldwork encounter. New philosophical reflection often takes the form of what we above called puppeteering—the staging of dialogues between past and present, between theorists, or between theorists and native interlocutors—instead of grappling with the actual dialogues that go on in the field: episodes of asymmetrical conversation, argument, misunderstanding, agreement, mutual sharing, affection, aggression, and manipulation.

Though philosophers throughout the first part of the twentieth century often looked to ethnographic accounts and non-Western concepts for critical inspiration, the relationship has since been inverted. Many anthropologists now subsume their specific ethnographic fieldwork or histories into whichever philosophical concept, theory, or methodological approach appears most in fashion. These are many, and they come in and go out of vogue quickly: for example, juxtaposition, governmentality, assemblage, materiality, agency, resistance, biopower, postcoloniality, deterritorialization, sovereignty. We are not pleading here for a *particular* balance in the relation between ethnography and philosophy, but we want to draw attention to how this relationship, which has been unstable and mutually productive over the past century, has now stabilized into a kind of slavish subservience of the anthropologist to particular philosophical schools. To equate theory making with the illustration of specific philosophical trends is a travesty of the kinds of articulation possible between High Theory and anthropology, and it suggests inattention to the range of views and open questions about human consciousness and action. With its exclusive attention to language and the written, it partakes of "neo-scripturalism": the dedication to and worship of texts.

Today ethnographic experience and discovery rarely stimulate philosophical thinking, but such was not always the case. From medieval scholars to the eighteenth-century *Encyclopédie* edited by d'Alembert and Diderot, the confrontation with cultural difference and, in the latter case, with the "noble savage" unencumbered by civilization was integral to undertaking a project of self-definition and to formulating a concept of humanity. Some philosophers, such as Lucien Lévy-Brühl, subsequently even became ethnologists. Moreover, one cannot overestimate the importance of ethnographic work on sacrifice for the theories of Marcel Mauss on the gift or of Georges Bataille on expenditure, not to speak of the debt to ethnographic accounts of the philosophical doctrines of phenomenology and existentialism.

In the 1960s, the work of E. E. Evans-Pritchard formed the substance for arguments about the relativism of belief by Peter Winch, and about rationality and the commensurability of moral systems by Alisdair Mac-Intyre. This reflection leads us to ask, Is any equivalence between the highly productive relationship of, for example, Lévi-Strauss with Sartre in the 1950s and 1960s and that, a half century later, of anthropologists with Homi Bhabha or Judith Butler? The point, we emphasize, is not to warn anthropologists against learning from philosophers and social theorists but rather to bring to consciousness the fact that we are no longer producing much work that challenges them and their concepts. The tendency of anthropologists to deploy their work only as illustrative cases for philosophical trends or concepts threatens to make anthropology into a sterile intellectual exercise.

To be sure, following the lead of philosophical schools has alerted us to themes and objects either absent from or marginal to classical anthropology. In mimicking the movement of the globalizing world itself; developing a multiplicity of fieldwork sites in ways that include following people or objects on the move; concentrating on borders, borderlands, and the interstitial; and focusing on instability in objects and relationships, anthropologists have in this critical moment produced a massive body of work. When considered up close, however, these innovations merely remind us, over and over again, that everything is moving, unstable, and embedded in globalizing processes—meager theoretical insights from such a large output. Both in theories of fieldwork and in theorizing about contemporary societies and cultures in flux, the claims seems to boil down to the usual criticisms of essentialism and naturalization, and to a repetitive insistence on the constructedness of cultural norms. No doubt such critiques are a salutary antidote to hegemonic stereotypes rampant in the first world, but they can hardly be taken as new theories that can inform how we can learn from, with, and about the contemporary world.

Likewise, while one should applaud experimentation with forms of writing (no two ethnographies today seem comparable), one should also question whether experiments in form are matched by conceptual innovations in the use and organization of evidence and by the depth to which questions are explored. Ethnographies do not, after all, constitute a genre, despite various attempts to standardize them. They are better characterized as belonging to an antigenre that nonetheless builds on all others. They take up the challenge of novelization theorized by Mikhail Bakhtin, as "drawn to everything that is not yet completed," open to an "inconclusive future," affirming that the "author [is] in a zone of contact with the world he is depicting" (1981: 27, 28, 30). But a narrative that wanders and jumps about in order to depict an inconclusive future needs even more experiential depth than does a simple story subsumed under a sophisticated theoretical frame.

Writing not based on much experience in the field, much acquaintance with people or with the questions that concern them, cannot fail to show a certain vagueness no matter how theoretically competent the writer. Rhetorical and performative virtuosity can rarely compensate for the lack of fieldwork experience, which provides an opening to dilemmas in the contemporary world. One consequence of their lack of experience is that many anthropologists instead look for evidence chiefly in archives. For them, consequently, fieldwork as a series of human encounters in communicative events has become subsidiary—the Derridean supplement, necessary but also a substitute—and therefore mimicked or replaced by surrogate rhetorical techniques.

EXPERIENTIAL ENCOUNTERS

In this volume, our concentration on the possibilities in experiential encounters leads to an exploration of questions about understanding how subjectivity is assumed in an inconclusive present, and it suggests modes of engagement in generating the knowledge and social and political action that enable ongoing relationships. We highlight fieldwork encounters in which experiential insights are arrived at not only through visualization and observation but also through linguistic exchanges, (mis)translations, feelings of attraction and repulsion, discussions and arguments, and fights and power tactics, as well as through the study of knowledges that societies have produced about their past and present. Although our encounters no longer focus on the revelation of passive interior states within cultures, we also do not think that their primary function is to yield evidence of Western hegemony. What specific kinds of insight, then, do they provide?

Fieldwork encounters, we hope to demonstrate, are modes of ethical engagement wherein the ethnographer is arrested in the act of perception. This arrest can lead both to a productive doubt about the ongoing perception of the phenomena in interaction and to the possibility of elaborating shared knowledge. We thus explore fieldwork experience mainly not as a geographical orientation to the mapping of place or personhood but as engagement with both Being There and with forms of distancing that help make cultural difference visible. That is, fieldwork is the registering of sensory impressions in a (temporal) process of mutual subject-discovery and critique, an engagement with persons, groups, and scenes that takes into account the dynamics of our interactions as well as the differences between our locations and those of our interlocutors.

We open a discussion anew about the status of visualization, observation, and description by emphasizing the thorough mediation of exchanges, linguistic and otherwise, in interlocution, and we explore what opportunities fieldwork experience provides for a special kind of reflexive experience and perception. We do not, in this venture, wish to return to an innocent understanding of fieldwork experience as a transparent transmission of impressions; rather we seek to reconceptualize the relation between observation, experience, and representation as one of dialectical objectification. Along these lines, the relation between subject and object may be more unstable and variable than critiques of colonialism or power/knowledge allow for, and there may be specific arenas or modes of interaction in which knowledge is more at play and its consequences less predictable.

In explicating notions of experience and subjectivity from this perspective, we hope to recast the understanding in anthropology of what "theory" does and can do, with an emphasis not on prescriptions of what cannot or should not be done but on possibilities of sharing experience that lead to objectivities-in-progress and to interpretations that might converge into historically situated propositions and double-edged critiques. Objectivities-in-progress are possible only if ethnographers reestablish a critical distance from the people and processes they study.

The "abolition of critical distance," as Fredric Jameson reasoned in his seminal 1984 essay "Postmodernism, or the Cultural Logic of Late Capitalism," resulted from the disappearance of "the old-fashioned ideological critique" (86), as well as from an inadequate historicization of the present. Also, loss of confidence in an older, mostly Marxist-inspired apparatus of concepts such as *ideology, alienation, progress,* and *objectivity* led to assertions of an "I'm okay, you're okay" or even "I'm okay, I'm okay" subjectivism and to the use of languages of mutual affirmation, effacing the necessary analytical break from the "native's point of view." Double-edged critiques would require the anthropologist to integrate a more dialectical understanding of historical encounters—in their extremes, catastrophic or emancipatory—that might lead to mutual, intersubjective questioning rather than smug assertions of identity rights or untraversable differences.

NOTES

1. The term *gaze* is most frequently taken over from Foucault, who initially uses it to describe surveillance and disciplinary techniques in medicine: observation as a means to exert control over a subject (see Foucault 1978).

2. For some early notable examples of this trend—which combine field-work encounters with historical investigations, along with study of the national and subnational—see the work, in France, of George Balandier and François Heretier on Africa, and of Pierre Bourdieu and Jean Favret-Saada on France; in England, on England, see Marilyn Strathern, Judith Okeley, Helen Calloway, and Anthony Jackson; and in Denmark, on Iceland, see Kirstin Hastrup.

3. This introduction is not meant as a survey of the discipline—an outline of its theoretical, national, topographic, and area-specific fields—which would require a more lengthy treatise. We sacrifice breadth of coverage in order to focus on several dominant perspectives, and therefore restrict our criticisms only to the work of some particularly prominent authors. And we limit our analysis largely to debates about anthropology as they have taken shape since the mid-1980s within the United States. Among the many publications that critically examine the practices of fieldwork specifically, or the state of theory and the discipline of anthropology more generally, the following collections of essays provide some orientation (we apologize for the unavoidable omissions): Jongmans and Gutkind (1967); Golde (1986); Smith and Kornblum (1989); Sanjek (1990); Bell, Kaplan, and Karim (1993); Hastrup and Hervik (1994); Lewin and Leap (1996); Nordstrom and Robben (1995); Greenhouse, Mertz, and Warren (2002); Kalb and Tak (2005); Sluka and Robben (2007); Mimica (2007). Along the lines of the present volume, see Cerwonka and Malkki (2007), a bold attempt to draw theory out of ethnographic experience as it unfolds.

4. Edward Said offers a typical case in point: he praises Orientalists such as Louis Massignon, Jacques Berque, and Maxime Rodinson—towering figures who were steeped in textual knowledge but at the same time engaged with Muslim individuals and societies, supporting their anti-colonial struggles—while strongly criticizing others like Bernard Lewis, who authorizes himself with textual commentary from the power-laden distance of the so-called objective analyst.

5. Issued in four editions in France between 1947 and 2002, Mauss's text appeared in English only in 2007.

6. For an example of puppeteering, see the recent review by Rosalind Morris (2007) of Derrida's "legacy" in anthropology. Rather than asking what Derridean reading might bring to anthropologists when we read, which is one of the things we all do, she subsumes all anthropology into an act of Derridean reading, and then bats away anthropologists (and others) who have had the temerity to cite Derrida critically or

who claim to have understood him but, according to her reading, have not. Deconstruction might be construed as a particular form of reading that complements fieldwork, but Morris instead insists that it radically undermines the two "epistemological commitments" of anthropology: "phenomenology and empiricism" (356). Indeed, most ethnologists have found these approaches, of which there are many versions, necessary. What takes their place, for Morris? Reading Derrida reading, of course. And a correct reading of Derrida by anthropologists, she concludes confidently, will make us "tremble," because the human, our object, "is under erasure" (382). To be fair, Morris does not simply praise Derrida but encourages us to "lament" that Derrida "passes over Marx's sociologically significant questions" (367). Lament? And what are those questions for which we are to collectively mourn? What is the *socius* to which the Master's disciple prefers to apply her *logos?* Questions regarding the "historical organization of productive relations"—specifically, "the labor of women" (366). But really, why should Derrida be specifically concerned with "the labor of women"? In this chiding of and for Derrida, Morris reintroduces an empirical or phenomenal object—women's labor (a set of experiences: we might even confide, in our unguarded moments, human, all too human, experiences)—and thereby arrests the free play of signifiers (which might, if we dare an unconscious wish, bring the Master to his knees). Women of the World, Unite!

7. For an example of the absence of critical engagement with the societies debated, see Asad (1993). For an example of how the dominated become invisible in a colonial history, see Rabinow (1991).

8. For a prominent example of a writer who links authority within culture to textualism, see Messick (1996).

REFERENCES

Appadurai, Arjun. 1990. "Disjuncture and Difference in the Global Cultural Economy." *Public Culture* 2(2) (Spring): 1–24.
Asad, Talal. 1993. "Ethnography, Literature, and Politics: Some Readings and Uses of Salman Rushdie's Satanic Verses." In *Genealogies of Religion: Discipline and Reasons of Power in Christianity and Islam.* Baltimore: Johns Hopkins University Press.
———. 2003. *Formations of the Secular: Christianity, Islam, Modernity.* Stanford: Stanford University Press.

Bakhtin, Mikhail. 1981. *The Dialogic Imagination: Four Essays.* Ed. Michael Holquist. Trans. Caryl Emerson and Michael Holquist. Austin: University of Texas Press.

Bell, Diane, Pat Kaplan, and Wazir Jahan Karim, eds. 1993. *Gendered Fields: Women, Men, and Ethnography.* New York: Routledge.

Cerwonka, Allaine, and Liisa Malkki. 2007. *Improvising Theory: Process and Temporality in Ethnographic Fieldwork.* Chicago: University of Chicago Press.

Clifford, James. 1986. "Introduction: Partial Truths." In Clifford and Marcus 1986.

Clifford, James, and George E. Marcus, eds. 1986. *Writing Culture: The Poetics and Politics of Ethnography.* Berkeley: University of California Press.

Dirks, Nicholas B. 2001. "The Crimes of Colonialism: Anthropology and the Textualization of India." In *Colonial Subjects: Essays on the Practical History of Anthropology,* ed. Peter Pels and Oscar Salemink. Ann Arbor: University of Michigan Press.

Fabian, Johannes. 1983. *Time and the Other: How Anthropology Makes Its Object.* New York: Columbia University Press.

Foucault, Michel. [1973] 1978. *The Birth of the Clinic: An Archaeology of Medical Perception.* Trans. A. M. Sheridan. New York: Vintage.

Geertz, Clifford. 1973. "Deep Play: Notes on the Balinese Cockfight." In *The Interpretation of Cultures.* New York: Basic Books.

Golde, Peggy, ed. 1986. *Women in the Field: Anthropological Experiences.* Berkeley: University of California Press.

Greenhouse, Carol, Elizabeth Mertz, and Kay Warren, eds. 2002. *Ethnography in Unstable Places: Everyday Lives in Contexts of Dramatic Political Change.* Durham: Duke University Press.

Hastrup, Kirsten, and Peter Hervik, eds. 1994. *Social Experience and Anthropological Knowledge.* London: Routledge.

Jameson, Fredric. 1984. "Postmodernism, or the Cultural Logic of Late Capitalism." *New Left Review,* no. 146: 53–92.

Jongmans, D. G., and P. C. W. Gutkind, eds. 1967. *Anthropologists in the Field.* Assen: Van Gorcum.

Kalb, Don, and Herman Tak, eds. 2005. *Critical Junctures: Anthropology and History Beyond the Cultural Turn.* New York: Berghahn Press.

Lewin, Ellen, and William Leap, eds. 1996. *Out in the Field: Reflections on Lesbian and Gay Anthropologists.* Urbana: University of Illinois Press.

Marcus, George E. 1986. "Contemporary Problems of Ethnography in the Modern World System." In Clifford and Marcus 1986.

Marcus, George E., and Michael M. J. Fischer. 1986. *Anthropology as Cultural Critique: An Experimental Moment in the Human Sciences.* Chicago: University of Chicago Press.

Mauss, Marcel. 2007. *The Manual of Ethnography*. Trans. Dominique Lussier. Ed. N. J. Allen. New York: Berghahn Books.

Messick, Brinkley. 1996. *The Calligraphic State: Textual Domination and History in a Muslim Society*. Berkeley: University of California Press.

Mimica, Jadran, ed. 2007. *Explorations in Psychoanalytic Anthropology*. New York: Berghahn Books.

Morris, Rosalind. 2007. "Legacies of Derrida: Anthropology." *Annual Review of Anthropology* 36: 355–89.

Nora, Pierre. 1996. "General Introduction: Between Memory and History." In *Realms of Memory: Rethinking the French Past*. Under the direction of Pierre Nora. English language edition ed. Lawrence D. Kritzman. Trans. Arthur Goldhammer. Vol. 1. New York: Columbia University Press.

Nordstrom, Carolyn, and Antonius Robben, eds. 1995. *Fieldwork under Fire: Contemporary Studies of Violence and Culture*. Berkeley: University of California Press.

Rabinow, Paul. 1991. *French Modern: Norms and Forms of the Social Environment*. Cambridge, MA: MIT Press.

Said, Edward. 1978. *Orientalism*. New York: Pantheon.

Sanjek, Roger, ed. 1990. *Fieldnotes: The Makings of Anthropology*. Ithaca: Cornell University Press.

Sluka, Jeffrey A., and Antonius C. G. M. Robben, eds. 2007. *Ethnographic Fieldwork: An Anthropological Reader*. Malden, MA: Blackwell.

Smith, Carolyn, and William Kornblum, eds. 1989. *In the Field: Readings on the Field Research Experience*. New York: Praeger.

TWO

Textualism and Anthropology

ON THE ETHNOGRAPHIC ENCOUNTER, OR AN EXPERIENCE IN THE HAJJ

Abdellah Hammoudi

So much has been said about anthropology as writing, discourse, texts, and pretexts that the task of reconsidering the ethnographic encounter might be likened to a recourse to magic in order to resurrect the dead. A focus on experience and deep acquaintance might well prove to be essential, however, to engage with our current and future predicament, in which we can no longer manage not to be *in each other's way*. One paradox of the present situation is that (in many quarters of our discipline) the more globalized the world, and thus the greater the circulation of people, goods, and ideas, the less favored is the approach based on meeting people (on the ground); or, when such experience is sought, it is limited, transient, and mobile. *Do not linger* seems to be the motto or, if you insist, *hang out* for a moment—and remember, everybody you happen to cross paths with is on the move. So, move on!

I want to focus on the specific form of textualism that moves away from fieldwork, in the sense of a prolonged encounter and conversation with some people, and privileges encounter through the reading of texts and the use of textual strategies. I will focus on the textualisms of the Foucauldian and Derridean sort—discourse and genealogy, deconstruction and dissemination. They have been applied to various topics; here, I pursue the outcome of these two strategies as I find them at work in the study of ritual.

Anthropologists who have used textual strategies over the past three or so decades are legion, but I will limit myself to one example of each textualism from the Middle East, the area where I do fieldwork on religious practices: Talal Asad's study on ritual, in his *Genealogies of Religion* (1993), and Michael Fischer and Mehdi Abedi's study of the hajj, the Muslim pilgrimage to Mecca, in *Debating Muslims* (1990). My comments will revolve around three points:

1. The textualisms I deal with move away from the people who have produced the discursive tradition and the practices that that tradition authorizes. Designed to avoid the messy politics of traditional fieldwork encounters, they inadvertently end up rendering invisible how people practice their traditions and the experiences they have of the ritual process. In the Derridean type of textualism, only literate elite Muslim writers and commentators are visible.

2. Despite their move to text, in the examples I am considering the authors seem to feel it necessary to evoke some kind of action on the ground. Accordingly, they introduce a form of surrogate ethnography: textual strategies that produce a reality effect, or an effect of the concrete (to paraphrase Roland Barthes).

3. Those employing both strategies miss what I call *practical articulation:* the relation between discourses/texts and institutions. In conclusion, I draw on my own ethnography of the hajj (Hammoudi 2005, 2006) to illustrate this notion, using the idea of double articulation in language.

RITUAL THROUGH TEXTUALISM: THE DISCURSIVE TRADITION

Although Talal Asad has addressed a broad range of issues in his work, his early textualist approach to ritual, highly indebted to Foucault, has perhaps found the largest audience, and has permitted him to elaborate other topics in subsequent writings.[1]

He uses the notion of genealogy to accomplish three interrelated tasks: first, to show how the concept of ritual has been used without consideration of how it came to be; second, to examine the genealogy of ritual, as category (i.e., its belonging to a particular tradition, that of Christian hermeneutics); and third, to point out the inadequacies of the concept with respect to the study of different traditions—here, a relatively undifferentiated Islamic tradition (as he depicts it) and the medieval monastic moment in Europe. His analysis is unbalanced, however. He historicizes Europe by comparing two moments (modern and medieval ritual), without undertaking similar research on Islamic equivalents in forms of worship. He compares European to Islamic traditions, in order to put forward a view of ritual as rules practiced to build specific virtues through exercising the body. He presents both these traditions as an alternative to a hermeneutics, deemed a specifically modern production.

Asad's work is of interest to me because of his use of the Islamic tradition, whose practice of worship and rule for mystic self-accomplishment he juxtaposes to hermeneutics. His encounter with ritual is not ethnographic and fieldwork-based but textual, a method that rests on several assumptions. First, a constructivist critique of the notion of ritual can be formulated only by reading and analyzing a body of textual writings on rituals—an effort to which Asad devotes most of his book. But a focus on *ritual* can highlight a particularistic genealogy and thereby point to what is left out. In this case, what is left out is found by contrasting one tradition with others. However, such a move cannot reveal what may be left out by the discursive tradition that Asad sets against the one he questions, or what this genealogical approach itself leaves out. Asad therefore contests only a generalized use of ritual as category: other traditions did not evolve a hermeneutic approach in their understanding of their own religions. He insists that the Islamic and the medieval monastic traditions relied on the notion of correct worship, or the rule for correct observances. This argument is highly debatable, given the enormous diversity of hermeneutic commentaries produced by Christian monks and Muslims over several centuries.

According to Asad, ritual as rule, exercise, and correct observance was occulted by a Western and modernist discursive tradition, which constituted ritual by means of such dichotomies as thought/action, hidden subjectivity/outward appearance, subject/object, and so forth. Thus, ritual actions became identified with codes to be deciphered instead of being approached as codes for conduct (Asad 1993: 59, 72–74). In studying these rules and practices for cultivating the virtuous self, Asad draws on the rule of Saint Benedict and Benedictine exercises for approaching the divine and developing a specific morality. For Islam, he invokes Muslim mystic practices, and again he relies on written accounts, though the body of texts that present Islamic mystic thought and practice is much smaller and sometimes elusive.

Asad attempts to show that ritual acts do not so much encode meanings as produce them through systematic bodily exercise. For example, virtue is achieved as *competence*—a *habit* achieved by training and disciplining, by the application of *disciplines*. Yet he does not discuss the possible and actual discrepancies (for example, in Muslim mystic endeavors)—the gap—between effort and achievement. Nor does he discuss the difficulties and ambiguities involved in translating the Muslim use of the words and notions of *education, exercise, struggle, effort*, and so on, as well as words in the Foucauldian vocabulary, such as *training* or *disciplining*. Moreover, Asad never pursues genealogical analysis regarding what he calls the "Muslim discursive tradition." Thus, he takes that discourse at face value; words coming from the Muslim tradition seem never to be subject to the Foucauldian bifurcation between what is said and what could possibly be meant at different or successive readings and encounters.

Asad derives the rules and exercises that are said to produce virtuous subjectivities not from firsthand encounters, observation, and description but from the study of ritual in anthropological texts and in texts produced by the Christian and the Muslim traditions. Like an entire generation of anthropologists, he moved away from the fieldwork tradition in order to draw rather stark conclusions about the unequal power relations between scholars and the people studied, about objectivism, and about orientalizing, which stems from, among other things, the "colonial encounter." In other words, Asad's work actually presents practice as inferred from written discourses to which he gave a certain order, thanks to a set of architectonic concepts taken as the implicit structure and structuring principles of Christian and Muslim texts. Thus, the ritual practices themselves fade away.

To study ritual as a cultivation of virtuous selves, one would have to turn away from instructions for action to concentrate on how men and women put those instructions into practice to change themselves. I hasten to add that for me, *practice*, as a category, is not limited to habitus, resulting from a perception of the possibilities within a specific environment (a naturalized social structure). It also involves customs of discussion, understandings and misunderstandings, that constantly refuel the dynamics of action, ritual or otherwise.[2]

A second example is Asad's reading of Mauss's celebrated reflections on *techniques du corps* (body techniques), in which he introduces a modified and surrogate sort of ethnography to illustrate conclusions drawn from the study of discourse and genealogy (as the cultivation of the self and the production of subjectivities)—conclusions that were supposed to be about real life, not simply the discursive domain. Here, I think that ethnography is deployed to produce a *reality effect*. His modification consists of suppressing Mauss's effort at approaching the formation of meaningful bodies (meaning as embodiment). Asad uses Mauss instead to illustrate the notion of a functional dependency of the subjective on the objective—an accommodation of discourse and genealogy, a variant of the dependency of superstructure on infrastructure. Indeed, he goes so far as to take Mauss's piece as evidence for his proposition that "consciousness becomes a dependent function" (Asad 1993: 77).

In his reading of Mauss's *techniques du corps*, Asad emphasizes the mechanistic, disciplinary implications over the experiential-phenomenological ones. He interprets formulas such as "the body as instrument" and the body as a "technical object," as a "technical mean" (*moyen technique*) or as "embodied aptitudes," to mean that the body is an "assemblage of embodied attitudes" (Mauss [1936] 1950: 372; Asad 1993: 75). Asad ignores Mauss's insistence on learning and imitation as a process in which an operative consciousness is at work toward a total accomplishment and perfected form. Mauss never takes totality as something that can be realized in practice; rather, there is an incipient orientation toward totality, an incipient form of aspiration toward something made ever more perfect. For him, unlike Asad, the learned body is not an "assemblage of embodied aptitudes." Thus, beyond the trained dancer there is always a better dancer: that is, the first foreshadows the second. Asad's concept of production of self is too close to mechanical production to be congruent with Maussian body techniques. Moreover, unlike Asad, Mauss recognizes periods of breakdown and reform of practice (Mauss [1936] 1950: 385). In a nutshell, Mauss's approach insists that *techniques du corps* and bodily articulation of competences compose "symbolic figures" (372). Mauss uses texts and observations made by himself and others (on swimming, military drills, bodily attitudes, and configurations of bodies in settings such as lectures and hospitals where patients are cared for). *Techniques du corps* involve ambiguity, and bodies are ambiguous beings—part object, part subject, to use an expression of Bruno Latour (1993).

Asad's approach to ritual opposes interpretive approaches, specifically those developed by Clifford Geertz. The critical point here is the confrontation between two major concepts: *reading* and *production*. Reading is infinite, whereas production points to the limit to interpretation in something Asad takes for a fact: the extant repertoire of the practices and disciplines intended to produce virtuous selves (Asad 1993: 78–79). Asad never considers the hierarchy or the order of the elements in the repertoire. In fact, variations in the ordering are possible, so that the same repertoire includes different paths to virtue. This fact of variation is a well-known feature of Muslim mystic practices; in the monastic orders in medieval Christianity as well, rules differ from one order to another. Such variation in *vocation* is a function of circumstances and interpretation. Vocations are symbolic of different worldviews (as well as of other things), in the sense that monks and mystics pursue and embody them, as symbolic forms of themselves, as selves to come.

What is more, Asad replaces the admittedly intellectualist metaphor of reading action through cultural frames with the no less figurative activity of reading and interpreting books, which he takes for the only activity that matters, an activity that is apparently immune from the critical operations of discourse theory. Reading is the major and/or the exclusive activity of intellectuals pursuing discursive and textual theories, and

Asad is no exception. However, his studies of religion use certain books only, especially those that seem to follow the model of rules dealing with inmates or of blueprints like those of the panopticon—he includes hardly any biographies or autobiographies of mystics or monks, though there is an abundant literature on them, and hardly any discussion on the encounters of mystics or monks with their contemporaries. Thus, just as can be seen in the succession of epistemes in knowledge production, here too there is an illusion of reversibility, to the point that the writing performance effect is treated as something reproducible in a laboratory.

Moreover, Asad, in his treatment of mystical initiations from the study of books, hardly touches on the ways in which Muslims may disagree among themselves on what is and what is not Islamic practice, and how they differ in the interpretation of the correct way of observing their religious duties and in the interpretation of those duties themselves. A consideration of how these discourses evolve in specific discussions, in oral exchanges within particular contexts, is excluded by an approach such as his. An important consequence of this approach, though certainly not the only one, is that we learn nothing about rituals as ongoing processes with stable or shifting institutional articulations. In any view of Asad's writings, as well as in Michel Foucault's, there is a problem in dealing with the process of institutional articulation as an aspect of practical articulation.

To summarize, what we have noted here is the complexity of what Asad, as an anthropologist, does. First, he *reads* anthropological books about ritual and religion and, second, he reads Mauss—in both cases, reading through the paradigm of discourse and the paradigm of the so-called coalescence of power/knowledge. However, Mauss is read as an alternative to interpretive theories of religion, and this is done after Mauss's text is emptied of its theorizing based on ethnography. Entangling the situation even more is Mauss's effort to bring together practice with the production of self. Asad uses the notions of habitus and body techniques to outfit genealogical theory with something concrete. Whereas Pierre Bourdieu (1972) elaborated these concepts on the ground of real encounters and concrete circumstances—that is, in fieldwork in Algeria[3]— Asad turns whatever ethnography he finds in Mauss into models of disciplinary practices found in texts that define blueprints. Encounters with and through books are extremely varied: books can be read with ethnographic sensibilities, and an ethnography of textualism might produce interesting results. The point here, again, is that discourse analysis is one encounter among others—perhaps appropriate for certain tasks, but certainly of limited relevance for developing a theory of ritual.

That ritual works at forming and transforming the self is evident; that "the Muslim discursive tradition" confirms this truth of ritual is also evident. One has to immediately add that intention and conformity in these matters are hotly debated, and thus one should speak of Muslim discursive *traditions*. Such conceptual elaborations create serious tensions in Asad's framework, though he by no means presumes a unified, enclosed, and consensual field. The point I want to stress is that ambiguities, contradictions, absurdities, and paradox are best described in situational encounters: in them, the anthropologist remains focused on people's actions, speeches, views, and theories in order to go, in a second stage, into a metalanguage, with the aim of constructing a synoptic view of things. Otherwise, we may be stuck with languages of the traditions themselves.

RITUAL THROUGH TEXTUALISM: THE WRITING VARIANT

The textualism I have considered so far ends up being a mouthpiece for the traditions under consideration, whether the medieval monastic in Christianity or the Islamic. Despite its premises, it appears to conflate utterance and discourse. At the same time, what may be silenced (left unspoken) by differing Muslim discursive traditions is left untouched.

The second variant of textualism I now turn to is the one that is familiarly called deconstruction, the critical approach famously championed by Jacques Derrida. I focus on Michael Fischer and Mehdi Abedi's *Debating Muslims,* perhaps the first attempt to use this kind of textualism in the study of a mandatory observance in Islam—the hajj. Their book will serve as an illustration of *deconstruction* and *writing* applied to ritual practice.

This self-styled, more radical form of textualism does not present practices as they are enunciated in verbal performances extracted from texts
and classified under a set of implicit architectonic concepts. Here, writing
is the only practice. In the face of this textualism, no alternative paradigm
would be left standing: not discourse, epistemes or power/knowledge
coalescences, or practice, in discursive form or otherwise.

Deconstruction—as is well known—is but one approach to writing.
Many others have been tried since Roland Barthes initially formulated
the view that reading and writing were not to be thought about separately. The line that traditionally separated them was blurred, becoming
instead a line of *suture* (in Lacan's parlance). To be sure, desire and
encoding were, for Barthes, still within the matrix of writing (notably
in his *S/Z* [1970]), leaving aside the writing of the event, which he also
practiced.

But for the Derrida-inspired theoretician of generalized writing (*écriture*), even this blurring of reading and writing would seem to retain categories typical of the transcendentalism of reason, which is at the
foundation of structuralism. There will have to be pairs of opposites (one
such opposition is reading/writing) defined only conceptually—that is,
as abstract forms, inseparable from an assumption of the Hegelian
"objective spirit." True, as Claude Lévi-Strauss put it (1963), phonemes
are material: sounds form signifiers by opposition and contrast to one
another. However, the contrast breaks down as soon as one notes that the
same sounds may sometimes correspond to different signifiers: for
example, in the celebrated Derridean pair *différence/différance* (Derrida
1982: 3–27). Moreover, the *dichotomy* signifier/signified that forms the
sign collapses as soon as one notes that signifieds tend themselves be signifiers, something that operates within speech as well as within written
discourse (Derrida 1976, [1978] 2001). When I say *différence* (difference),
différance (deferral) is also there inscribed: one or the other meaning is
retained as speech develops, and appears in different speech contexts.
Here contrast or opposition are not at work; rather, words sit on top of
each other as in a palimpsest. Moreover, this double inscription of differences has a tangible material existence in the letter itself: in both the
graphic form and the sound form. Thus, according to Derrida, the

graphic could no longer be identified with a written trace: the notion of *trace* subsumes both the sound trace and the graphic one.

In this theory, the oral, in the sense of communication on the ground, loses its significance; and the radical textualism the theory proposes, when its logic is extended to ethnographic fieldwork, authorizes writing from other writings as a partial or total substitute for fieldwork. This substitution is motivated by more or less the same considerations mentioned above in the case of discursive textualism, to which Derridean anthropologists add radical doubts regarding the sense of co-presence in interlocution.

As I already said, Fischer and Abedi's work on the hajj presents itself as an implementation of such a program in the domain of ritual. To be sure, this work is rather eclectic, a quality that allows it to capture some of the political meanings of the ritual by introducing a very traditional and rich description of political context. Moreover, a combination of deconstruction and feminist theory informs their effort at showing the tension of meanings that ceaselessly cascade through all traces that an anthropologist may put together and call hajj, ritual, or for that matter religion, culture, consciousness, politics, and so on. Indeed, every trace, every signifier, has its signification only in differing from a previous one, and in its ability to defer others yet to come. Deference/difference. Fischer and Abedi choose, in one formulation, to frame a section with the title "Fear of *Différance*, the Hajj 'Rodeo,'" announcing their *vaguely* Derridean approach: "*Différance*, Derrida's pun, playing on *difference* and *deferring*, is a key term in his analysis of the way language and writing operates: language depends on oppositions or differences to make meaningful sounds (phonemes) and utterances, yet each utterance or writing can be allowed by subsequent contexts, so that final meaning is always deferred. This is most obvious in puns like a *différance*, where meaning disseminates in multiple directions, and where an attempt to freeze meaning through an initial writing or context can be undone by reviving alternative meanings" (Fischer and Abedi 1990: 152).

Feminism, combined with the play of difference, finds an ally in the notion of *abundance*—disseminations in multiple directions—as differentiated from *scarcity*; these notions are metaphorized, according to Luce Irigaray (1985), by the female and the male body, respectively. The first is described in contrast to the second, in the following terms: "The inherent plurality and multiplicity of the female sexual body is opposed to the singular sexual organ of the male, centralizing and hierarchizing his desire. The metaphor provides a political allegory: a decentered form of generous and omnipresent communication nurturing all parts (an economy of affluence rather than scarcity) . . . to more centralized forms appears 'hysterical' and 'uncontrolled' and threatening" (Fischer and Abedi 1990: 153). Hence the strategy adopted: the female body as metaphor is brought in to "neutralize" oppositions, for the purpose of offering a "critique à la Derrida" and of pointing to the alternative female body at the core of Islamic ethics, by invoking Hagar's centrality in the hajj. This deployment of the female body would destabilize community and nation, male and female roles, and bring unsettled discourses to the play of national and class differences (Fischer and Abedi 1990: 153).

I will limit myself to an outline of the hajj, as it is disseminated in the text of Fischer and Abedi, by summarizing the multiple and always differing and deferring meanings of the hajj. In this summary I will concentrate on two points: first, on the absence/presence of ethnography, which keeps this text unconsolidated and for me unpersuasive; and second, the relevance of the discourse of *différence/différance* to Hagar's predicament. This focus will enable me to use the notions of *unconsolidation* and *decentering*, as they appear in this textualist encounter in contrast to the ethnographic one, to drive my exploration.

After beginning with a relatively brief and eloquent section on the hajj, the authors devote the bulk of their work to the hajj as presented in writings, mostly by Shiite thinkers who theorized in support of an Islamic (Shiite) revolution. These writings, in turn, are put into the larger context of a sort of political history of the relations between Iran and the Sunni world of the Middle East (Saudi Arabia in particular), centered on four pilgrimage seasons: 1964, 1968, 1971, and 1987. Those years were key to the developments and dynamics that led to the 1979 overthrow of the shah and the founding and establishment of the Islamic Republic of Iran; it was a time of intense competition for leadership of the Muslim community, which played itself out, among other loci, in the struggle over control of the hajj as a mediatic scene of global scope.

The play of deference/difference is documented through the instability of words and meanings, and illustrated here by key words such as
nation and *umma;* through ritual and religion as traces of unconsolidated
meanings that are disseminated in salvation, the politics of ritual and ritual politics, Shia-Sunni competitions, and struggles for the center of
Islam; and through sacrifice and other rituals disseminated via metaphor
into paradigms of Muhammad-Ibrahim and of Muhammad-Ibrahim-
Ismael-Isaac-Hussein, with the latter given Shiite inflections. And in the
discourse of the *umma*/nation, male heroes are unsettled by Hagar, the
woman who saved Islam by ensuring the genealogical continuity of
the Abrahamic foundation (i.e., averting the death of Ismael—the biblical
Ishmael—from thirst). She represents life-giving nurturance and generosity, saving father and son, constituting the father as father. Also, the discourse of religious identity disseminates in the direction of other religious
identities (Judaism and Christianity are present yet occulted, i.e., deferred);
community disseminates in the direction of class and stratification (especially in the biographies of elite thinkers, such as Shariati and Mutaharri).

Instead of a notion of individualized authors and texts, all are put on a
carousel that makes them disseminate—one may as well say disseminate—within each other, to the point of authorizing a "text." Con-
textual readings/writings proliferate in this miraculously fecund text
signed Khomeini, Shariati, Mutahhari, Fischer, and Abedi, to mention just
a few writers who—like others, according to the Derridean view—should
be considered as pure "signatures," not authors, either striving toward
organic exclusiveness or willingly forgoing such exclusiveness through
what can be called *penial* practices (from pen, pennes, pen-nis, penial sac,
penial sheath).

The other sort of context brought to the attention of the reader refers to
events documented by historians, journalists, and others. Here, an event,
or set of events, is taken as reported in texts, and presented by the anthropologist as a context, which thus organizes a sort of existence that is not
purely textual: the reports range from eyewitness descriptions to synthe-
ses of previous accounts. One might wonder how the structural context
described in this part of the work is related to proliferation and dissemination, but I choose only to touch on such matters of contextualism here.

Let us now turn to ethnography—a move that might seem paradoxical, given Fischer and Abedi's seeming rejection of the field. Yet texts and their various employments can be integral to ethnography. Fischer and Abedi employ texts in at least three ways. Two, which may be unwitting, we have already encountered: a vaguely Derridean-feminist critique and a classic chronicle of events from which a structural, political, and social context is inferred. These two do not sit well together.

The third usage of texts can be documented from the first part of their work, where the authors follow the rituals through episodes excerpted from narratives of a few pilgrims—the Shiite writers and some others already mentioned. All were exposed both to traditional Islamic learning and also to some modern school systems (the Iranian ideologue Shariati attended the Sorbonne, for example). Consequently, no discourse of individuals who lacked any schooling was considered. The dichotomy literate/ illiterate can be unsettled through special attention to the scriptural and discursive practices of society. Such attention makes possible a critique of distinctions and dichotomies of the kind that appears in the typology posited by Jack Goody: preliterate/literate, presence/absence of writing, or generalized/limited literacy (Messick 1993: 24–25). But these unsettlings—important as they are with regard to changing quasi-stereotypical images of societies (here Islamic ones)—do not address the almost total absence from textualist anthropological studies of people who lack the skills associated with literacy and textuality.

I suggest that in the text by Fischer and Abedi (and many others), writing and rewriting operate as surrogates for ethnography—more specifically, for an encounter with people who do not know how to read and write in the ordinary sense of these terms, a sense that at this point cannot be destabilized either by discourse theory or by differing/deferring (despite digital technologies, a subject to be treated elsewhere). Fischer and Abedi's account of the hajj details the successive steps together with the meanings attributed to them by literate Muslims, especially Shiite writers. The description is drawn partly from manuals, partly from narratives of individual Muslim pilgrims. Three features are particularly striking about it: the abundance of quotations, its reliance on editorial techniques, and the use of words that appeal to the reader's imagination. The long evocation of the intricate and complex ritual becomes a series of vignettes that the reader is meant to find striking, and perhaps intimidating.

I will briefly develop these points before returning to ethnography. The plethora of citations and quotations make for a particular sort of reading: many Iranian voices of mullahs and writers are put together, respond to each other, develop and add detail to important themes. The major rituals are thus enumerated and given the form of an ordered succession, with interpretive openings in different registers of meaning. Some names stand out, though: Ali Shariati, with his insistence on sacrifice and on Hagar's effort, portraying her trials and sacrifice as an exemplary moral struggle (Fischer and Abedi 1990: 159–60); Falsefi; and Yusuf Ali, specifically in the register of identity and politics of separation from kindred religions and communities (Judaism, Christianity). According to Ali Yusuf, they note, "Cain stands for the Jews, the 'elder brother' Semitic religion, who tried to kill Jesus and exterminate the Christian . . . to kill Mohammed and put down his people" (165). Ismael is, in effect, the younger brother of Cain, the sacrifice of Abel in this context being also the sacrifice of Ismael and Mohammed. Fischer and Abedi also cite Ali-e Ahmad, Khomeini, Abdulai Chenef, and Mutathari.

In several respects, the authors are performing ethnography instead of doing it. First and most prominent is the density of citations and quotations, intended to bring in the *voices* of Muslims—particularly writers, as I noted, some of them prominent. From a Derridean perspective, what matters is not voice as speech but writing as trace, which subsumes any oral articulation. However, in the authors' strategy, citation works as voice: specifically, as voices heard in conversation, and from all classes, ethnicities, races, and genders, as if listening were involved.

However, we know that this is not the case, and the density of quotations cannot replace anthropological description even though the authors borrow descriptions, such as the following from the famous Ali-e Ahmad: "several times, I saw people cutting up carcasses just for fun, and such gleam of delight in their eyes. You'd think they were all studying anatomy" (quoted in Fischer and Abedi 1990: 170). Passages like this one, and they are numerous, come in bits and pieces and substitute for the much-criticized culturalist perspectives that are situated and thickly descriptive. But the quoted sentences and passages are selected according to the unstated writing strategies of the anthropologist. Excerpting pieces of prose signed with other names, and fitting them together, accomplishes the *reality effect* that the anthropologist desires. Thus quoting from surrogates works as description, and seeing through somebody else's eyes is somewhat conflated with seeing through one's own eyes without positioning the anthropologist in the undesired role of describer.

Implicit in this writing is an editorial strategy, in the literal, journalistic sense. Here the titles of the chapters and sections are very important, announcing the main points before arguments are made for them: "Fear of *Différance*," "The Hajj 'Rodeo'" (with a footnote explaining that "rodeo" was the code name for the hajj among Moors who in post-Reconquista Spain legally converted to Christianity but secretly continued to be Muslims), "Hajj as primal scene," "Four hajj seasons," and so on. Add to this technique the use of iconographic material (mostly drawings from older Persian books but also a modern painting and a stamp), not commented on except in captions, and an abundance of quotations from James Joyce, Emmanuel Lévinas, Virginia Dominguez, the Qur'an. The recourse to so many authorities, including divinely inspired ones, protects the authority of the anthropologist. Very often the excerpt also evades interrogation and discussion. Quotation and excerpts evade deconstruction itself.

Finally, a word on other rhetorical devices, such as the use of vignettes. A passage from the section I am analyzing can serve to illustrate my point. An account of the hajj, under the title "Hajj as primal scene," it includes two excerpts from the Qur'an and one from Lévinas. Fischer and Abedi open this section:

> Imagine the crowds of Muslims from all over the world for the annual hajj pilgrimage to Mecca: (1) Fellow Muslims present, actually visible, number in the millions: what more impressive sense of spiritual community (*umma*) overriding status, national and other mundane distinctions? (2) The crowds are separated into national units and small units by hajj guides. "Iranians carry *aftabehs*; Turks have long tubes with bulbous ends[;] . . . Lebanese and Syrians carry *aftabehs* that are smaller than ours—and Indians and Africans carry kettles." Iranian mullās lead their flocks in distinctive prayers such as the *duʿā komeil*, and the prayers (*duʿā*) include curses of the first three Sunni caliphs. (1990: 157)

The *duᶜā komeil* is a long invocation believed by the Shiites to have been dictated by Imam Ali to his disciple Komeil. Fischer and Abedi mention this dramatic practice in the context of the Shiite hajj, which differs, in this respect, from the Sunni one. A footnote refers to a month of fieldwork "among the faithful," during which Abedi recited the *duᶜā* to Sunnis who "were very impressed, some even crying" (Fischer and Abedi 1990: 476n18). But this month of fieldwork was undertaken in Houston, among Muslims fasting during Ramadan. There is no indication that any firsthand experience informed the writing of the chapter of their book dealing with the hajj. So, we do not know what actually happened in the four hajj seasons when Shiite pilgrims performed the famous *duᶜā komeil*. Another chapter reports on the recitation performed in Houston and takes up themes related to Hagar that overlap with what Fischer and Abedi write about her in connection with the hajj.

Again, details mentioned, like national emblems, are taken from the Iranian author Ali-e Ahmad. The use of the verbal form *imagin* in the imperative and the casting of the sentences in interrogative form (with the most powerful affirmative effect) are some of the rhetorical devices that call on our imagination and call for our initiative. Again, within that rhetorical space descriptions are inserted in quotation (especially from Ali-e Ahmad, who wrote a famous narrative of the pilgrimage he made in 1964). The vignette, widely used in new anthropological writing, functions here as a substitute for firsthand ethnography, itself now relegated to the margins (i.e., a footnote). In the text signed by Fischer and Abedi, the vignette form works like something that is not deferred/differed. The sort of mimicking the writing deploys suggests a ghost ethnography haunting the text. Textualism might well be simultaneously triumphant and on the defensive.

WRITING HAGAR: ETHNOGRAPHY AND EXPERIENCE

In this section, I want to reflect on textualist practices and experience from the perspective of my own ethnography of the hajj, in order to question some of the grounds on which fieldwork, as a source of firsthand accounts, has been marginalized or replaced by textualist practices. In so doing, I do not assume that we are in the presence of two clearly demarcated strategies, setting textualism against firsthand experience; combinations of the two have been tried (for example, in the work of Lila Abu-Lughod [1997] and Smadar Lavie [1990]). However, such combinations tend either to produce more knowledge about writers, journalists, various media, and debates than about the lives and social conditions of the anthropologist's interlocutors, or to result in stifling eclecticism. In extreme cases, such as can be found in the study by Fischer and Abedi, where the firsthand encounter is either irrelevant or absent, the enterprise achieves some success only as writing about other writings.

I will concentrate on the motif of Hagar in the hajj, in order to show how an approach that relies on a Derrida-inspired textualism elides what I call *practical articulation*. This is an elision we find in all discursive approaches (already addressed in my reflection on surrogate ethnography).

The name Hagar—more obviously in its Arabic form *Hajar* or *Hajer*, derived from a Semitic root—is related to migration, displacement, traveling, and leaving. One may also think of the migration of the Prophet (the Hejira, in English) from Mecca. Hajar/Hajer is the mother of Ismael, the female ancestor of the Arab peoples; their father is Abraham/Ibrahim. Muslim sources, unlike Jewish ones, do not linger on her status—spouse, concubine, servant: she is simply the mother of Ismael. In the hajj there is a cult devoted to her. Pilgrims perform the *sayᵖ* (the running) between two emergent rocks, much as she ran back and forth in search of water to save her baby Ismael from dying of thirst.

The story of Ismael takes us into a rather involved family saga, familiar to Westerners from the book of Genesis. As a servant of Ibrahim and Sarah, she had intercourse with the patriarch at the instigation of Sarah, because Sarah was barren, and bore Ismael. As it is well known, a few years later, despite their advanced age God gave Sarah and Ibrahim a second son, Isaac (in Arabic *Ishaq*)—a name that, according to commentators, refers to inextinguishable laughter upon receiving an unexpected, providential gift.

At some point, Ibrahim, at the urging of Sarah, sent Hajar and Ismael into exile in the desert. The Muslim story has it that Ibrahim took mother and child to an inhospitable desert valley, which we understand to be the place where Mecca was founded. That is where Hajar, abandoned by the father of her son, saved Ismael from death and reared him alone. Ibrahim eventually returned and decided to sacrifice this son in obedience to an order he thought he received from God in a dream. The ordeal took place (in the absence of Hajar) at Mina, another barren and rugged valley in the vicinity of Mecca. Ultimately, God substituted a ram for Ismael, and father and son came back to the city and reerected the Kaaba, the cubic "House of God." For Muslims, Islam is the restoration by the Prophet Muhammad of the original monotheism founded by Ibrahim and the reestablishment of its observances and their sacred spaces.

Fischer and Abedi cite Muslim sources (mainly but not exclusively Shiite) in their account of this ritual episode, and Shariati is sometimes their main source regarding Hajar. They label Adam, Eve, and Cain the heroes of the "theater of creation," and Abraham, Hagar, and Ismael the heroes of "history" (1990: 159). Shariati says that the actor who plays all these heroic roles is the pilgrim: "You! whoever you might be, woman, man, old, young, black, white" (quoted in Fischer and Abedi 1990: 159). Following Shariati's etymological play, they connect *ummat* (Muslim community) with *imamat* (spiritual direction) and *umm* (mother). "Abraham was indeed an 'umma'" (Shariati, quoted in Fischer and Abedi 1990: 163). Still another quotation from Shariati connects Eve to the central rite of the hajj, the famous station of Arafa (Fischer and Abedi 1990: 164). According to him and to other Muslim sources, the name Arafa must be understood in connection with the Arabic verb *ʿarafa*, meaning "to know." Such an etymology would support speculation that gives Eve, the female figure, not Adam, the male figure, the initiative and the power of knowledge and recognition. Indeed, in this story it is Eve who recognized Adam ("man") after their fall from Paradise, and not vice versa. To know the self and recognize your fellow participant in this dyadic venture, as in others, is understood as a significant privilege (Hammoudi 2006: 257–58). Among these heroes, Hagar enjoys a special honor, as she alone is mentioned as being on par with Abraham. Fischer and Abedi also quote from the Libyan leader Mu'ammar Qadafi in a way that makes his discourse converge with Shariati's on the theme of *ummat* (1990: 163).

In these quotations, Fischer and Abedi register the advent of new and incipiently feminist discourses in the circulation and dissemination of meanings of the name and actions of Hajar that emerge at the heart of the Islamic ethics of effort, persistence, and sacrifice. They note that this "Hajar voice" keeps male, nationalistic, and centralizing discourses unconsolidated (Fischer and Abedi 1990: 220, 484nn100–2). However, Fischer and Abedi omit any reference to other discourses developed by other powerful currents within the Muslim nations, most notably the ones that draw on secular and liberal philosophies. Nor do they pay attention to the circulation of Western texts within the texts of the Muslim writers they cite. As is well known, many Muslim thinkers, militants, and leaders have been promoting versions of feminism, inspired by the widely circulated philosophies of human rights, within many Muslim constituencies. It would be easy to show that the texts cited by Fischer and Abedi remain *unconsolidated* precisely because of the dissemination of the avowedly European-inspired ones.

On the one hand, Hajar's voice appeals to audiences far beyond textual exegetes and hermeneuts, as it energizes the ongoing social and political struggles that are transforming Muslim societies. On the other hand, Fischer and Abedi foreground a notion of "alternating submission/self-assertion of alternative discourses" (Fischer and Abedi 1990: 220)—thereby guiding an analysis quite different from a critique that would have found a deferred inscription of Hajar in the writing of Muslim thinkers. And indeed, even Shariati's and Qadafi's texts may well be analyzed as an attempt to trace the advent of Hajar's voice, controlled and contained by a global discourse of *ummat* liberation.

But a Derridean play on words such as *umm, ummat,* and *imamat* should also have included *imam*. Characteristically, Fischer and Abedi discuss *imamat* as leadership (1990: 163) but not *imam*, which can refer to the male leader, such as Shariati or Qadafi or many others who might direct the *umma* (community) and *umm* (mother). As long as *imamat* is explained only as "leadership," however, we remain blind to the possible pun within *imama*, which (as the feminine of *imam*) can also represent—for differing and conflicting constituencies—a possible, a desirable, a necessary alternative yet to come: a female prayer leader and political leader. The pun would be supremely Derridean. Indeed, it has already occurred in a New York City mosque—but in reality, not in rhetoric alone (see Elliott 2005a, 2005b). We might conclude that languages do not completely overlap with action, struggle, possibility, and creativity, and vice versa, and that there is something to be discovered outside the text.

What happened in New York, where, for the first time, an African American Muslim *imamat* presided over Friday prayer—supported by some, opposed by others—in the large Muslim *ummat* has religious as well as political implications. One is a reorganization of worship and a reordering of the idea of mosque, as it might end up being directed by a Muslim woman, a female person and body. Can a devout body at prayer still be talked about as a gendered body or even as a body? In point of fact, a group of Muslims accepted or even advocated praying behind a woman, which meant a reorganization of the mosque not imagined within the traditional male order of the prayer space.

By comparison, Shariati and Qadafi, the authorities cited by Fischer and Abedi, pay homage to the exemplarity of Hajar. Was Hajar—this name— written by these prominent Muslims precisely to capture or limit the name's unforeseen powers? Shariati was a serious reformer, but reading him, one must keep in mind the politics of discourse—he was writing in the context of the power struggles in Iran during the crucial decade or so that lead to the 1979 Islamic revolution. Moreover, Qadafi's revolution helped change the condition of women in the workplace, and he even surrounded himself with a feminine guard. In both cases, the exemplary Hajar is kept in her place, often one that is repressed and, in the legal systems and the unwritten codes of the Iranian and the Libyan revolutions, circumscribed.

The change that happened in the New York mosque may encourage similar action elsewhere. In Mecca, as I experienced it in 1999, I came across many praises of Hajar. When I undertook the famous running, I did so in the company of the women of our group of six (three women, three men; I was without my wife, and one of the three women had temporarily left behind her husband and children to travel with us). After the sevenfold running back and forth—men wearing the seamless *ihram*, women in ordinary long robes with hands and face uncovered— hair is clipped in a gesture that marks the end of the ritual. It was Aicha, a teacher from Beni Mellal whom I had helped on a few occasions, who completed the clipping of my hair (after a female member of our group had done a poor job). Noticing my hesitation, she said: "What? . . . I can do it!" and, after further discussion, added: "We are in the presence of Mother Hajar, and in the neighborhood of the Kaaba." Aicha was accomplishing the pilgrimage under the guardianship of a man who took care of a group of women without men, as the law required that women be accompanied by a tutor.

I had realized at that point how far the *masʾa*, Hajar's path, was physically off center, tangential to the Kaaba and the Mosque. As it stands now, it is a covered gallery stretching over several hundred meters, the space between the two rocks. Aicha did not want to engage in a conversation about this spatial arrangement: "We are in the hajj here. Men and women. . . . The afterlife comes first." I pushed her, and all I got was "I am here for hajj, and so are you . . . aren't you?" I thanked her for clipping my hair and left when she rejoined her group.

Before the running, I had drunk from the Zamzam spring; it is located underground within the Mosque, very close to the station of Ibrahim, which is aboveground. Drinking from that spring also recalls the story of Hajar and Ismael, and so does the semicircular low wall adjacent to the Kaaba that marked Hajar's space (called *hijr*). This space was packed with women, but not exclusively. The circumambulation itself was *mixed* and the gender separation in the most sacred Mosque of Islam was not as stringent as in the Medina Mosque, where a wooden barrier completely isolated women from men, leaving them only two access points to the prophet's shrine.

The concentric circles around the Kaaba, women and men together, powerfully confirm the ultimate erasure of gender difference in their crucial part of the ritual cycle. Moreover, the *hijr* (the place of Hajar) is attached to the structure we circled. At the other crucial phase of the pilgrimage—its sine qua non, the station of Arafat—the crowd that numbers in the millions stands in prayer, men and women, around the Mount of Mercy (Jabal al-Rahma). We should also remember, as noted above, that this place is associated with Eve, the female primordial figure of human genealogy (for further discussion, see Hammoudi 2006: 217).

Similar observations can be made about other ritual actions, although many women from our camp did not attend the stoning of Satan or the sacrifice. Undoubtedly, fear of a stampede, which sometimes has resulted in deaths during the hajj, played a large role in their decision; yet their absence also mirrored the circumstances of the sacrifice being commemorated: Ibrahim and Ismael journeyed alone, without Hajar, to execute God's order. And at Arafat, at Jabal al-Rahma, even though the words *rahma* (mercy) and *rahm* (womb) are closely connected, men act as if this cornerstone of the pilgrimage (i.e., the standing, the prayers, and the invocations there) required the strictest separation of men and women, and the most stringent enforcement of male preeminence in worship. Elsewhere I have described men displaying this attitude. One example was at Arafat:

It was four o'clock in the morning when I opened my eyes. I left my improvised bed, made my ablutions, and went out for some fresh air. I took a short stroll in the direction of the Mount of Mercy outlined in the first light of dawn, then returned to lie down and wait for the others to awake. Men and women emerged from sleep slowly, and then the familiar bustle of activity began. We did our dawn prayers separately; then, a little after five o'clock, we performed the morning prayers together, in our vast shelter. The crowd swelled with fresh arrivals of pilgrims. Volunteers were already monitoring the organization of prayers. Abbas fretted about the ranks, which were poorly formed and not close enough, according to him. Another man demanded that the women be sent back behind the men. "Our neighbors"—he pointed at another group—"prayed behind our women. Their prayer is invalid." Without a word, my companions' wives and the other women went to join the "neighbors' women." The two groups thus united in the correct order, "women behind men," we prayed under the guidance of an Arab tribesman from the countryside south of Rabat, discreet and very pious, educated in Qur'anic matters. From all sides, the clamor of invocations, prayers, and sobs arose, even though the station, as we knew, only began with the Friday communal prayer at midday. (Hammoudi 2006: 207–8)

Aicha's reluctance to discuss with me the subject of space and gender may be interpreted in several ways. I found the same reticence in Fadma, the wife of my friend and assistant, Lahcen, although we were very close. Fadma, who had some schooling but had forgotten how to write and never could read, told me that "those things came after the saving of the soul. The person must first save the soul" (*lwahd inajji ruhu ba*ᵓ*da*). This sort of prioritizing was very common; but the women I met (they were very few, I admit) were not submissive, as the following incident that I witnessed in Mecca illustrates:

> In the hallway, we were surprised to smell a "tajine" simmering in the next room. A group of men were staying there who had come on pilgrimage without their wives—a technician from the Ministry of Agriculture, a driver who worked for a hospital in Skhirat, and a cattle breeder-dealer from the Rabat region. They shopped and cooked in turn.
>
> "Goodness, the women had better start cooking!" Abbas remarked to Salah. "We've got everything, for God's sake! Couscous, canned meat, oil, and all sorts of olives. Everything's from Ouezzane—the best!"
>
> We had talked about cooking with the women. Farida, the physician, had argued that our time in Medina should be devoted to prayer, that piety demanded we satisfy ourselves with simple food from the cafeterias. Abbas had insisted that the women, "as in the other groups, could make an effort" to prepare meals. Some Moroccan women did wake up before their men, make breakfast, and tidy the rooms before going off to the mosque. When they had done their morning prayers, they came back and got lunch started before going to the shops.
>
> Salah agreed with Abbas, but he wanted to avoid direct conflict with Farida, a bourgeois lady whose good opinion he sought. As for me, I said little, but every time someone asked, I supported the anti-cooking party. The issue was poisoning relations between women and men, though, and between Abbas and Salah. Because he was illiterate and from a modest background, Abbas felt dominated by Salah, a high-ranking engineer and the owner of a "splendid villa," as he described it. (Hammoudi 2006: 89)

In the many discussions we had in my group, Hajar often surfaced in a leading role. Yet none of the women, two of whom were highly educated (one a medical doctor, the other a lab specialist), accorded her the same status as Ibrahim—though they did not necessarily argue that the two were unequal. When I talked to Lahcen and Fadma, my longtime friends who had gone to Mecca with another group, I found that they had added greatly to their previous knowledge about the story of the hajj and about Hajar. For example, Fadma told me: "By saving Ismael, Hajar saved

Islam"—a statement to which Lahcen responded, "So, now, you want more?" After some laughter, Fadma replied, "What more? . . . Hajar did *jihad* and saved Ismael." We talked about her *jihad,* and Fadma, who frequently expressed opinions and asserted her rights vis-à-vis Lahcen, this time spoke only of her happiness and the peace that the hajj had given her.

No general conclusion can be drawn from these episodes; I introduce them here simply as conversational encounters that reveal both dissent and admiration for Hajar that is framed in very different terms than we find in texts such as Shariati's. Women, dissenting voices, and feminist voices are numerous and powerful across the Muslim world. However, their diversity and the source of their power lie outside the realm of the textual, relying in part on institutional and social dynamics. Finally, women's and men's voices for change articulate new meanings and aspirations from within the Muslim discursive traditions and practices. The latter are not mere disciplines. Often these voices oscillate between submission and self-assertion, as well as engaging in many other registers. As one African American Muslim woman whom Abedi interviewed in Houston made clear, the struggle for institutional and normative change involves shaping new meanings from the scriptures along with concrete plans for social and political action (Fischer and Abedi 1990: 317–19, 326).

EXPERIENCE, ENGAGEMENT, AND ARTICULATION

By "experience" I mean an ethnographic encounter in which the anthropologist meets people as they engage in their own activities. Here I have been trying to highlight certain differences in outcome between textualist strategies and firsthand ethnography in the study of ritual. In this case, the ethnographer deals with the experience of people engaged in the ritual, including his or her own predicament of feeling engaged and distanced at the same time. Such an approach obviously does not take us to the realm of the ineffable; indeed, experience here involves what my interlocutors say and do, as well as what I say and do with them. It also involves our use of nonverbal media. Examples of such media in my study of the hajj ritual are the Kaaba, the cloth of the Kaaba, the black stone, the mosque, the *jamarats* (the columns stoned during the stoning of Satan ritual), sacrificed animals, and the *ihram*. Whatever these nonverbal media may be—media that both convey messages and perform mediation—they are ambiguous, part subject and part object. Experience thus involves interlocution, observation, and action with, around, regarding the nonverbal media.

Experience further involves sharing what the ethnographer infers from interlocution, observation, and action with and around the nonverbal. I borrow from William James the approach by inference, and redirect it toward sharing experiences through communicating my inferences and descriptions to my closest interlocutors, or to others engaged in the same action (in this instance, in the hajj).

Finally, a dynamic such as the one I outline here presumes moments of co-presence of subjectivities in communication, debate, controversies, and conflicts beyond what is possible through simply writing—the reading of frames of meaning, the discursive construction of subjectivities, or the discarding of subjectivities altogether. The engagement of subjectivities, in contrast, promotes the emergence of knowledge of phenomena that the subjects engaged had not consciously grasped. This approach assumes that the ethnographer shares his or her observations, interpretations, fears, and skepticism—that is, a subjectivity—with a counterpart that contests it and is entitled to its own metalanguages. For example, I was repeatedly told or asked in one form or another: "You are far from religion," "Anthropology is a Western science; can't you liberate yourself from it?" or "Why are you here looking at sacrifice while Muslims do it with members of their family?" (The last question I was asked many years ago in the Moroccan High Atlas, while I was studying sacrifice; see Hammoudi 1993.)[4]

Now, consider the difference between theorizing on the basis of a *common* experience (although partial, contested, conflicting, and conflictual), as knowledge in the making, and theorizing on the basis of any version of textualism. The relation between ethnography and theory is especially telling here. It is quite obvious that in Asad's work, as in much contemporary anthropology that employs this brand of textualism, the *surrogate* ethnography never works through engaged experience or pays any heed to action as a process being realized. Instead, it is Mauss's subtle and phe-nomenological observation and writing, in which the *techniques du corps* are seen as imbued with a sense of direction, that Asad turns into disci-plines, excluding all intentionality. In this approach, the relation between ethnography and theory is the same as that of illustration to a set of ideas. The two are tailored to fit each other. Surprise is ruled out; nothing is irre-versible, unexpected, or susceptible to taking unforeseen directions.

This characteristic is heightened when the radical Derridean textual-ism of Fischer and Abedi theorizes on the basis of ethnographic detail drawn from texts. It is possible (and why not?) to mean by ethnography the collection of information on the hajj from some Muslim writers and their rather lofty biographies and autobiographies. But although such collection is useful, it seems to assume a very narrow scope for ethnogra-phy and experience. The writers quoted by Fischer and Abedi rarely nar-rate the hajj as it happened to them and to other pilgrims around them (the most notable exceptions are Abdulai Chenef, a Nigerian writer, and Ali-e Ahmad, an Iranian). There is no evidence of firsthand ethnography in the work beyond Abedi's interviews in Houston, as already men-tioned. Having thus markedly narrowed the scope of what might be called ethnography, Fischer and Abedi comment on it and on what they think the proper relation of ethnography to theory should be. They note the utility of intertwining biography with "ethnographically rich por-traits with historical descriptions of taxation, economy, and their social features," citing the work of Walter Benjamin on Baudelaire; but they also use Benjamin to reflect on the relation between ethnography and theory, pointing to his difference with Adorno: "He insisted (against Theodor Adorno) on not making the ethnographic portraits mere illus-trations of pre-posed theory, but rather on keeping the ethnography close to descriptive reality, on embedding it with traces of theoretical interest, so that in a culminating decisive context, there would come a sudden illumination. Theory should be like a sudden ray of light, but one that prismatically deconstructs, so that one sees its sources and structure. The method of this 'philological attitude' ('unfolding' mean-ings) is a way of bringing the resources immanent in social history to bear on readers" (Fischer and Abedi 1990: 221).

What Fischer and Abedi combine, perhaps unwittingly, is genealogy and deconstruction. Moreover, their approach seems to mistakenly identify both with "unfolding meanings," a process better understood as using fragments of ever deeper description and translation to work in the direction of meaning. Thus, to go back to the theme of Hajar, one may see new meanings of the words *woman, man, marriage, love, sexuality, work,* and *property* unfolding through fragmentary descriptions and repetitions of encounters, losses, and gains. This is not a process that derives much benefit from deconstruction. And to undertake an anthropological study of the hajj, in pursuit of critical knowledge and a theory of ritual, the resources of social history need to be analyzed in the light of the description of current social and political dynamics. Only such an approach can touch the discourses and, I would add, practices of the street, the lower classes, and oral lifeworld, which Fischer and Abedi claim to include in ethnography while merely invoking them rhetorically: they draw on the writings of a Muslim intelligentsia and not on encounters with streets, classes, groups, or men and women actually undertaking the hajj. Finally, one cannot overlook their strategy of using the hajj to illustrate fear of difference and anxieties about the *ummat* discourse, the *ummat*/nation discourse, the secular, the Judeo-Christian, authority, and power.

I end by emphasizing the importance of the notions of *articulation* and *practical articulation*. They direct our attention to concrete situations and institutional structures such as the order of ritual actions, their rules, spatial and temporal arrangements, and so on. Also, they point to what is said or recited (i.e., uttered) within these arrangements and processes. Thus in the realm of language, the notion of articulation implies that language is best approached through instances of its enunciation or speech, rather than as a set of structural differences on the model of phonological binaries. In "Instances of Discourse and Enunciation," Émile Benveniste (1966–74: 1.226, 251) argues that language expresses the positions and positionalities of a speaker. This view is at odds with Foucault's notion of discourse as a medium through which power relations produce speaking subjects. The approach I am arguing for here focuses instead on speech and sentence articulation—saying something to someone about something—which requires an understanding of sense and reference. The said may be clear, but the reference (what is meant in saying) needs interpretation (Ricoeur 1981). Finally, interpretation is a function of time (past and present), as the said is understood only thanks to convention and tradition, and what is meant (reference) is contingent on present and anticipated contexts.

There are objects and objectives articulated in action and interlocution that textualisms of the sort considered here dissolve. People (pilgrims, anthropologists, and others) pursue these objects, and through them many concrete concerns regarding their lives, including power relations as well as the ever-shifting experiences of the self. Above all, I insist on the study of practical articulation, although I do not use the notion of practice in Bourdieu's sense—that is, as opposed to intellectual and intellectualist habitus. More to my point, I have suggested above that what is important is to consider the articulation between written and spoken (oral) forms of discursive traditions in an ongoing practice of debate, discussion, and dynamic rearticulations. For example, oral rearticulations involve literate and illiterate people, rural and urban populations, lower and higher classes, and women and men. These practices of articulation account for the ability of Hagar's voice to unsettle oral discourse while for a time leaving mainly intact important articulations of rituals and institutions.

NOTES

A first version of this paper was edited by Leo Coleman, to whom I extend sincere thanks. I owe a special debt of gratitude to my colleague John Borneman, whose insightful remarks helped me clarify my ideas. In addition, his editing of the final version improved the writing significantly.

1. See, for example, Asad (2003, 2007); also, the essays in Scott and Hirschkind (2006b), especially the editors' introduction (Scott and Hirschkind 2006a), the responses (206–41), and Scott's interview with Asad (Scott 2006).

2. I have recently discussed in some detail (Hammoudi 2007) Bourdieu's concept of habitus in relation to his arguably inadequate ethnographic

practice, especially with regard to conflicting views and practices within the same tradition (in the article, a Kabyle one), as well as with regard to differing perceptions of the environment as it is socially constructed.

3. Bourdieu's elaboration is not without severe limitation, as I have tried to show elsewhere (see Hammoudi 2007).

It is surprising to me that Asad faults Bourdieu for not citing Mauss's famous *techniques du corps* in his exploration of habitus. Scholars generally understand Bourdieu's work to be based, among other things, on Mauss's widely read article of 1936 (republished in a collection of 1950 with a long introduction by Lévi-Strauss).

Also, Bourdieu used and cited Mauss's piece in an article titled "Célibat et condition paysanne" (1962), republished recently in Bourdieu (2002).

4. Here I summarize some aspects of an approach I tried in my work on the hajj (Hammoudi 2005, 2006).

REFERENCES

Abu-Lughod, Lila. 1997. "The Interpretation of Culture(s) after Television." *Representations*, no. 59: 109–34.

Asad, Talal. 1993. *Genealogies of Religion: Discipline and Reasons of Power in Christianity and Islam*. Baltimore: Johns Hopkins University Press.

———. 2003. *Formations of the Secular: Christianity, Islam, Modernity*. Stanford: Stanford University Press.

Barthes, Roland. 1970. *S/Z*. Paris: Seuil.

Benveniste, Émile. 1966–74. *Problèmes de linguistique générale*. 2 vols. Paris: Gallimard.

Bourdieu, Pierre. 1972. *Esquisse d'une théorie de la pratique: Précédé de trois études d'ethnologie kabyle*. Paris: Droz.

———. 2002. *Le bal des célibataires: Crise de la société paysanne en Béarn*. Paris: Éditions du Seuil.

Derrida, Jacques. 1976. *Of Grammatology*. Trans. Gayatri Chakravorty Spivak. Baltimore: Johns Hopkins University Press. [Originally published in French in 1967.]

———. [1978] 2001. *Writing and Difference*. Trans. Alan Bass. London: Routledge. [Originally published in French in 1967.]

———. 1982. *Margins of Philosophy*. Trans. Alan Bass. Chicago: University of Chicago Press. [Originally published in French in 1972.]

Elliott, Andrea. 2005a. "Muslim Group Is Urging Women to Lead Prayers." *New York Times*, March 18, B1.

————. 2005b. "With Women at the Forefront, a Muslim Service Challenges Tradition." *New York Times,* March 19, B3.

Fischer, Michael M. J., and Mehdi Abedi. 1990. *Debating Muslims: Cultural Dialogues in Postmodernity and Tradition.* Madison: University of Wisconsin Press.

Hammoudi, Abdellah. 1993. *The Victim and Its Masks: An Essay on Sacrifice and Masquerade in the Maghreb.* Trans. Paula Wissing. Chicago: University of Chicago Press.

————. 2005. *Une saison à La Mecque: Récit de pèlerinage.* Paris: Seuil.

————. 2006. *A Season in Mecca: Narrative of a Pilgrimage.* Trans. Pascale Ghazaleh. New York: Hill and Wang.

————. 2007. "Phénoménologie et ethnographie, à propos de l'*habitus* kabyle chez Bourdieu." *L'Homme* 184 (October): 47–84.

Irigaray, Luce. 1985. *This Sex Which Is Not One.* Trans. Catherine Porter with Carolyn Burke. Ithaca: Cornell University Press.

Latour, Bruno. 1993. *We Have Never Been Modern.* Trans. Catherine Porter. Cambridge, MA: Harvard University Press.

Lavie, Smadar. 1990. *The Poetics of Military Occupation: Mzeina Allegories of Bedouin Identity under Israeli and Egyptian Rule.* Berkeley: University of California Press.

Lévi-Strauss, Claude. 1963. "Introduction: History and Anthropology." Chapter 1 of *Structural Anthropology.* Trans. Claire Jacobson and Brooke Grundfest Schoepf. Vol. 1. New York: Basic Books. [Originally published in French in 1958.]

Mauss, Marcel. [1936] 1950. "Les techniques du corps." In *Sociologie et anthropologie.* Paris: P.U.F.

Messick, Brinkley Morris. 1993. *The Calligraphic State: Textual Domination and History in a Muslim Society.* Berkeley: University of California Press.

Ricoeur, Paul. 1981. *Hermeneutics and the Human Sciences: Essays on Language, Action, and Interpretation.* Ed. and trans. John B. Thompson. Cambridge: Cambridge University Press.

Scott, David. 2006. "Appendix: The Trouble of Thinking: An Interview with Talal Asad." In Scott and Hirschkind 2006b.

Scott, David, and Charles Hirschkind. 2006a. "Introduction: The Anthropological Skepticism of Talal Asad." In Scott and Hirschkind 2006b.

————, eds. 2006b. *Powers of the Secular Modern: Talal Asad and His Interlocutors.* Stanford: Stanford University Press.

THREE The Suicidal Wound and Fieldwork among Canadian Inuit

Lisa Stevenson

Once, while sitting by a smoking fire of arctic heather and drift-wood, a young boy, Paul,[1] told me the story of his best friend's death. He was racing his snowmobile when he hit a guide wire. It caught him at the neck. Paul had been to the hospital to visit his friend, and his friend had tried to speak to him but no words would come out.

Our conversation around the fire soon moved to other deaths and other stories. But a little while later, reflecting on what happens after death, Paul remarked, "My sister used to say my uncle came back to life as a raven, and that raven is living behind our house."

"Does she still think that?" I asked.

"I don't know. It's still there."

The raven is still there. Is the raven that lives behind the house really Paul's dead uncle? Perhaps, perhaps not. But it's still there.

In what follows I will reflect on the status of the raven in fieldwork and how we come to relate to it as a figure of a kind of productive and even hopeful uncertainty, one that stubbornly remains (*it's still there*) even as it refuses to be neatly resolved. I want to think, then, about the possibility in fieldwork of listening for hesitation—listening for that which persistently disrupts the security of what is known for sure. Doing so entails taking uncertainty as a legitimate ethnographic object.[2] Fieldwork in uncertainty would be less about collecting facts than about paying attention to the moments when the facts falter. Such attention to moments of doubt, of hesitation, dissolves the professional distance between the ethnographer and her subjects. For a moment both are thrown into the same existential frame: it is not simply that I am documenting the uncommon things my young friend believes, but I am arrested by his uncertainty. I am arrested by the fact that he may never know for sure whether the raven is his dead uncle, but something about the raven's *thereness* is important to him. I would suggest that such uncertainty must be experienced rather than simply known. It also seems that doubt, like pain (Das 2007), requires not resolution but acknowledgment; and thus in the case of my young friend, his doubt, and my acknowledgment of it, implicates us in a mutual project of discovering the world.[3]

Fieldwork in this sense, as an act of listening for uncertainty, blurs any easy distinction between the epistemological and the methodological. It becomes a practice of the self in which, in the interest of understanding another, we allow ourselves to be shaken, displaced from our customary dispositions and beliefs, even from our familiar ways of loving. This raises a series of theoretical questions: What do we know for sure and what is persistently in question? How does doubt manifest itself, become material, in the process of fieldwork? When does certainty preclude certain conversations, preclude other kinds of knowledge? How do we move forward without certainty, acting as if particular things were true, even as we continue to test their truth?

LIFE IN QUESTION

Fieldwork often occurs in the shadow of discursive certainties—ways of knowing and acting in the world that work to prevent doubt or uncertainty from emerging. In my own research among Inuit youth during a suicide epidemic, I was struck by how quickly attention turns to preserving life. The value of life becomes the ground from which all efforts and arguments stem. Elsewhere (L. Stevenson 2005a) I have described the colonizer's consuming desire that the colonized *cooperate* in the mutual task of survival. In the Canadian Arctic this desire for cooperation is most ardently given voice in what I call the suicide apparatus—the network of researchers, caregivers, teachers, and bureaucrats that have joined forces to confront suicide and keep Inuit alive.[4] The individuals who make up this apparatus are caring, thoughtful people dedicated to improving the lives of Inuit in Nunavut. In what follows I don't want to diminish the intensity of their efforts or the decency of their intentions. I was often humbled by the energy and perseverance of people who work in this field. I do want to point out, however, what I consider to be a blind spot of their discourse. The self-evident truth of the suicide apparatus, its unquestioned certainty, is that life is worth living, that life itself is its own value. As colonial subjects Inuit must come to understand that death is not a thinkable option, that death is instead the unfortunate consequence of aging or diseased bodies. Inuit must cooperate by staying alive—or at least by valuing life above all.

Yet death, by accident, violence, or suicide, is something Inuit teenagers know intimately. While undertaking my fieldwork in Iqaluit—the capital of Nunavut, one of Canada's northern territories—on Baffin Island, I worked closely with a group of about twenty Inuit youth. Several of them attempted suicide while I was there. All of them had witnessed suicides or suicidal acts in their lifetimes. One of them was constantly asking to die. A 13-year-old girl I worked with was raped and murdered. Rather than being a philosophical decision or a liminal act, suicide had become part of their everyday fabric of life, and death was something that had to be attended to—again and again.

Toward the end of my fieldwork in Iqaluit I received a letter from a young Inuk man named Jacques. Composed in a state of exhaustion after he had spent days pleading with his 17-year-old girlfriend not to kill herself, the letter read: "How do we know that suicide is not the answer? Has anyone talked to people who have committed suicide? How do we know their lives aren't better now? . . . I guess we'll never know until we see all the people that have died." Jacques' dilemma— "How do we know that suicide is not the answer?"—left me wondering just what the unstated question might be to which suicide serves as a possible answer. For most professionals concerned with Inuit suicide, there is no question. Their goal is straightforward: prevent death and maintain life. To imagine doing otherwise, even for a moment, would be to think life differently.

Yet thinking life differently may be crucial when Inuit youth suicide is described both as epidemic (M. Stevenson 1996) and as a "routine part of life" (Brown 2001). The suicide rate among Inuit males ages 15 to 24 is almost 40 times higher than the Canadian average for that age group (Hicks 2006: 19). Each year there seem to be more suicide task forces and conferences, political campaigns and prevention trainings. But, as a long-term resident and politician of Nunavut shouted at a group of mental health practitioners and civil servants gathered to discuss suicide in a circumpolar perspective, "You experts don't have the answers. We don't know what to do about suicide. If we did we would be doing it!" Despite all the attention and resources directed toward this issue, the suicide rate among Inuit youth in Nunavut continues to rise and Inuit have, to a large degree, lost faith in the ability of professionals to help.

This sense of defeat around combating suicide is a crucial component of the lifeworlds of Inuit and non-Inuit living in Nunavut. Suicide prevention campaigns constantly rally people to have faith, and to make a difference. But for anyone who lives with it, including the anthropologist, suicide is no longer just a problem about which something must be done but a wound. As a medical anthropologist, committed to listening to those often ignored by the suicide literature,[5] I soon became less concerned with improving the techniques of suicide prevention and more interested in understanding the affective and normative fields in which suicide, and the "lifesaving" interventions it inspires, occurs. I hope, ultimately, that such an approach clears the ground for an alternative conceptualization of what it might mean to attend to the pain of others.

Danny, a youth I worked with, recounted his experience with suicide. From his words, which pour from his mouth, we can get a sense of the way suicide saturates his lifeworld:

> I seen somebody suicide. I couldn't do nothing. I tried stopping it. I was too late. My cousin. She killed herself at . . . our old house. That time I went there . . . I can hear somebody from upstairs crying or something. So I started going up, thinking that nobody's there. I was kind of scared. Nobody's there. And then when I went upstairs I see my cousin holding a gun on her face. Shotgun. I tried stopping it. She pulled the trigger. I ran out of the house. I was scared. I couldn't do anything no more.
>
> . . . I couldn't talk. I couldn't move. I couldn't do nothing then. Too scared. I didn't leave my room for three days straight. 'Till the funeral we went. They were telling me to come out. Go eat. I couldn't move, I couldn't do nothing.

Danny continued telling his story a little later:

> I almost killed someone too before. My sister's boyfriend. He was beating up my sister. They wouldn't open the door when I tried going there. I could hear my sister crying, shouting, getting beat up. So I just kicked the door open. Then I grabbed a harpoon. And then I started hitting him on the head and on the back. All over with the harpoon. Just started hitting him. [The description continues.]
>
> I went to my grandparents. I was thinking about it. Long time. Then I just started saying, I should just kill myself. I'm going to go to jail for sure. I should just kill myself. Something like that. . . .
>
> Then I started talking to my grandparents telling them that I almost killed my sister's boyfriend. I was trying to beat him up to death. And they started freaking out and they started telling me lots of shit about killing people's no good. And I just told them I'm going to kill myself. They started telling me not to think like that.
>
> I just told them I can't help it. After what I've seen I can't help it. He was trying to stab my sister. My sister too.

A few years after the incidents he recounted, and during the time I was in Iqaluit, both Jacques and Danny participated in a suicide-prevention training course. Danny was really proud of himself for sticking it out, for hauling himself out of bed to get there every day. After the course was over, Jacques told me a little bit about their experience. He told me about the time the organizers had been "talking about how lots of people when they commit suicide, they think their life will get better. When they said that, Danny just looked at me and we both said, 'It probably will,' and we just started cracking up. Everybody else was just looking at us. We couldn't stop laughing."

Suicide prevention functions as a structuring discourse in Iqaluit. It inflects much of the daily work that goes on. A kind of sociality has sprung up around suicide prevention, which some Inuit see as a white person's club. Government bureaucrats (the large majority of whom are transplants from southern Canada) have described themselves ironically as in a competition to see who "cares the most" about suicidal Inuit. Indeed, all government departments are charged with "suicide proofing" their programs. So intense is the media attention surrounding the issue that when a national suicide prevention conference was held in Iqaluit, one woman guiltily confided in me that it seemed as if there were "a suicide cruise ship just cruising through town."

The laughter of these two young men challenges the confidence of that discourse. It indexes a darker and perhaps less certain way of thinking about life and death, one that such suicide prevention trainers usually disavow. After what Danny has experienced, it is not so clear that life always trumps the possibility of a life after death. The status of any future is uncertain, and not necessarily bright.

BRIGHTER FUTURES

Working amid a suicide epidemic I came to believe that our relationship to "tomorrow," and to the future in general, reveals much about "the hold which life has" on us—to redeploy Bronislaw Malinowski's ([1922] 1961: 25) phrase. In fact, I would propose a reading of Canadian colonialism that suggests that the transvaluation of "tomorrow" was the ground on which occupation was sought. Canadian bureaucrats of the postwar period were preoccupied with getting Inuit to promise to come to work *tomorrow,* to save their money and food for *tomorrow's* scarcity, and to generally live their lives as if tomorrow were something to bank on. To take just one example, the *Book of Wisdom for Eskimo,* published in 1947, promised to teach Inuit "how to make your rifles and boats last a long time, how to save the food animals from becoming scarce, and how to plan for times of scarcity" (Ford 1947: 1)—as if Inuit hadn't been living with periods of scarcity for generations. Even today, the brochure for Canada's National Aboriginal Foundation's scholarship fund is titled "Building Brighter Futures." In its opening paragraphs, it declares: "Futures don't 'just happen' . . . they are created through hard work, creativity and perseverance" (National Aboriginal Achievement Association 2006: 2). I will argue, however, that the work ethic that is being promoted in both cases relies on a particular relationship between self and future that Inuit do not always adopt. That is, in order to make a promise about the future—for example, that one will be at the meeting at 9 A.M. two months from today—one must have the sense that the future is predictable and that one's current self will extend into that future.[6]

It was an Inuit friend, Daniel Tulugaq, who eloquently described for me the introduction of calculable tomorrows and committed futures into Inuit lives: "The school had a big effect because everything we were taught in school was *qallunaat*—you know—white history. And the white people did a lot of amazing stuff and here the Inuit did *nothing*. It wasn't taught that way, but subconsciously it seems like it was. You know, Inuit never had anything. We didn't know nothing. . . . We didn't *do* anything with our lives until *qallunaat* came and saved us."

Not doing something with one's life is read by the *qallunaat* (non-Inuit) as a failure of character rather than as a divergent sense of self or of one's relationship to the future. Arguably, however, the very idea of "doing something" with one's life depends on a coherent, stable self projected into a manipulable future—something that would have been nonsensical to Inuit in precolonial times and still is rejected by many Inuit today.

In a suicide epidemic, tomorrow is always at stake. Suicide is an affront to the government's promise of brighter, happier, healthier futures. Suicide stands as a rejection of any claim the future makes on the present. Consequently, plans for the future are often conceptualized as buffers against suicide. A psychiatrist from Toronto, for example, some-one with a long history of doing consultations in the North, once told me that the most disturbing thing about his psychiatric interviews with Inuit youth was that when you asked them what they would be doing in five years very few had a ready answer. Such commitments—contracts with the future—would, it is hoped, shield Inuit youth from the pain and dis-appointment of the present.

After my conversation with the psychiatrist I began to ask youth about such plans. In an extended conversation with Pauloosie, I tried without success to probe him for details about his future, promises to himself about what he would become: "So when you are 90 years old, an elder . . . what's going to make you feel like you've led a good life?"

"I don't know. I'll wait and see."

"You're 18. When you are 20 . . . do you have any plans for what you want to be doing, where you want to be?"

"It will just happen, I'll just wait and see what happens."

Struck by his apparent lack of imagination about the future, I pressed him even more: "Well, what do you eventually want to *be?*"

"Just myself and be happy and not do bad things, just have a good life and teach young kids, and, like teach them, land skills and stuff."

In contrast to these telegraphic refusals of my questions, when I asked him whether he got bored when he was out on the land, he was eloquent and assertive. "Nope. Out hunting is a lot different than staying home," he said, and after pausing to reflect he continued: "Like when we go out hunting, it's more peaceful and more quiet and there's not that many people out there, just us, and we're all trying to have fun and try and catch some caribou or seals or anything, or go berry picking or go for a walk or something. And play some games and listen to music or talk on the *uva* [bush radio] to your relatives or friends."

One of the concepts that the colonial administrators conveyed to Inuit was that lives were something you did something with: they were entities to be constructed, manipulated, and, importantly, projected into the future. For Pauloosie, life reveals itself rather than being anxiously chore-ographed. Out on the land you are not doing anything with your life. Life is unfolding in the company of a community of family and friends.

A desire to secure the future, for ourselves or those we care about, is not something from which fieldworkers are exempt. Even setting a time and a place for an interview anchors the future to the present. Peter Kulchyski, who has worked for many years in Pangnirtung, describes a scenario familiar to ethnographers working among the Inuit: "'Can I interview you?' '*Ii* [Yes], but not today, try me tomorrow.'" When the ethnographer returns the following day, he discovers that the person to be interviewed has "gone 'onto the land' for three weeks" (2006: 160).[7] Kulchyski, in his interpretation, focuses on the fact that perhaps *yes* did not really mean yes, something that is certainly often the case. It is also possible that *tomorrow* was not a promise, but a marker of radical uncertainty. Who really knows where I'll be or what I'll be doing tomorrow? Thus the significance of the familiar phrase *Aamai qauppatqai*—"Who knows, maybe tomorrow?" Tomorrow remains in the realm of possibility and uncertainty, that for which I can give no account, that for which I am ultimately *not* responsible. Planning the future, then, is not the same as being open to its multiple possibilities.

"Time," as Jaypeetee Arnakak, an Inuk policy analyst and a good friend explained, "is not an object—there is no term for 'time' as such in Inuktitut." And planning "in real Inuktitut" means something more like "if the conditions are right." Time is simply not "subject to personal will and power." Rather, as Arnakak puts it, "dynamics beyond anybody's control are at play, and an Inuk would . . . wait for conditions to become right" before embarking on any project. For Inuit, the future is often both uncertain and unknowable.

What difference does it make if one refuses to make promises about tomorrow? or fails to keep them? or never intends to keep them in the first place? What kind of an image of self and what kind of possible worlds open onto such a relationship to tomorrow? I want to argue that the way we think about the future is linked to the way we think about death. To promise, or even just to plan, is a way of flouting death. It is in this sense that suicide may also be read as a radical refusal to make (or keep) a promise.

Thus while we can (and often do) talk at length about a future-orientation that might be a "risk factor" for suicide, the very discourse of risk remains caught in a temporal orientation that presumes the solidity of a self being projected into the calculable future. The modern "denial of death" (Ariès 1974; Becker 1973; Freud 1953) serves to consolidate a particular sense of self, one that extends confidently and indefinitely into the future. Sigmund Freud described this attitude as "living psychologically beyond our means" (1953: 299). Yet epidemiological and even, it must be said, anthropological understandings of suicide rarely escape such a framework—seeing death as preventable and viewing present selves as, in some sense, "guaranteed" or "insured" by their orientation to a risk-reduced future.

What different shades does a life assume when it is not calculated to evade death but rather is improvised around death? What happens to well-laid plans when tomorrow is no longer taken for granted? Rachel Qitsualik (2004), an Inuit columnist, observes, "It was being at peace with death that enabled Inuit to be at peace in life. In feeling that death was a reality, inevitability, for every living thing, they were free to maximize the quality of their current existence." Qitsualik writes in the past tense, marking this way of experiencing death as "traditional." The youth I worked with, while very much a part of medical modernity, continue to see death as beyond their control. One young man told me,

> It's healthy. Death is healthy. Everybody is meant to die sooner or later. Everybody was born, so everybody's got to die. Nobody's going to live forever. So it is healthy. If you die, you die. You can't really do anything about it. . . . No offense—but you've lived your life, now it's somebody else's. That's why we have namesakes. I was named after my grandpa Jamesie, he died, so I was born, it's my turn. When I die my descendants will be named after me. I don't know—it's *healthy*.

What's more, the possibility of immortality—becoming a raven, living on through one's name—means that suicide is never simply about the absence of meaning. The dead continue to act on the world.

UNE AUTRE ÉCOUTE

In addition to engaging in discussions about what to "do" and how to "solve" the suicide epidemic, I have been trying to listen with a different ear, to provide what Stefania Pandolfo calls "une autre écoute" (2006: 262–63), as she describes a way of listening that does not fix the other in place but is open to the possibility of questioning, of change, of reformulating lines of debate. "Thinking life differently" is how I formulate this.

As I have shown, one way of beginning to rethink suicide in the Canadian Arctic is to place it in the context of the colonial attempt to enforce particular ways of thinking about tomorrow, in which the present is ransomed to the future. For the Inuit, colonized by a bureaucratic state that is preoccupied with planning the future, suicide may be seen as a response to a colonial obsession with the future—a response that calls attention to the poverty and pain of the "now." It is a response to the pain of living in the future's wreckage—a now that becomes unlivable.

It became evident to me that presuming the value of life, staging it as the ultimate good, could be as dangerous as negating it. If listening to the pain in the lives of suicidal youth is merely a means to the end of keeping Inuit youth alive, then there is no authentic listening. Listening—when life is radically in question—means taking uncertainty about life very seriously. Only when I was able to hold life as a value in abeyance could I listen more faithfully, and the outlines of a more indistinct, perhaps darker, and definitely more uncertain way of thinking came to the surface.

For instance, Saila, an 18-year-old who sometimes wanted to die, described for me a series of deaths that had marked her life. First her neighbor, Sarah, committed suicide. One month later, Saila's own brother was involved in a shoot-out with the police. One month after that, the daughter of the woman who committed suicide died: "I don't know—from thinking too much or something. Her temple exploded or something." Saila continues with the litany of deaths. "And then one month later it went back to my house, that thing happened with my brother, that accident [in which he died]. That was freaky."

"Completely freaky," I agree.

"It just went from my house to next door, to my other next door, and then back to my house."

"What was going on?"

"I don't know."

Saila never says precisely how these deaths were connected, or even that they definitely are, but she does say that it was "freaky" that the deaths ricocheted between three adjacent houses over a period of months. In this description, the suicide of Sarah was not separated from her older brother's act of violence or from the tragic deaths of her younger brother and Sarah's daughter. Instead Saila talks about something freaky that came over those houses. What exactly that is—what it means to be freaky—is left untheorized, unresolved. It is clear, however, that death is not fully in our control, that death is more like a visitation or a possession from elsewhere, something that comes over a body, a family, or even a home. It is a question not about knowing or believing x about death, but about pointing to the facts, the events, the ravens that don't fit into our established ways of knowing.

That freaky quality of death also pervaded the dreams of the youth I worked with. Such dreams were offered to me in the same way they were offered to other family and friends—as events to be weighed, considered, reflected on. Nuurlu tells me about a dream she had after her cousin killed herself.

"I had a dream I was in this dark place and there was a couple of people, they're like, 'Nuurlu, help me!'" She describes being surrounded by, and tangled in, thorn bushes. Her cousin and a friend were hiding behind the bushes. "They were like, 'Nuurlu, help me, help me, please, get me outta here!' And there was this deep scary voice laughing freakily. And they kept saying, 'Help me, Nuurlu!' And after, I dunno, this freaky voice said, 'Nuurlu, kill yourself, your cousin did.' That was fuckin' scary."

In this dream, it is the voice calling her to commit suicide that is "freaky" and "fuckin' scary," a voice that seems to have a kind of power to get you to do things you don't necessarily want to do, or don't fully understand. What emerges from these narratives is unsettling. Rather than unquestioningly feeling a duty to live, which Hannah Arendt (1958) saw as characteristic of the Christian era, Inuit youth sometimes feel an obligation to die—to answer the call of family and friends who have appeared to them in dreams asking them to join them in the afterworld. For most Inuit youth, while "life" as an abstraction has little value, specific relationships to others, both dead and alive, matter profoundly.

Furthermore, many Inuit youth understand quite well what is expected of them, that their duty to live runs parallel to their duty to attend school, to stay away from drugs, to plan for a brighter future. Even the most despairing can recite the axioms of suicide prevention and count the signs of suicidality on their fingers. It is in this context that Monica—a 13-year-old girl who lives with her alcoholic uncle and whose friend was murdered minutes after they parted for the night—can say to me, almost pleadingly, "It's not that I'm suicidal, it's just that I don't want to live anymore."

Monica refuses the language of suicide prevention and searches for another language to describe what she experiences. *I don't want to live anymore.* The distinction Monica makes between being suicidal and not wanting to live is subtle, yet it is this distinction that removes her, if only temporarily, from the suicide apparatus. The distance she achieves from the suicide apparatus allows her to acknowledge the ways in which her young life is marked by pain, anger, and injustice. It is not the possibility of death that she wants removed, but her pain in life.

Without suggesting that it should be otherwise, I simply want to point out the intense policing of the suicidal body. Not only is every Inuit youth seen as potentially suicidal, but there is also a desire for constant surveillance of the suicidal body. The director of the youth center admitted to me that for her, the most important suicide prevention programming would be someone available twenty-four hours a day. She, understandably, hated having to go home without being able to hand suicidal kids off to someone else.

For frontline youth workers, the fear of someone dying on their watch is terrifying. One of the aspects of suicide interventions that makes them so complicated is that the caregiver, whether he be a doctor, teacher, or school counselor, is constantly faced with the brute fact of the agency of another human being. That is, in the case of suicide disease is marked primarily by the intention to carry out a particular *action* rather than by an organic imbalance or the deviation from a norm. One way to manage the uncertainty of such an encounter (in which health is defined negatively, as the absence of an action or its desire) is to have a set of procedures ready that, if carried out, will in some sense absolve the practitioner of any "responsibility" toward the patient's future actions. While I was doing fieldwork, various government agencies were working on protocols that enumerated the steps for workers to take when confronted with person at risk for suicide and what to do after a suicide occurs. These are important attempts to find a way out of the chaos of a world where suicide is an ever-present possibility. Such protocols are also an example of what Charles Taylor (1994: 174) calls the "bureaucratic ways of proceeding," characteristic of modern state forms. These bureaucratic ways of proceeding, which lift the burden of decision or responsibility from us, are generally designed to mitigate the failure of the state or its agents.

Suicide prevention efforts, along with attempting to reduce the risk of self-harm, generally strive to ensure that practitioners cannot be implicated in the death of their charges. In my experience, Inuit suicidality has much to do with excess and repetition, and the crisis it represents usually occurs after the procedures and protocols have long since been followed, after the nurses and doctors have already been seen. How to proceed is terrifyingly uncertain. That is, even when I insisted in desperation that my young friends visit a doctor, to relieve me of some of the responsibility I felt, things didn't always go the way I anticipated.

STATE OF EMERGENCY

We were finally sitting in the hospital waiting room, which was actually two banks of molded plastic chairs in the middle of a hallway. There was a small television hanging from the ceiling, its volume muted. Faces of Michael Jackson were spinning past, black hair against a pasty whiteness of skin. Beside me was a young girl, 13, a headband pulling her hair tightly back across her forehead. Beside her was her brother. She had pleaded with him not to leave her, not to commit suicide, and had insisted on coming to the hospital. Behind a countertop, two male staff in scrubs were standing hunched over a computer, talking in the languid cadences that mark an after-hours shift—waiting only for the time to pass between emergencies.

But even as they talked, they were observing us with both blank glances and short furtive looks—deftly preserving the required sense of distance and disinterest while consuming our pain: assessing, cataloging and ranking it. Yet for all the distress collected in our bodies—the one asking to die, his younger sister pulling him back, and me, wanting a reprieve from responsibility—we were not an emergency. Looking back on that time, months later, Jacques would say, "Everything was going wrong with me. Everything. I wanted to die. I told everybody, 'I don't care, I wanna die, I wanna die, I wanna die, I wanna die.'"

"And do you think you really did?"

"I think I really did. I think I *really, really* wanted to die."

When I arrived at Jacques' house earlier that night the door had been locked. I drew my breath sharply. Doors aren't usually locked. People don't usually have to knock. But the dog must have barked, because someone came to open the door. Jacques was sitting in the dark, listening to a song by Ja Rule called "Murder Reigns." Playing it over and over. He told me about writing 112 letters to MuchMusic[8] in Toronto, describing why he wanted to meet Ja Rule: "He writes exactly what I feel." Jacques rips his suicide note out of his notebook and hands it to me. It says that no one's to blame and that he already misses his sister. The music continues. We listen:

> What can I say? I was raised as an only child, lonely
> Poppa disowned me, so the streets raised me
> To call me crazy is not unheard of
> Now it's gonna reign down murder. (Ja Rule 2002)

That wasn't the first time, though. A few days earlier, Jacques telephoned me at home. "If I tell you something, will you promise not to tell the others?"

"Yeah, what?"

"I just tried to commit suicide."

"What do you mean? Why?"

He tells me more specifically that he tried to hang himself. Twice. The rope broke both times. He is telling me that he won't go to the training the next day because of the marks around his neck. His back and arm are bruised from falling. His left side is numb, and he can't see properly out of his left eye.

"Can I call an ambulance?"

"No. I don't want to go there, they're going to know what I did."

"I'm coming to get you."

"Okay."

When I get there he is waiting for me at the door. I don't even have to honk. I try to hug him when I see him but it's awkward. Without saying much, we drive around. I know he likes driving around; he's told me that before. We go to Apex, then toward the dump, but it's too dark, out Federal Road, around the Road to Nowhere. I ask, "What were you thinking?"

"I wasn't thinking. I wasn't thinking anything."

At a certain point, his mood starts to shift; he starts talking about girls, some I know, some I don't. His voice is metallic, matching the warehouses and barking dogs we are driving by. He keeps talking about girls, about the size of their boobs and the ways he flirted with them. I am disgusted and yet I let him go on talking. This is about desire, after all. Then I change the subject.

The next day, as we walked together to a friend's house for caribou stew, he told me about the dreams he was having of the angel of death. The angel of death appeared in his dreams every night telling him that he, Jacques, was next. I looked up at the fingernail moon and the stars as he spoke: "Every time I closed my eyes I could see him. Whether it was just because my head was playing mind tricks or whatever. I realized that if I died I wouldn't have *anything*. I wouldn't even have family, I wouldn't have my deceased family. I wouldn't have anything. Nothing. Except death. That's the only thing I would have. And that's where he came from. Because I didn't think I would have anything if I died."

We were taking the shortcut to Tundra Valley through the cemetery. The white crosses looked bluish in the night. As we walked up the hill from the cemetery, he told me that this was his favorite place to come and sit and think. He pointed out a huge swath of northern lights that looks like a snowmobile trail.

At that moment a small plane banked before going in for a landing at the airstrip. It caught us in its lights. We stopped, unable to see anything, except the plane heading toward us. At what seemed like the last minute it banked left against the cliff.

It was very cold, minus fifty with the windchill, and Jacques told me he could feel his nose and ears getting frostbitten.

"It don't matter, it happens all the time. I just feel a little tingling."

"Doesn't it swell up?"

"Sometimes, but it's okay." So we kept walking, the granular snow blowing like sand, creating eddies of snow. We don't say anything. Later he draws the angel of death on a small piece of paper. A man with no feet, carrying a scythe, in a hooded dress. "It wasn't just a voice in my head. It was someone telling me something. You know what I mean? Maybe that sounds crazy."

Once, as a teenager, Jacques walked in on his mother and one of her boyfriends. They were smoking up.

> I walked in the house and I started shouting at her, "All you want to do is be with different guys, all you want to do is smoke up. All you want to do is drink." She started yelling at me in front of that guy. Started to shout that I was an accident, that I shouldn't have even been born. I said, "Well, that's your fuckin' fault, you wanted to be a slut, you wanted to be this and that." By that time, that guy tried to get involved and that's when I stopped caring. The cops came and I spent the night in jail. The only thought that was going around in my head is why should I be here? I was an accident. I should just leave.

Jacques' mother had been in Montreal, going to high school, staying with her mother, Jacques' grandmother, who had moved to Montreal to be with her boyfriend. When Jacques was eleven months old, his mother decided to return to Iqaluit to take a job at the Frobisher Inn. His grandmother pleaded with her not to leave, not to bring up her grandson in "that shithole." She would adopt him, care for him herself. But Jacques' mother wouldn't listen. She left Montreal for Iqaluit as fast as she could, taking her newborn baby with her. A few months later, the police found his grandmother's body by the side of the road leading out of Montreal.

Jacques learned what had happened to his grandmother by chance on a visit to Montreal. He had been hanging out at the mall, and out of the blue a woman came up to him and asked what his name was. He told her and she said she had known his grandmother. They sat down in the food court and started to talk.

She told me all these stories about my grandmother that I didn't know. And one of the stories that she told me was that they were out drinking one night at the Legion in Montreal and apparently my grandmother used to love darts, she always used to play darts. And she was at the Legion with that friend that night and told that friend that she wanted to come see me, and my mother. So that night, when the Legion closed, she starts hitchhiking to Ottawa, because it would be cheaper to get a plane ticket from Ottawa to Iqaluit, instead of Montreal to Iqaluit. So as she was hitchhiking—nobody really knows how far she made it—and apparently she was . . . when she was hitchhiking . . . she was hit-and-run. So I never got to meet my grandmother, and from my understanding, she died because she wanted to come and spend time with her grandson.

Jacques knew what to tell the doctor. He knew that if he said he wanted to kill himself—if he spoke of the angel of death—that he would end up confined to a hospital bed. He had been there before, had long since regaled me with stories of breaking into the medicine cabinet, overpowering the guard to get at the drugs. After he ingested them, "You could see the whites of my eyes." His stomach had had to be pumped, after a tussle with the guards from the front door who had been called in for reinforcement. The bravado of the story erased any shame.

He didn't want to spend the night in the hospital again. Therefore he had to pull himself together, make a lighthearted joke to the doctor, focus on his lack of sleep (if only he could get enough, things would be okay), on his girlfriend leaving him (really it made him feel like shit), on the predictability of his emotional turmoil.

Of course, anyone would feel like that in your shoes. What about some pills to help you sleep?

Yeah. That sounds good. How many do I take?

Two tonight, and I'll give you enough for three more nights. That should do the trick. Come back if you're still feeling bad.

Yeah. Okay.

Before I knew it, we were walking back down the hill we had climbed, expectantly, just an hour before, six pills in a package tucked into Jacques' inner pocket. I think about the way people say, after the fact, wracked by guilt, "Oh, I wish we had known, I wish he had said something"; mostly it isn't that he never said anything but that he was always saying it, and that the saying turned into a drone, which had no meaning except exhaustion, which became the background of life. It's not that we never knew—it's that we always knew, and so it didn't seem real.

There we were. The irrepressible Jacques, alternately dreaming and then nightmaring. The absurdly hopeful fieldworker, who could no longer say why she was there. A young girl, who was supposed to be at school the next morning, going with her brother to the hospital.

After accompanying Jacques to the hospital I still could not be certain he wouldn't commit suicide. In the place of hope there was something else. We had spent ourselves, and in that there was a solidarity. A going and a coming that had not had any describable effect. But each of us knew that the other was willing somehow and that we could be together in the face of another night, with thin northern lights and dry powdered snow, dogs barking, snowmobiles revving. Late at night, without any emergency except as a state of being.

.   .   .   .   .

As I came to know Jacques, Danny, Monica, Nuurlu, and Saila, I came to love them and, in the process, to desire their life. Fieldwork thus became a mutual project of reflection on the impenetrable residues of daily life— the things that persist, like the raven, in their uncertainty. I soon came to believe that when staying alive becomes an end in itself, and the good life is seen merely as a means to that end, a distinctive feature of being human is obscured—that we live with regard to someone or something, or, in Martin Heidegger's sense, that existence entails taking a stand on one's being (Dreyfus 1991).[9] In the face of suicide, this has led me to ask whether it is possible to articulate my own desire for the life of an other without making that desire an imperative, allowing that other to risk his or her life. It has also led me to ask whether there are different affective and political bonds to be formed—different ways of loving that presume neither the certainty of life as ultimate value nor the discreteness of life and death.

NOTES

This research was funded by a Social Sciences Research Council International Dissertation Field Research Fellowship and a National Science Foundation Dissertation Improvement Grant, as well as a Hornaday Fellowship from the University of California, Berkeley. This article has benefited tremendously from conversations with John Borneman, Parvis Ghassem-Fachandi, Byron Good, Mary-Jo Good, Nancy Scheper-Hughes, and Lawrence Cohen, as well as the encouragement of Abdellah Hammoudi. I am especially grateful for the insightful comments of John Borneman and Stefania Pandolfo. Eduardo Kohn's patience and critical insight have made this chapter far better than it would have been without his generous help. Finally, I want to thank the Inuit youth who shared their lives and stories with me. I hope they will recognize what they taught me in these pages.

1. Throughout this essay, names and identifying details have been changed, except in the case of Jaypeetee Arnakak.

2. This is not to say that uncertainty is the only or most important possible object of ethnography but simply that recognizing it and taking it seriously as an ethnographic object opens up a whole world beyond the "factual" and implicates the ethnographer in the testing of reality.

3. In the same vein, Good et al. provide an important description of how narrative both "explores the indeterminacy of reality and stimulates a comparable exploration on the part of the reader" (1991: 838).

4. A more detailed analysis of this suicide apparatus, including a discussion of its historical emergence, can be found in L. Stevenson (2005a).

5. One of the ways Inuit youth are ignored by the literature is by being transformed into bearers of risk. I am advocating a different kind of visibility, one that is attentive to the complex discursive worlds in which Inuit youth live and imagine their lives.

6. Nietzsche claims that to make such a promise about tomorrow, "Man himself must first of all have become *calculable, regular, necessary,* even in his own image of himself" (1967: 58).

7. For clarity, capitalization has been added to Kulchyski's original.

8. MuchMusic is a Canadian cable television channel dedicated to music and music-related programs.

9. Dreyfus (1991: 23) writes that for Heidegger, "To exist is to take a stand on what is essential about one's being and to be defined by that stand."

REFERENCES

Arendt, Hannah. 1958. *The Human Condition*. Chicago: University of Chicago Press.

Ariès, Philippe. 1974. *Western Attitudes toward Death: From the Middle Ages to the Present*. Trans. Patricia M. Ranum. Baltimore: Johns Hopkins University Press.

Becker, Ernest. 1973. *The Denial of Death*. New York: Free Press.

Brown, DeNeen L. 2001. "Culture Corrosion in Canada's North: Forced into the Modern World, Indigenous Inuit Struggle to Cope." *Washington Post*, July 16, A1+.

Das, Veena. 2007. "Language and Body: Transactions in the Construction of Pain." In *Life and Words: Violence and the Descent into the Ordinary*. Berkeley: University of California Press.

Dreyfus, Hubert L. 1991. *Being-in-the-World: A Commentary on Heidegger's "Being and Time," Division I*. Cambridge, MA: MIT Press.

Ford, Samuel G. 1947. *The Book of Wisdom for Eskimo*. Ottawa: Bureau of Northwest Territories and Yukon Affairs, Land, Parks and Forests Branch, Department of Mines and Resources, Canada.

Freud, Sigmund. 1953. "Thoughts for the Times on War and Death." In *The Standard Edition of the Complete Psychological Works of Sigmund Freud*. Trans. under the editorship of James Strachey, in collaboration with Anna Freud, Alix Strachey, and Alan Tyson. Vol. 14. London: Hogarth Press.

Good, Byron J., Mary-Jo Del Vecchio Good, Isenbike Togan, Zafer Ilbars, A. Güvener, and Ilker Gelisen. 1994. "In the Subjunctive Mode: Epilepsy Narratives in Turkey." *Social Science & Medicine* 38(6): 835–42.

Hicks, Jack. 2006. "The Social Determinants of Elevated Rates of Suicide by Inuit Youth." PowerPoint presentation made at Public Policy Forum seminar, "Economic Transformation North of 60°," Ottawa, December 13.

Ja Rule. 2002. "Murder Reigns." On *The Last Temptation*. © Def Jam.

Kulchyski, Peter. 2006. "Six Gestures." In *Critical Inuit Studies: An Anthology of Contemporary Arctic Ethnography*, ed. Pamela Stern and Lisa Stevenson. Lincoln: University of Nebraska Press.

Malinowski, Bronislaw. [1922] 1961. *Argonauts of the Western Pacific: An Account of Native Enterprise and Adventure in the Archipelagoes of Melanesian New Guinea*. New York: E. P. Dutton.

National Aboriginal Achievement Foundation. 2006. *Building Brighter Futures 2006–2007: Bursary and Scholarship Awards for First Nations, Inuit and Metis Students*. Ohsweken, ON: National Aboriginal Achievement Foundation.

Nietzsche, Friedrich Wilhelm. 1967. *On the Genealogy of Morals.* Trans. Walter Kaufmann and R. J. Hollingdale. In *On the Genealogy of Morals and Ecce Homo.* New York: Vintage.

Pandolfo, Stefania. 2006. "'Bġīt nġanni hnaya' (Je veux chanter ici): Voix et témoignage en marge d'une rencontre psychiatrique." *Arabica* 53(2): 232–80.

Qitsualik, Rachel Attituq. 2004. "Carry Me Away." *Yes!*, Summer; www.yesmagazine.org/article.asp?ID=872 (accessed on May 14, 2008).

Stevenson, Lisa. 2005a. "Life in Question: Inuit Suicide, Biopolitics and Visions of Community." Paper presented at Annual Meeting of the American Anthropological Association, Washington, DC, November 29–December 3.

———. 2005b. "Life in Question: Inuit Youth, Suicide and the Canadian State." Ph.D. diss., University of California, Berkeley.

Stevenson, M. G. 1996. "Inuit Suicide and Economic Reality." Unpublished report, Inuit Tapirisat of Canada, Ottawa.

Taylor, Charles. 1994. "Philosophical Reflections on Caring Practices." In *The Crisis of Care: Affirming and Restoring Caring Practices in the Helping Professions,* ed. Susan S. Phillips and Patricia E. Benner. Washington, DC: Georgetown University Press.

FOUR

The Hyperbolic Vegetarian

NOTES ON A FRAGILE SUBJECT IN GUJARAT

Parvis Ghassem-Fachandi

DISGUST AND VIOLENCE IN INDIA

Scholars of Hindutva have argued that in the context of communal violence in India a heightened sense of vulnerability among members of the
Hindu middle and lower middle class is integral to the legitimization of
violence, where a "majority" feels threatened by a "minority" (Jaffrelot
1996; Hansen 1999; Nussbaum 2007). In the state of Gujarat, this process
includes the projection of a lack of vulnerability onto Muslims, expressed
and rationalized by reference to diet, worship, and sexuality.

In this essay, I explicate how the affect of disgust relates to violence by
focusing on a case study of an upwardly mobile member of what is generally conceived of as a "lower" social category, a proponent of Hindu
nationalism who was complicit in the 2002 anti-Muslim pogrom in the

city of Ahmedabad. I hope to shed light on the unique communicative aspect of meat, in which my own participation was central to my arrival at an understanding, and the threat it can pose in central Gujarat. More specifically, I will focus on the role disgust plays in creating new forms of identification by enabling a successful externalization of those aspects of the self that have to be denied.

This case study should not be read as an attempt to displace macrohistorical or sociological explanations for violence—powerful approaches to explain ethnic and political violence in India that have much merit.[1] To do so would reveal a fundamental misunderstanding of the predicament, the possibilities, and also the limitations of ethnographic knowledge derived through fieldwork encounters. In competitive academic settings such misunderstandings are frequently caused by automatically and erroneously equating description and analysis, on the one hand, with plausible explanation on the other. Many fieldwork insights are not likely to feed directly into explanatory frameworks; they instead compel a detour through *Verstehen,* a process of interpretation that lacks closure.

This essay seeks to extend and complicate current paradigms by focusing on processes of identification that I found to be prevalent in Gujarat during the events of 2002. These processes are, in the literature, insufficiently understood and inadequately taken into account. I hope that my own insights may open up new approaches, but for now the overall picture remains fragmentary and incomplete. While no single perspective allows for self-satisfied epistemological posturing, each carries a promise of shifting the focus onto different intellectual and theoretical grounds.

BHARAT'S DISGUST

It was an inauspicious moment for a vision of *maas* (flesh) when, on February 8, 2002, Bharat, one of my Hindu roommates in the city of Ahmedabad, described to me the first time in his life that he saw raw meat. Earlier that year Chief Minister Narendra Modi had begun a campaign to close down illegal slaughterhouses, and newspapers alleged illegal cow slaughter by Muslim butchers.[2] On February 24, in Tankaria village near

Bharuch, the police killed a young Muslim man during a raid in which cows were allegedly slaughtered during the Muslim Bakri-Id festival (the Muslim commemoration of the Abrahamic sacrifice in the Old Testament).[3] Things would get much worse. The stage for sacrifice was set.

Bharat's encounter with raw meat had happened in 1998 in Ahmedabad. Though raised in the country, he explained, he had never before seen uncooked meat. Hence his shock one day when he went to Lal Darwaja in the old city center, and by accident walked right into the chicken market at Patwa Sheri, a small lane with Muslim-run fish and meat shops: "I got sick [bimaar], disgust overwhelmed me [traas thai chhe]. I saw a raw chicken. I had no idea what I was getting into. I walked right into the area. Suddenly I saw something hanging from a hook, just next to me. I looked up and I saw it hanging. 'This is a chicken,' I thought. 'This is a chicken.' Then I began to gag."

Bharat's face turned serious as he narrated; he portrayed his reaction graphically, gagging several times to demonstrate. The light steel armchair on which he sat cracked under his movements. "I sat down after the gagging [uubako]. I had to catch my breath. Then I vomited [ulti], and someone brought me a glass of water. . . . I sat there for 5 minutes. Then I returned the same way I had come, and I have never gone back into this area of the city again. For three days, I could not eat. I always saw the chicken on my plate."

Bharat exited the lane the very same way the food exited his body: that is, he went backward (bekwad), much as his vomiting (ulti) was meant to reverse ingestion, to turn something inside out.

Almost three weeks after Bharat told me of this harrowing first encounter with meat, on the morning of February 27, 2002, fifty-nine passengers on an overcrowded train—including many Hindu activists returning from the holy site of Ayodhya—were burned to death in a ghastly fire. In Gujarat this incident came to be known as the Godhra massacre (hatyakand). In the pogrom that followed, more than 1,000 Muslims were killed and more than 150,000 displaced. Bharat understood the fire on the train in Godhra as having been provoked and instigated by Pakistan in collaboration with local Muslims who, in his view, had acted as proxy agents of the enemy state. He described the scenes on the streets of

Ahmedabad that followed as a legitimate punishment of the Muslim community as a whole, something that had to be done. The ongoing pogrom violence, he said, was a "purification" (in English). Several months later, he illegally purchased what is locally called a "country-made revolver."[4]

HINDUTVA AND VEGETARIANISM IN GUJARAT

In central Gujarat, the substance of meat in its production and consumption not only provides an idiom for stigmatizing the Muslim but also channels visceral and affective expression. Meat, as I will show, both is a tempting taste and can be experienced as disgust, anxiety, and hate; in both senses, it enables stigma to become corporeal. At the same time, meat also indexes intimate questions of sexuality and renunciation, *himsa* and *ahimsa* (violence and nonviolence), sacrifice and incorporation—features of substantial importance in contemporary identity formation in Gujarat.

The analytic concept of "Hindu nationalism" is locally called *hindutva*, which literally means "essence of the Hindu." Residents of Ahmedabad sometimes say "mane hindutva thai chhe" or "mane hindutva ave chhe," phrases that loosely translate as "Hindutva rises up in me" or "Hindutva is happening to me." Such idiomatic expressions—and there are many—express nationalism as an *experience* akin to a sentiment, even an affect, of a very different nature than is ordinarily assumed in academic analyses. In Gujarat, *hindu-tva* frequently describes an awakening of something sleeping deep within the subject, which can be stirred to the surface and shaped into political form. Whoever can control this amorphous secret within the subject holds a key to mass politics.

The state of Gujarat itself is strongly identified with vegetarianism in its diverse practices and ideologies. It is particularly salient because all dominant social and religious elites espouse strict vegetarianism, as did, of course, Mahatma Gandhi, who was born in Gujarat. Its importance is largely due to recent historical transformations, which made more prominent communities such as *vaniya* (merchants), mainly Jains and Hindu Vaishnava, as well as the influences of the Swaminarayan *sampradaya*, a Hindu reform sect of the nineteenth century (Mallison

1974; Desai 1978).[5] As a form of renunciation, vegetarianism extends not only to abstention from meat but also to the exclusion from worship of animal sacrifice, performed traditionally in the context of kingship and Mother Goddess worship (H. Basu 2004). Today in central Gujarat, vegetarianism is the most unambiguous and immediate expression of *ahimsa* (nonviolence). A manifestation of a long cultural tradition, it has become more significant because of the collapse of the traditional social order and the rise of the *vepari* or merchant ethic (Tambs-Lyche 1997).

It is equally crucial to note that the doctrine of *ahimsa* and the figure of Gandhi have become the most successful spiritual exports out of India into the global marketplace of ideas. Gujarati elites are acutely aware of the attraction *ahimsa* holds for the Westerner, and many local pronouncements on *ahimsa* implicitly address the West. In this way the West has become internal to India—and to things experienced intimately in the body.

A point of ethnographic distinctiveness for central Gujarat, as compared to nationalist stirrings elsewhere, is how the political usages of disgust today are linked in complicated ways to *ahimsa* and *hindu-tva*. As a fieldworker, I was compelled to follow this line of inquiry by repetitive encounters with eating and vomiting in the context of communal posturing, which I identify as forms of visceral nationalism.

MODI'S VIBRANT VEGETARIAN GUJARAT

In 2003, Chief Minister of Gujarat Narendra Modi, weakened by the international critique of his actions during the Gujarat pogrom in the previous year, commemorated the 135th anniversary of Mohandas K. Gandhi's birth with a speech in Porbandar, the town in Gujarat where the Mahatma was born. The chief minister meditated on "Bapu's principles"—Gandhi's unique blend of emphasizing social reform, village economy, the removal of untouchability, and the Khadi movement—and in the speech he devoted considerable time to the "hidden strengths" of Gujarat: that is, to the treatment of animals and vegetarianism.

Modi, who is sometimes rumored to enjoy eating chicken now and then, explained:

Gujarat's main strength lies in its vegetarianism. Most Gujaratis are strict vegetarians. The concept of "Chhappan Bhog"[6] or 56 different dishes is native only to the Indian context, and more especially to the Gujarat culture. The beauty of the Gujarat palate lies in its variegatedness.

Vegetarianism is the first step for a healthy society. When Gandhiji went abroad at a young age, he took a vow that in any event he would not indulge in the consumption of animal flesh. According to the ancient Vedic texts of India, . . . there is "fire" or "Agni" in the stomach (kund).[7] It is this fire or heat that digests the foods and provides nourishment, and strength to the body as a whole. According to our Sanskrit scriptures, if a vegetable, or fruit, or food grain is put in fire, then that fire and its container is called a "Yagya kund" [vessel or pit for sacrificial fire], but if dead flesh is put in fire, then that fire becomes the fire of a "shamshaan bhoomi" [still earth, ground of death, burial ground] or the fire of the funeral pyre. The fire of "Yagya" [sacrifice] gives life, energy, strength, and piety, while the fire of the "Shamshaan" [cremulatory fire] consumes and converts dirt to dirt and ashes to ashes.

As per Bapu's principles, vegetarianism is unavoidable for the purity of thoughts and action. It is a kind of purity of means. You reap what you sow. . . . From all viewpoints, vegetarianism is the perfect food. Vegetarianism is also the solution to protection of animal life. We have to listen to and understand the pain of speechless animals being taken to the slaughterhouse.[8]

Modi is widely understood to have supported, if not orchestrated, the anti-Muslim pogrom in 2002. His rhetorical approach—evoking Gandhi's words in the famous leader's own birth town—is common to contemporary Indian politicians. But even more significant is the invocation of diet, sacrifice, and death: three phenomena that not only are significantly linked conceptually but were relentlessly cited during the Gujarat pogrom.

Gandhi was assassinated in 1948 by a former member of the Rashtriya Swayamsevak Sangh (Association of National Volunteers, or RSS), Nathuram V. Godse, who claimed he was motivated to kill because he opposed Gandhi's doctrine of nonviolence, which would lead the country into certain ruin (Nandy 1980).[9] In India, the assassination of the Mahatma is often referred to as a "sacrifice for the nation," but in Gujarat this expression is highly ambiguous. Some residents might explain that the Mahatma's assassination was necessary so that Hindus could be emancipated from this superhuman father figure.

Modi himself is a former RSS functionary. From the moment he assumed political office in 2001, he deployed a micropolitics of *ahimsa* whenever convenient (see Ghassem-Fachandi 2006). In the first week of February 2002, as mentioned above, he campaigned against illegal slaughterhouses (most of which were Muslim-owned) throughout the state, a campaign that incited local acts of violence during the annual Muslim festival of Bakri-Id. Moreover, within weeks of the anti-Muslim pogrom, the Modi government cynically proposed to develop "Ahimsa tourism" and to open a modern "Ahimsa University."[10]

Modi's politics of vegetarianism, acutely attuned to the sensibilities of Gujarati elites and cautious not to alienate the rest, would be inconceivable without the international acclaim for *ahimsa*. As Gandhi and *ahimsa* are those aspects that the West loves about India, to speak from the position of the vegetarian father preempts protest as it employs an international figure who is venerated and whose influence does not seem to dissipate. Although Gandhi is frequently ridiculed locally—an entire genre of jokes about him reveals the ambivalence regarding this larger-than-life figure—his name still carries power when invoked publicly.

Hindu nationalist thought can easily dispense with any of the real content of Gandhi's ideas, because what counts are no longer his ideas but the *mana* of what one might call "global Gandhi": the recognition that a condensed form of the figure of the father of the nation commands internationally, and the way that this figure can be used as an emissary of all things "Hindu."

In what follows I will deal with one of the smaller though socially significant effects of this sort of political idolatry, mainly with reference to a specific new form of cultivated digestive disinvestment—Bharat's identification with and of disgust.

EDUKATION IN THE CITY

I first met Bharat in 1999, when his *guru* and academic adviser at Gujarat University recommended that he share a room with a foreigner from America who was going to do research and language study in Gujarat.

He was a thin, meticulously groomed man, with a closely trimmed moustache and oiled hair smoothed to one side. Bharat was in his mid-20s at our initial encounter, and wore his best, gold-embroidered *kurta* and brand-new sandals. He spoke no English, nor did he address me in Gujarati, but he ceremoniously handed me a red rose, a token of our future friendship and gesture of welcome to India. The shy farmer with the red flower is a memory that has stuck with me.

At that time, I had already completed an intensive field study between 1995 and 1996 in rural Gujarat, organized by the Institut für Ethnologie of the Freie Universität Berlin. I was, however, unfamiliar with urban Gujarat. Bharat and I began to experience Ahmedabad together. In the following years, whenever I lived in Hindu neighborhoods I invited Bharat to live with me for free. He always thankfully accepted the offer, as the student hostels were in lamentable shape, and became especially hazardous after a devastating earthquake in 2001.

Bharat comes from a family of farmers (*khedut*), but he left the farm business behind to live in Ahmedabad. He never told me so, but I suspect that this decision was reached shortly after the sudden death of his father, which elevated him prematurely to being the male head of his extended family household. At around the time his father died, in 1994, Bharat joined the RSS in his home village—"mara imej mate," as he explains, for his image.

For the RSS, he at first only served food at marriage functions and did kitchen work, activities he calls "social work." But today he has become the most successful export from his home village to the big city. Farming needs water, and after years of drought in Gujarat water has become scarce. Degrees are readily available, however, and therefore for someone like Bharat they are more accessible than is water for farming. To send the oldest son off to become a teacher, while the younger one stays home to tend the fields, is the first step in obtaining an urban foothold in government service.

Bharat's kin tried to emulate what they had seen many Patel farmers do in generations before them. The Patel of Gujarat, the Patidar, were once classified as *shudra,* the fourth *varna* associated with servant status (Pocock 1972: 29), a fact alluded to today only with circumlocutions. The two main caste branches of Patel now belong to the most economically successful as well as politically powerful groups in all of Gujarat. Many are members of the middle classes and have relatives in the United States, especially in New Jersey.[11] When talking to members of the Patel community in Ahmedabad, one will often hear "Edison," "Elizabeth," or "Metuchen," place-names that have a spectral ring to Bharat but are definite destinations of relatives for members of the Patel (and are near Princeton, where I moved in 2003).

Our life together, always in strictly vegetarian Hindu middle-class housing societies, and often joined by friends and caste brethren from the countryside, soon became routine. Bharat related to me as his *mota bhai* (older brother); he usually prepared food and took care of the household, while I paid the bills. Given my prior field experience in rural Gujarat, I insisted on occupying a separate room where I could work at any time of day or night—drawing my boundary. Bharat soon complained that whenever I was traveling he felt lonely in the large apartment building, especially at night, when the quiet darkness of a large middle-class apartment caused him to have nightmares. Bharat consequently invited Pratap, a fellow caste member and friend from a neighboring village, to live with us, and I agreed.

Bharat had soon delegated all housework to Pratap. Although the youngest of us, he was no bachelor. His wife and children remained in his home village with his parents, while he pursued a degree in Hindi at Gujarat Vidhyapit, a university founded by Mahatma Gandhi. Pratap, who planned to write something on *ahimsa*, treated both Bharat and me as his *guru*s and older brothers. We three, then, lived together for about seven months.

At Gujarat University, where I was still studying Gujarati, the knowledge that Bharat and Pratap were cooking daily for me, the Westerner, soon led to a series of inquiries among my teachers, as well as suggestions for alternatives. When I once complained about a stomachache, for example, they questioned Bharat's cooking with medical, if not alchemical, precision. At another time, I grumbled in passing about the excessive oil in the food that I had eaten (which caused me considerable weight gain). I was advised with sudden sternness to seek out another cook.

One teacher explained that the overuse of oil (*tel*) in food was a sure sign of the *guna* of *tamas* (attribute of darkness): that is, of typical *tamasi* food. Food that is considered *tamasi* in Gujarat carries negative associations, as it is linked with poor intellectual abilities (mental slowness and inertia), lustful thoughts (sexual rapaciousness), and proneness to violence (bloodlust) in those that consume it—signs of weak control of the passions. I initially found these reactions puzzling, but I came to understand that while Bharat and Pratap kept strict vegetarian diets, their academic superiors nonetheless continuously ascribed to them typical lower-caste practices, such as the consumption of nonvegetarian food, which for them has unambiguously negative connotations.

For example, one day my Gujarati language class was rescheduled to the early afternoon. My professor, a young and attractive Jain woman who was divorced and was finishing her Ph.D. in linguistics, commented on the smell of onions on my breath—an intimate remark that took me by surprise. Indeed, I had eaten lunch in the university cantina together with Bharat, as I normally did, shortly before the class. The cheap lunch was purely vegetarian and included two dishes: *khichadi* (rice and lentils) and the usual salad of raw onions mixed with lime juice. For my Jain professor the smell of raw onions (or garlic, for that matter) was not only disgusting but also, and more importantly, indicative of nonvegetarian food habits. While she was sought to ease my embarrassment, she was less generous about someone like Bharat, whom she considers "rough" (*asanskari*). The incident reminded me of my first German girlfriend, whose parents complained that their daughter smelled like garlic after she spent time at my place.[12]

According to Bharat, his initial motivation to come to the city and enter a university was a desire to teach and aid the educational progress of his community, the Jadav, whom he considers largely "illiterate" (*abhan*). For Bharat "educashun" is the attribute that distinguishes Jadav from those groups whom he calls "unchusthan" and describes as "higher-level upar," such as the successful Patel, Vaniya (Hindu Vaishnava and Jain merchant groups), and Brahmins. I once asked Bharat why out of all possible disciplines he chose to study the subject of Gujarati, given that it is the least likely degree to translate easily into a prospective job. He replied, somewhat indignantly, "But I *am* Gujarati."

He used the same intonation when saying, "I *am* Hindu"—as if these two identities were intertwined, if not the same, and could be taken away from him. To Bharat it makes sense to study what one is, that is, *gujarati.* The claim to be "Gujarati," however, meant much more than simply membership in the state of Gujarat as a linguistic and political entity. Today, being a Gujarati also unambiguously denotes being a Hindu. Members of the numerous Muslim communities of the city would not call themselves "Gujarati," as this term is exclusive of the term "Muslim," even though many Gujarati Muslim communities identify strongly with the state, speak fluent Gujarati as a first language at home, and are distinguishable in many ways from Muslims in other parts of India.

Bharat's academic advisers explained to me that language study for someone like Bharat is an appropriate discipline because with language comes cultivation, which he lacked (*sanskar*—"politeness, respect"; and *sanskruti*, "civilization," like the German *Kultiviertheit*). Bharat's main academic adviser, his *guru*, told me bluntly, "Bharat is not smart, but loyal." In other words, Bharat is still in the process of becoming a "Gujarati" proper.

Bharat aspires to be considered a successful man from a locally respected family. And indeed he seems to command considerable respect in his home village. When I visited his family and kin in his natal village, his younger brother Mahesh proudly showed me sacks full of stored grain (mostly *baajri*, or millet) worth tens of thousands of rupees. We visited a school friend who decided to become a *sadhu* (renouncer). He lives as a *brahmacharya* (celibate) at a local Hanuman temple and worships as a *pujari* (temple priest). Bharat talked to his old friend as if they were two entrepreneurs meeting after many years of separation; one is successful in the business of religion, the other in the business of academia.

We rode on a fancy blue tractor to inspect the fields, and to do *puja* (worship) for Bahucha Mata—the family *kuldevi* (lineage goddess)—at the small temple in the middle of a sizable piece of land. At night, the usually very taciturn Mahesh offered me the *hukkah* and cigarettes to smoke, but made me promise not to tell his brother. All the neighbors laughed and giggled, as Bharat had acquired the annoying habit in his new life in the city of calling everyone to order for their habits.

When Bharat is in the city, however, he evokes a different sense of origin. Despite landownership, savings from stored agricultural produce, and a high status among his village peers, Bharat calls himself "poor" (*gharib*) and many of his kin at home "backward." The Jadav are *nadoda rajput,* a subsection of a subcaste that is a *pachhaat varg* (a backward class), classified among the OBC (other backward classes; see Parikh 1998: 75). Since the implementation of the Mandal Commission recommendation in 1990, 27 percent of government-related jobs are reserved for other backward classes such as his.[13] In the city, Bharat's insecurity about the status to which he can aspire leads him to calibrate his behavior strategically and with caution.

When speaking of the social status of his community, the Jadav, Bharat employs no Gujarati term; he instead uses the English word with a local twist, "bekwad." Gujarati contains many adjectives associated with groups considered backward: for example, *halka loko* (inferior people; *halku* means "low, thin, light"), which is usually contrasted with *ujliyat loko* (high people; literally, "the radiant people"), denoting members of either traditionally higher castes or successful communities. For Bharat, the term *halku* conjures up something dirty and disgusting, from which he always wants to distance himself. Bharat stresses that the Jadav are *bekwad,* not *halka* (i.e., backward but not inferior); they are perhaps *abhan,* but not *nich* (i.e., illiterate but not low). While he will never call his own community low or inferior, but only *bekwad,* he is less careful when describing other groups.

Although both Bharat and Pratap come from the same community, they have different personalities. While Pratap has a friendly nature, an almost effervescent jolliness all around and about him, which allowed him to befriend easily the daughter- and mother-in-law in the neighboring Patel apartment (for example, cutting vegetables for lunch together with them), Bharat is a more solemn figure, with a stiff demeanor, and is overly self-conscious. Although he does have a sense of humor, his laughter is rarely contagious.

Once when we visited by foot the drive-in cinema in the north of the city, he almost provoked a fistfight with a terrified young man who accidentally touched his arm with a cloth while cleaning the tables of an eatery. At another time, when a street tea seller overcharged me, Bharat threatened him with violence by his entire community. To be fair, these are exceptions to his usual behavior. But they reflect his tendency to take his own masculinity seriously, perhaps because he then was still unmarried, while Pratap, who already had two children, felt more confident in that respect.

Both, however, shared a rejection of Muslims, and saw in Hindutva the logical extension of proper democratization—the fact that the majority should have its way in the face of a recalcitrant minority, the Muslims. In the competitive atmosphere of Ahmedabad, Hindutva seemed to prop up who they wanted to be: Hindus. But while Pratap often voiced the circulating stereotypes and rumors about Muslims, he was nonetheless uninterested in political matters and somewhat immune to a more aggressive anti-Muslim rhetoric. Bharat, however, took things much more to heart, especially the events surrounding the 2002 pogrom.

In the many years we knew each other, Bharat never found it important to tell me that he was a member of the RSS, although he knew perfectly well my interest in the organization's ideology and national-ritual practices. This, it turns out, is an experience I share with many Gujaratis, especially with Muslims. Many local Muslims told me that more than anything else that happened, the discovery of a Hindu friend, neighbor, or colleague working in the RSS led to strong feelings of betrayal. For many, betrayal began years before the violent events of 2002, or even before similar events in 1992–93. One Muslim acquaintance traced its origins back to the aftermath of the 1969 communal violence in the city, when he realized that one of his best friends was encouraging his son to engage in RSS activities. Yet I have met no Muslim who ever actually confronted his friend or neighbor with these feelings, which in any case are only rarely expressed directly. Whenever I suggested to Muslims that they break their silences, and address suspicions and concerns about RSS membership openly, I was accused of being naive. Insistence, they said, could lead only to the eruption of a dangerous cycle of disputes among neighbors and "friends"; they were satisfied with an uneasy but peaceful calm.

Shortly after the pogrom had begun, Bharat told me how his involvement with the RSS had started. I had expressed shock about the absence of the rule of law on the streets of Ahmedabad and the organization's obvious involvement in the violent mob scenes that I personally witnessed.

Consequently, our discussions became more directly political and confrontational. Busy with his studies, he had not visited a local branch of the RSS for some time; but after the pogrom he became involved again, and proudly showed me his khaki uniform. At around the same time, Bharat's academic advisers told me that they, too, had formerly been members of the RSS, but no longer agreed with all of the organization's goals.

ASSIMILATING LACK

Like many of his peers, Bharat does not speak English well, and his lack of marked improvement while living with me became part of the stigma associated with his social background. Yet he is very astute in his selection of English words. Some listeners perceive his selective use of English simply as betraying his low educational status; despite his studies, his use of foreign words and concepts reveals a fundamental unfamiliarity with a wider English-speaking world. In this regard, he is quite unlike many bilingual professionals; at the same time, he is also unlike the large number of residents in the city who, despite weak active English skills, will nonetheless fall into what a linguistics professor in Baroda has referred to as "Gujarezi."

Gujarezi is used mainly in Ahmedabad and Baroda, in varied forms that depend on the English vocabulary and general linguistic competency of the speaker. For the most part this linguistic practice is incomprehensible to a non-Gujarati speaker, as English words are transported into Gujarati syntax and pronounced in accordance with Gujarati phonetic rules. By contrast, in Bharat's use of English words, there is a more decided semantic shift at work, with an even stronger indigenization of concepts and words whose similarity to English can obscure differences of meaning.

Bharat has never attended a school where English is taught or taken an English-language course at the university, nor does he ever enjoy a movie in English. He takes in English words through the Gujarezi that he hears practiced on the street. For Bharat the selective appropriation of new words—a practice he shares with his peers, like Pratap—is a formidable technique for incorporating the modern world of the city, as he essentially assimilates its power in order to overcome his relative lack. Although these words will not appear in standard Gujarati or English dictionaries, their experimental and creative use evolves into collective understandings.

For example, Bharat refers to techniques of dress and style in the city as productive of "personaliti"; to communal conflagrations, marital conflict, or sexual frustration as "tenshun"; the wished-for effect in first encounters for job interviews, class presentations, marital negotiations with affines, or first scenes in Bollywood movies, as the power of "entri"; and all sorts of transgressive behaviors involving wasteful expenditure as "enjoi."

The term *enjoi* was widely used by young men like Bharat on the streets during the 2002 pogrom to refer to rape, looting, and the destruction of Muslim bodies and property. Initially taken from the very successful Coke commercial "Enjoy, Enjoy!" that entered India some time in the 1990s, *enjoi* is incorporated into typical Gujarezi constructions, such as in *enjoi leva mate* (in order to enjoy). *Enjoi* reaches into the semantics of the Gujarati verb *bhogavavu* (to enjoy, to suffer) and the noun *bhog* (pleasures, the victim of a sacrifice), and expresses the idea of excessive and wasteful consumption. The deployment of this term suggests how economic liberalization, the circulation of new goods in an atmosphere of accelerated consumption, is experienced and assimilated by a younger generation. Its semantic differences from English point to ways in which the term reaches deep into the collective unconsciousness of Gujaratis.

The words *personaliti* and *entri* are employed in different but not completely unrelated ways. Bharat often insisted on borrowing a leather belt of mine, bought in an expensive traveler's store in Berlin many years earlier, that he fancied. The belt had an elongated hidden pouch on its inner side where I used to keep my *Notgroschen*—emergency cash kept ready in case of sudden illness or accident. Many of my Gujarati friends were fascinated with the secret device and fantasized about what else could be hidden in it. Whenever Bharat had to give a presentation in class, he asked to borrow this belt.

Bharat enjoyed his class presentations, in which he declaimed wise sayings and recited poems with spiritual value. With great concentration, he practiced at home in front of the mirror for hours, memorizing the smallest details of gesture, rhythm, and tone: then he stood in front of an attentive audience wearing a clean, freshly pressed white shirt, a black leather belt, a watch with a golden wristband (he did not like mine, which was a silver Sonata watch), and spit-polished shoes. Naturally, I was Bharat's audience.

Entri is the power of catching someone else's gaze. It can be wielded by a fancy belt, an expensive pen in one's shirt pocket (a symbol of literacy), or an impressive motorbike. This desire to stand out and be gazed at is the inverse of the traditional threat of being looked at desirously, the fear of *najar* (the effect of the evil eye): both belong to the same class of phenomena. The gaze is powerful, whether feared here or desired there—be it in *entri* or *najar*—and loses none of its potency. Bharat is not afraid of jealous looks. In fact, he often desires to be the recipient of a gaze that might betray the jealousy of others.

When I asked Bharat to offer me another example of the phenomena of *entri*, he mentioned Bollywood movies in which the actors' frequent entries to and departures from the screen are highly stylized. Within the same movie, the main hero or heroine may make many different entrances, each time in new clothes and with a different musical overture. Audiences frequently welcome these scenes with a sigh of pleasure, a call, or some other sound of recognition. The staging of the entry has a particular aesthetic importance.

The cinematographic practice is also reminiscent of the sequencing of Vaishnava worship in Gujarat, in which love and care for the deity take the form of an elaborate *puja* (worship ritual). The human-shaped image is undressed, bathed, and then dressed and adorned again with clothes and jewelry. And the practice by which Bollywood superstars such as Amitabh Bachhan, Shah Rukh Khan, and Ashwarya Rai are divinized in their own right through temples and shrines is regarded with amused detachment by Bollywood fans.

Bharat's *personaliti* and *entri* concern first appearances in encounters, which manifest the essence of a person (*vyaktitva*) expressed through a mark, sign, or symbol of recognition (*olakh*). The fetishistic power of the object that promises to produce such *entri* is supposed to cancel out the initial impression made by his name and appearance, permanent qualities linked to caste and class. Bharat tries to get rid of *bekwad* and does not want to be confused with *halka*. He tries to take control of the identification to which he is in danger of being subjected. The point is that the techniques to produce *personaliti* and *entri* can be learned, managed, and manipulated. They are supplemental devices that seem to make possible control of what Bharat is in constant danger of signifying in the city.

When Bharat stood in front of the tiny mirror that he had been able to save from the student hostel (where items change owners so frequently), his skin dark against his freshly pressed and starched white shirt, he reminded me of my father, an Iranian who immigrated to Germany, as I had known him in my childhood. Standing in front of his own reflection, Bharat performed *entri* to himself, imagining the way he might appear to others, trying to perfect that magic of charisma that might allow him entry into the world of the city. Whereas my father had picked up the obsessive practice of wearing dark ties, white starched shirts, and fancy suit jackets from watching black-and-white Hollywood movies in Teheran in the 1950s, Bharat took on the style of urban Indian university students, replacing his usual *kurta* with pants and shirt.

And like my father, when Bharat became aware that I was watching him at his most beautiful self, he could turn the fantasy into irony, joking about his smartness and sophistication in order to make me laugh. He often teased me about neglecting style in clothing (reminding me of my father's disapproval), a bad habit I picked up in the bizarre timeless space of the cold war Berlin of the 1980s. Only in the mirror, with the belt around his thin waist, did Bharat find a self that made sense to his aspirations and that enabled him to be generous. I really liked him in these moments.

BOUNDARY AND "WEAKNESS"

In our daily conversations Bharat often referred to his *maryada* (boundary, limitation, modesty) as his "weakness" (in English). This weakness—a space within him, which he maintained without reflection—found no expression in his village but must instead have developed, or taken concrete form, after he arrived in the city. His professor and *guru* at Gujarat

University had initially identified this "weakness" as a strong disdain for Muslims, which is why he explicitly told Bharat to live with me, a foreigner sporting a Muslim name. Over the years, Bharat himself repeated, "Muslims are my weakness."

In making this claim, Bharat means that he can lose his balance, his temper, in relation to Muslims. He can "lose it," so to speak, in relation to "them" (that is, lose grip over the boundary that separates him from them—*maryada*). Violence between Hindus and Muslims in Gujarat emerges when this boundary, which separates them by rules of modesty and limitation, is lost. Such violence is intimate, because it becomes possible when the boundary is being ignored—it is an effect of too much closeness, not too much distance. In cases of mixed marriages, for example, the transgression of marital boundaries is often considered a violent act in itself, thereby legitimating communal posturing (and the logic of "reaction"—*pratikriya* or *pratighat*).

The shocking positive attitude of many Gujaratis, Muslims and Hindus alike, toward violence cannot be comprehended if one fails to recognize the authority generally possessed by such boundaries. Community and caste boundaries are, from this perspective, a sort of frozen violence—petrified into structures that keep communities apart in some respects while allowing for innocent interaction in others.

But though Bharat followed his professor's advice to live with me, and thus struggled with his weakness, he did not overcome it. On the one hand, his views conform to the dominant discourse in central Gujarat, which stigmatizes Muslims as abject. On the other hand, he identifies me—his vice-ridden, higher-status, light-skinned, German-born, American-educated roommate—as a Muslim, and he initially had trouble making sense of me. In fact, despite all the vices I engaged in, some of which, like meat consumption, are stereotypically linked to Muslims, he came to treat me genuinely as a friend.

Like many other Gujaratis, Bharat views "religion" (*dharma*) as a matter not simply of "belief" (*manyata*) but also of group membership, which implies much more than just philosophical or spiritual orientation. *Dharma* is connected to social organization as well as to what one does, whom one marries, what one eats, and with whom one interacts on what

basis. Consequently, marriage and conversion are understood as synonymous. My insistence not to signify anything in the register of religion, despite my Iranian-born father, always seemed phony to Bharat
and others. He understands the marriage between an Iranian man and a
German woman as a "Muslim" marrying a "Christian," which made me
irrefutably "Muslim." In this regard, Bharat's perceptions of me did not
differ from those of local Muslims.

In retrospect, I must admit that he was correct, in a way, because I not
only sported what he considered a Muslim name and ate meat, but I also
constantly crossed into the local Muslim world without hesitation, visiting Muslim neighborhoods, religious sites, and houses. Although I initially asked him to accompany me, he never did (unlike other Hindu
friends). Muslims in Ahmedabad, in turn, seemed eager to incorporate
me as one of their own from overseas. Thus I became, in a very special
way, Bharat's "Muslim acquaintance"—the one Muslim he could deal
with despite his prejudices about those belonging to that category.

While touring Bharat's home village with him, I became aware that he
had already introduced me everywhere as a "Muslim." He did this again
in my presence, even after I had corrected him several times. Given the
extreme anti-Muslim atmosphere in the state, I was not too pleased with
this loss of control over my signification. Bharat, now a local success, had
obviously taken steps to overcome his "weakness," as his *guru* had
advised him to do. He was just showing off his "Muslim friend." Back in
the city, he introduced me to people as "Amerikan," a practice that I had
grudgingly assented to, as the category "Jarman" (German) seemed not
to make much sense to him.

That I could alternatively signify what is most desired or most despised,
"Amerikan" or "Muslim," speaks ardently to the intertwined logic of
stigma and phantasma at work in these identifications. Yet there might be
another factor at work. The Muslim population of Bharat's home village
consists of two houses of the Fakirani *jat,* a poor Muslim community in the
region whose members work as ritual specialists at Muslim shrines. Muslims today often ridicule this community for being too "Hindu," and it
occupies an unambivalently low social status. The only other Muslim presence in the village is spectral by contrast: the descendants of the former

royal family of a nearby regional town, who now live in America. While Bharat claimed that his own community was exploited and persecuted by the former Muslim rulers, his maternal grandfather told me that relations between the Jadav and the rulers were fine.

Although I was living mostly a vegetarian life with Pratap and Bharat, I did eat street food and visit nonvegetarian restaurants and Muslim homes. For Bharat, nothing signified "Muslim" more strongly than "meat," and his insistence on calling me a Muslim is consistent with his refusal to ever consider such dietary ventures "cosmopolitan," a common euphemism employed to excuse the consumption of nonvegetarian food in urban Gujarat. My own association with meat is mostly with a festive German *Sonntagsbraten* (Sunday roast) or *Weihnachtsganz* (the roasted goose for Christmas), which, deposited in the middle of a large table, is a symbol of extended collective commensality with friends and family—inclusive of wine, cigarettes, and late-night talk. For him, instead, meat connoted the absence of all humor.

Bharat, who thought of himself as a *pakka hindu* (a staunch Hindu), was annoyed by my inability to feel shame or hide my occasional indulgences. A middle-class Dalit professor whom Bharat knew dissimulated his own meat-eating behavior in Bharat's presence. Although we had eaten meat together many times, this friend frequently, in my presence, claimed to third parties that he was a pure vegetarian. For him, this behavior constituted not hypocrisy but a "smooth style" of social behavior: the absence of the desire to hurt religious sensitivities. I, by contrast, initially did not understand how to manage my "vices"; nor could I later bring myself to adhere absolutely to a strict vegetarian regime. In many ways my stubborn insistence on remaining utterly transparent in such matters was rude, and it did not give "Jarman" a good name.

To befriend and even live with a meat eater like myself, Bharat risked disapproval for his association with a "lower category." Yet I, frequently identified as Muslim, also commanded an enviable status when I interacted with academics, religious authorities, activists from nongovernmental organizations, neighbors, shop owners, and businessmen. This fact puzzled Bharat, and reminded him of what he lacked precisely because he so strongly aspired to it himself. Bharat's near reverence for some of the status that I commanded automatically led him to overlook the real reason for his own weakness: he was a farmer in the city, belonging to the OBC (other backward classes), in a society that harbors many silent prejudices against rural villagers known for their "roughness" (*asanskari, dhamaaliyu*). The attractiveness of categories such as "Gujarati" as well as "Hindu" lies in their promise to efface and overcome these stigmas.

For Bharat, nationalist organizations like the RSS or the Vishva Hindu Parishad (World Hindu Council, or VHP) are not simply protectors of Hindus and *hindu rashtra* (the Hindu nation), but also are knowledgeable about "culture" (*sanskrutini jaane chhe*).[14] He explained to me that if there exists any form of boundary (*maryaadaa:* "limitation," "boundary," "modesty"), then the memory of it should be kept ("je maryaadaa che ene jaanvi raakhvu"); and if there exists any custom, then that too should be protected ("ritrivaajo saachvi raakhvaa"). Thus "culture," for him, essentially consists of *rahenikarni* (the manner of living, the way of doing things) and *khaanipini* (the manner of eating and drinking, what is eaten and what is drunk).

Bharat's conceptions of commensality and traditional boundaries of caste coalesce with the discourse of the Hindu nation, in which the definition of "culture" is reduced to certain core symbols that can be conveniently deployed in electoral campaigns—the new politics of *yagya* and *yatra* (sacrifice and pilgrimage). In political discourse, this has led to a proliferation, even preference, for blatant Hindu kitsch—a fetishistic version of tradition, easily appropriated and used (Rajagopal 1999: 135).

Second-generation nationalisms often come in the form of an "awakening" to an imagined aboriginal essence that, even if historically associated with elites, is suddenly accessible horizontally to everyone (Anderson 1991: 195). Along these lines, the defensive and authoritarian use of identity and "culture" can be understood as a reaction formation against the experience of a self splintering, pulled in too many different directions by new temptations. Bharat's defense, his *maryada* (modesty, boundary, limitation), helps him fortify the sense of a self against the effects of capitalist consumer fragmentation, a self constantly attacked, and often defeated, by so many seductions, so many occasions to experience lack.

In the stern rage of the *pakka hindu* there lies a promise of something as yet unadulterated by the ugly compromises and corruptions of city life, where boundary maintenance can conflict with finding what one secretly desires.[15] An aggressive response to a perceived injury can, from this perspective, become a sign of authenticity, and complicity in violence can then be explained apologetically in terms of uncontrollable emotions or affects.

In short, Hindutva organizations not only protect Hindu neighborhoods from Muslims but also, and perhaps more importantly, protect Hindus from themselves, from the possibilities of their own desires. They fortify what Bharat refers to as his *maryada* regarding Muslims, an impulse to maintain an emotional distance that is his "weakness." Bharat *knows* he does not like Muslims, because they are identified socially as a threat, but his *feelings* concerning Muslims are more anguish about those aspects of himself that he shares with them as well as with members of lower caste or tribal groups, which differentiate them from proper Hindus. His academic advisers identify those same qualities in him: lack of restraint and self-control, unsophistication, inertness, illiteracy, and dirtiness (of mind and body).

These negative stigmas are not affixed to me, the "America-Muslim" who receives an automatic recognition that Bharat does not. Bharat is not invited into houses for dinner, or approached flirtatiously by upper-caste Hindu women of the middle class. He complains about this, realizing that it signifies a lack of *entri*.

I am unsure, even after the passage of time, how our friendship was able to sustain itself through these events. For me, the experience of the pogrom changed things dramatically. Bharat's self-conscious and calm affirmation of the pogrom violence angered me greatly at the time, and even made me mistrust him for a while. Following the advice of concerned friends, I moved away from Hindu middle-class Naranpura in West Ahmedabad, where we had been living, to Shah Allam, a Muslim area in the eastern part of the city. Although we met each other frequently, it took Bharat almost a year to come visit me in my "Muslim flat," as he called it, a middle-class apartment building not unlike the ones we had lived in together. By then, with the help of an RSS uncle, he had married, he had gotten the job of lecturer at a college, and his first child was on the way. In 2005 Bharat bought a fancy middle-class apartment with a large loan secured from the son of his former academic adviser, who owns considerable real estate in the city. Bharat, the shy farmer with the red rose, had finally achieved his *entri*.[16]

While I condemn Bharat for his complicity in the pogrom, I also believe that he went out of his way to protect me on the first day, when the violence in the city was unchecked. In the early morning hours, Bharat and I quarreled about venturing into the city. He did not want to accompany me, arguing that he was afraid that his brother's motorbike would be seized and burned, but also did not want me to go alone. I compromised by joining him on a visit to a Hanuman temple, where I received a *tilak*—a mark signifying "Hindu"—on my forehead. I felt confident wandering in the city alone, as I had some experience with urban violence in the city. I expected to be able to interview policemen and participants in a relatively controlled environment. I did not, however, entirely understand the magnitude of the events I was to witness: several hundred people were killed that day. I left the Hindu mark untouched, and I cannot help believing that it somehow protected me from harm.

MEAT, CASTE, AND THE NAUSEA OF MOBILITY

Vices come in clusters in Gujarat, and they are believed to reveal something about the essence of the person who engages in them. One vice always implies another, eventually leading to a series of addictions (*tevo*). If someone "takes drinks" (*daru le chhe*), it is likely that he will also take *gutka* (tobacco) or smoke a cigarette if offered. The most extreme vices in this series are the consumption of meat and the engagement in illicit sex. But vices (*vyasano*) do more than accumulate and collect around certain individuals lacking resistance to them. By extension, they also affect entire categories of people naturally prone to them. It is thus important for Bharat to be explicit about his adamant resistance to vices, because his surname, Jadav, reveals a caste that is potentially associated with stigmas. Jadav, who consider themselves *rajput,* are closely associated with alcohol, smoking, and, to a lesser degree, consumption of meat.[17]

Hence Bharat refuses tea even when it is offered by his academic superiors and other authorities of social importance. His superiors often show a certain astonishment at his refusal, to which Bharat will add that he also fasts three times a week, eating only *anaaj* (wheat), ghee, and *gol* (sweet molasses). Far from being disingenuous in such meetings, Bharat communicates a complete series of unspoken values beneath and between the few words that he utters shyly. In addition to pious fasting (*upvaas*) and abstention from tea, he is *implicitly* also communicating that he is *shuddh shakahari* (pure vegetarian); does not smoke cigarettes, *bidis,* or the *hukkah* (as do his uncle and brother); and is unlikely to take a "drinks" (he always uses the plural), or chew *gutka* (a stimulant with tobacco and betel nut) or *paan* (betel leaf).

When he first explained his caste to me, Bharat insisted vehemently that all Jadav are and always have been strict vegetarians, with a few impious exceptions. But on visiting his home village in 2001, I found that while most members of his community professed vegetarianism, older members openly admitted to nonvegetarian practices in earlier times as well as to distant contemporary relatives who would still indulge in meat. This history of dietary practices is shadowy and complicated by the community's sudden upward mobility. Even back in 1999, when we shared a house during my initial language training, Bharat was particularly offended when Tejendra, a *rajput* neighbor with a Rajasthani background, invited me to a chicken dinner at his place. Tejendra claimed that a real *rajput* (literally, "son of kings") eats meat, implying that Gujarati *rajput*s are not authentic because they are vegetarians. Behind Tejendra's claim is an Indian stereotype of Gujaratis—*rajput*, *vaniya*, and Muslim alike—which insinuates that they are particularly effeminate, lacking in courage and strength. Bharat's relation to vegetarianism and meat eating is, in one sense, an attempt to distance himself from this stereotype, to assume Gujarati-ness while remaining strong and firm.

Here, then, we must return to the incident with which I began: Bharat's bout of severe nausea at Patwa Sheri, which caused him to collapse in the aisles of a Muslim meat market. This was not the only time I heard of sudden afflictions in the face of meat. Restaurant owners of nonvegetarian restaurants in Ahmedabad have much to tell about such strange behavior, so-called hesitations and sudden averse reactions, especially among affluent Gujaratis, Jains, or members of the Swaminarayan branch of Hinduism. One owner, himself a vegetarian Hindu from South India, explained to me that something like a "vegetarian majority" has emerged in the city.

The severest form of these "hesitations" is what goes locally by the name of *allagi*, a condition in which the object (the allergen) puts the entire subject at risk. Abstaining from meat is one of those behaviors about which Bharat seems to have no doubt; he never seems to stray (in distinction to his actions regarding liquor or sex outside marriage). His affect of disgust appears brutally simple, yet remains highly ambivalent. Something in Bharat cannot let go of meat, and he obviously expends much more energy than do others to fend off its intimate address.

Pratap, Bharat's former roommate, laughs at Bharat's affliction with *allagi*. Although also politically conservative, and a vegetarian himself, Pratap has no problem with the sight or smell of meat and even encourages me to eat it. "It suits you" (*tamne faave chhe*), he says. He simply does not want to ingest the stuff himself; he remains in control in his relation to it.

Investigating the phenomenological nature of the abject, the nauseating power and the revulsions of the body when it seeks to turn itself inside out, Julia Kristeva maintains that "the abject is not an ob-ject" (1982: 1).[18] That is, the abject is not something that can be named, imagined, and thus tamed. It does not allow for the "I" to remain autonomous or detached. She adds, "The abject has only one quality of the object— that of being opposed to I."

What is Bharat attempting to relieve himself of as he retraces his way back through the lanes of Patwa Sheri in order to reverse his encounter with a raw chicken? What is opposed to the "I" here? Since he never actually ingested any meat, he seems to be trying to relieve himself of a sight that through his eyes penetrated deeply into his body. It is the very presence of meat that causes him to collapse in front of it, in the meat's sight. And, finally, why does he recall the chicken as being no longer on the hook but suddenly on his plate, as if he were poised to eat it?

PARALYZING CONFLUENCE

Despite the historical influences of vegetarian Vaishnava traditions, Jainism, the salience of Mahatma Gandhi in Gujarat, and its current index of the abject, meat eating is not simply associated with disgust. It also carries great potency, and can signify power. Anthropological theorists, from William Robertson Smith (1898) to Émile Durkheim (1995) to Mary Douglas (1966), have consistently shown that what is poisonous and impure in one context has magical potentiality (i.e., power) in the next. Such is the case with meat in Gujarat, if not in most of India.

This dual valence is acutely present in how members of lower-caste groups explain, legitimize, and rationalize their own practices of meat consumption or abstention (Hardiman 1987). During the numbing months of violence in 2002, I was told by Hindu residents in the most tense areas of Ahmedabad that Bajrang Dal leaders offered chicken and whiskey, as well as cash, to members of Adivasi and scheduled caste groups as incitements and rewards for attacks on Muslim neighborhoods.[19]

Along these lines, meat is equated with the need for strength (*tame joie chhe*) as well as sex, and its consumption has the quality of an excessive release, like that connected with sexual activity. Muslims, of course, are not the only ones to eat meat in Gujarat. I have seen many men from middle-class Hindu and Jain communities consume meat at night, out of the view of their wives, in the predominantly Muslim-owned meat stands and restaurants of the old city. But their meat eating, unlike that of most Muslims, is coupled with the consumption of illicit liquor, despite the fact that Gujarat is a state in which alcohol is prohibited. Muslim restaurant owners and meat stand proprietors, many of whom are religiously conservative, are not generally pleased about serving inebriated customers. What this middle-class consumption shares with the bribing of tribals with chicken and whiskey to incite them to attack Muslims is the desire for transgression. Meat seems to enable the Hindu consumer to cross a certain boundary and confront the image of the ever-powerful masculine Muslim, either as a co-conspirator in consumption or as a rival. The release of violence is akin to a relinquishing of the self to *enjoi*, an excessive expenditure and a form of letting go.

Two insights are important here. First, ingesting meat (or seeing blood) can result in, or is indicative of, power—heat—that, once summoned, has to be tamed or expended. Meat consumption defines not only the wretched but also the noble, the royal, the king. It is a form of heat, which provides power similar to the ritual heat of ascetic practices (*tapasya*). Second, as Harald Tambs-Lyche (1992) has demonstrated in contradistinction to the Dumontian dichotomy of Brahmin and king, caste complementarity in Saurashtra can be traced historically to the relation of the merchant to the king, the *vaniya* to the *rajput*, and to their respective regimes of value. These values culminate in what Tambs-Lyche (1997) calls a "Vaniya model of culture," which stresses vegetarianism (with an emphasis on *ahimsa*), asceticism, and a business ethic, whereas the "Darbar model of culture" stresses chivalry, honor, and animal blood sacrifices in the context of *shakti* worship, the rituals surrounding the Mother Goddess complex.

In Bharat's affliction of *allagi*, this complementarity has finally collapsed, leaving him with nothing but pure disgust and in a relation to the other as a *chalenj* to him. Needless to say, not all vegetarians in India, and especially in Gujarat, suffer *allagi* and fall sick when exposed to the sight of raw flesh. But for Bharat there is something still alive in the meat that takes cognizance of him, and his sensitivity marks him as a very special Jadav. His aversion is more radical than a mere "hesitation."

Caught within a confluence of historical influences, Bharat is arrested by contradictory impulses: the desire to ingest meat (in his account, it suddenly appears on his plate) and the visceral disgust at flesh, the substance of a being that was killed unnaturally for consumption. Ingesting meat risks the undoing of all that he has been so laboriously externalizing (vomiting): his backwardness (*bekwad*), inferiority (*halku*), and lowness (*nich*); his "hesitations" toward an enticing world, cultivated through fasting (*upvaas*) and abstaining from vices (*tevo*); and finally his claim to represent the "essence of Hindu" (*hindu-tva*).

At the same time, however, he claims proudly to be a *rajput*—a man fit to rule—and thus the holder of the exact power signified by meat. Bharat's desire for that power is so great that any open argument about his status as a true *kshatriya* (*rajput*, warrior) is a hostile challenge.[20] At the same time, meat signifies that part of himself that he wants to vomit out. It is when the raw meat looks back at him that something in him realizes what he is: the other side of power—that is, powerlessness, inferiority, and disgust. This "malady of *allagi*" is a manifestation of being caught in a maelstrom of impulses no longer neatly separate in a symbolic division of complementary values and roles.

If desire implies the wish to devour, then disgust takes the form of its opposite, revulsion and the impulse to vomit. As the symmetrical reverse of the desire to devour, now introjected and become corporeal, it has no language. It is pure affect. Yet how can something that has never been swallowed be vomited out? As we see in Bharat's case, the object to be evacuated is mental, not inside the body. That which is to be vomited is that which has been rendered unconscious: the desire to devour. Something in Bharat wants to devour meat and thus assimilate its power. But in the end, and quite ironically, this affliction of *allagi* enables Bharat to reinvent himself as a new subject in the context of Hindutva—a *pakka hindu*, a man with an identity, a man of action.

When Chief Minister Narendra Modi explained vegetarianism by alluding to Vedic sacrifice, in the speech quoted at the beginning of this essay, and when he insisted that those who ingest death become the death they are eating, whereas those who ingest vegetables attain life, he is doing much more than just engaging in empty Vedic phraseology. To be sure, Modi is neither philologically trained in Sanskrit nor a competent Indologist. Acutely attuned, however, as this chief minister always is, to his audiences and to the enormous prestige that anything "Vedic" and vegetarian has in Gujarat, Modi is making sure that people like Bharat keep on vomiting, even if they have not ingested anything in the first place.[21]

By contrast, persuaded by his Muslim friend Sheikh Mehtab, Gandhi himself famously ingested meat when he was young in order to appropriate the physical virility of the British. He even confessed relishing its taste for a while (M. Gandhi 1927: 18–20). Gandhi subsequently abandoned the practice and turned to *brahmacharya* (celibacy) in order to gather the strength needed to overcome political domination and later ethnic violence.[22] Although certainly a very strict vegetarian, and feeling guilty for his transgressions, Gandhi never expressed disgust for meat or for those who ate it, nor did he warn of contagion from those whose profession brought them into contact with it. In this way Gandhi's relationship to meat, and by extension his relationship to Muslims, always remained sovereign—not an act of bad faith.

There are many passages in Gandhi's voluminous writings that attest to his acute understanding of stigma in relation to diet. For example, discussing the nature of Sanatana Hinduism at the height of Hindu-Muslim conflict, he writes in *Young India*:

> Unfortunately today Hinduism seems to consist merely in eating and not eating. Once I horrified a pious Hindu by taking toast at a Musalman's house.[23] I saw that he was pained to see me pouring milk into a cup handed by a Musalman friend. . . . Hinduism is in danger of losing its substance if it resolves itself into a matter of elaborate rules as to what and with whom to eat. . . . [A] man eating meat and with everybody, but living in the fear of God is nearer his freedom than a man religiously abstaining from meat and many other things but blaspheming God in every one of his acts. (M. Gandhi [1921] 1987: 32–33)

Whereas Narendra Modi, a celibate who is rumored to have a secret girlfriend or wife, inscribes *ahimsa* and vegetarianism into the context of Hindu nationalism in order to mobilize disgust against Muslims, Gandhi's renunciation of meat was complete: the substance no longer exercised any power over him. Gandhi's strict abstemiousness, despite appearing obsessive to current observers, did not translate into the denigration of the character of members of lower castes, tribals, or Muslims. Though he needed to mobilize the masses for national independence, and though he did indeed connect this political activism to a regimen of bodily discipline, he at the same time maintained emotional sobriety vis-à-vis the inevitable cultural and individual differences that defined India then, as they do today.

The hyperbolic vegetarian, by contrast, vomits his own forbidden desires and feels disgusted by those who come to stand for what he himself signifies. Bharat's disgust is fueled by this fundamental proximity to Muslims owing to symbolic equivalences established between *him* and *them* by those from whom he desires *entri* (recognition). In this way disgust becomes a weapon used to establish a new relation to the Muslim, because it involves no argument or persuasion. Its rage is corporeal and instinctual, almost innocent. In short, Bharat's weakness of disgust, his malady of *allagi*, becomes a formidable power that Hindutva can harness. In turning this affliction into a sign of true "Hindu-ness" (*hindu-tva*), the expression of an uncompromising *pakka hindu* (staunch Hindu), the subject is made to externalize those elements of himself that are, for the moment, associated with the phantasmagoric figure of the Muslim.

NOTES

I thank James T. Siegel for invaluable intellectual discussion, close reading, and the felicitous expression "hyperbolic vegetarianism," suggested precisely when I needed it most; John Borneman for insisting on self-reflexivity; Abdellah Hammoudi for discussing interlocution; Benedict Anderson for cautioning me about disappointment with friends in Gujarat; Christophe Robert for referring me to Aurel Kolnai in English; David Holmberg, David Lelyveld, Igal Halfin, Leo Coleman, and Brenda Maiale for reading and commenting on drafts; and Sharon K. Weiner, Zia Mian, Billie Jean Isbell, Isabelle Clark-Decès, Arvind Rajagopal, Peter van der Veer, Thomas Blom Hansen, Aisha Khan, and Véronique Benei, as well as the audiences at the Yale conference "Visceral Nations" in 2006 and at the 2006 Annual Meeting of the American Anthropological Association in San Jose.

1.   See, for example, Stanley Tambiah (1996) on democratic form and crowd violence; Peter van der Veer (1996) on nationalism, ritual, and devotion; Amrita Basu and Atul Kohli (1998) on competitive politics, changing identities, and the state; Paul Brass (2003) and his detailed dissection of the theatrical production of violence, the diverse sets of violent actors, and analyses of media representations; Ashutosh Varshney (2002) on the decline of civic institutions; and Arjun Appadurai (2006) on globalization and violence.

2.   "Drive against Illegal Slaughterhouses in Cities," *Times of India*, February 7, 2002, p. 1; "Gauvanshni befaam katal: kaanun kartaa kasaaionaa haath laambaa chhe," *Sandesh*, February 9, 2002, p. 3.

3.   See "Gau maataanu jaahermaa katleaamthi haahaakaar: polis golibaarmaa 1 nu mot," *Sandesh*, February 24, 2002, p. 1; "Police Fire Kills One at Bharuch Slaughter Spot," *Times of India*, February 24, 2002, p. 1.

4.   Many local Hanuman temples in Ahmedabad, known for their communalist leanings, were openly selling *trishul*s (tridents—symbols of the God Shiva or the Mother Goddess, often used as weapons) and swords, as well as country-made revolvers during the days of violence.

5.   As Gujarat's largest Vaishnavite Hindu sect, the Swaminarayan *sampradaya* is associated with the rise to prominence of the Patidar in Gujarati politics (Hardiman 1988) and of "unequivocal vegetar-

ianism" (Pocock 1973: 80). It has been an active agent of a specific version of Sanskritization (Srinivas 1953, 1956, 1962). It is engaged in many social reform efforts, such as de-addiction programs, vegetarianism, and the complete abolition of all animal sacrifice, which was initially demanded in the context of suttee and infanticide (Mallison 1974: 463; Desai 1978: 368; Parekh 1980: 185). In 1981 the sect began removing caste barriers from initiation rituals for *sadhus* (Williams 2001: 171).

6. Though Modi is referring to a wedding feast, *chappan bhoga* is part of the Vaishanava feast cycle—one of the many food festivals at Mount Govardhan in Braj (U.P.), organized by the Pushti Marga *sampradaya* (see Toomey 1992: 139).

7. A *kund* is a pit, or a vessel, for a sacrificial fire.

8. "Speech delivered by the Hon. Chief Minister of Gujarat, Shri Narendra Modi[,] on the 2nd Oct. 03," at www.gujaratindia.com/Media/Speeches/Porbandar.pdf (accessed May 28, 2008).

9. The RSS was founded in 1925 as an all-male Hindu nationalist organization with the purported goal of unifying "Hindus" in a national movement (see Andersen and Damle 1987).

10. "Cabinet Nod for Ahimsa University," *Asian Age*, August 29, 2002, p. 11; "Gujarat Will Show the Way: Modi," *Indian Express*, August 29, 2002, p. 3.

11. The relations and competition between Gujarati Patel and those groups that have successfully managed to claim a higher status, *kshatriya* or *rajput*, are linked in important ways to the political developments of the Gujarat state (see Shah 1975).

12. During World War II, Germans referred to French enemy soldiers pejoratively as *Knoblauchfresser* (garlic eaters), which is also part of a classic anti-Semitic stereotype. Today, such labels are applied, if at all, mostly to Turks or other *Ausländer* (foreigners).

13. Until the Mandal Commission recommendations, the 31 percent quota had been divided between 7 percent for scheduled castes, 14 percent for scheduled tribes, and 10 percent for other backward classes. The commission suggested that the latter category be increased to 28 percent (Sheth and Menon 1986: 16).

14. The term *culture* here should not be understood in a relativist sense. The term *sanskruti* denotes "civilization," "social progress," as well as "culture" (see GED).

15. The term *paku* means "ripe," "mature," "firm," "without defect or flaw"; it is often used in dietary contexts for food cooked in ghee or milk, and hence "not liable to be polluted" (see GUCD). When used in

domains apart from food, a *pakka hindu* connotes not only a "staunch Hindu" but also something of a better, more pure Hindu.

16.   Bharat's "success" in using *educashun* for upward mobility is not being replicated widely, as the quality of government schools is abysmal. Contrary to the usual developmental rhetoric, rural Gujarat ranks in the bottom 25 percent of all Indian provinces in reading and writing. Among Indian children generally, in the fifth grade, for example, 40 percent cannot read at that level and 70 percent cannot even subtract (see Pratham Mumbai Education Initiative 2008). This situation is particularly dire for the rural poor, who increasingly appreciate the importance of education but who lack access to any proper educational facilities.

17.   *The Anthropological Survey of India* distinguishes between *karaida rajput* and *nadoda rajput* (Singh 2003: 992–95, 609–13). Whereas in the former branch men were listed as nonvegetarians (avoiding only beef and pork), women were listed vegetarian (609). By contrast, the *nadoda rajput* are listed as simply vegetarian (992). The Jadav are *karadia* of the *nadoda rajput* branch. Most established *rajput* groups question their claim to *rajput* status as *kshatriya* (Tambs-Lyche 1992: 21). According to Shah (1975: 10), they have only recently formed an endogamous group; they used to exchange women with *rajput* groups in Rajasthan. If we can assume that the exchange was asymmetrical (hypergamy), as Northern *rajput* groups are generally considered "more noble," the volatility of their status would be explained.

18.   For a phenomenology of disgust, see Kolnai ([1929] 1974). There is an English translation of this work (in B. Smith and Korsmeyer 2004), but its quality is uneven (I thank Christophe Robert for the reference). For more psychoanalytic reflections on disgust, see Kristeva (1982) and Freud (1930). Martha Nussbaum (2004) offers an interesting discussion of disgust in relation to law, but she is only marginally concerned with phenomenological and psychoanalytical approaches. For an attempt at a comprehensive study of disgust, see Menninghaus ([1999] 2002).

19.   The Bajrang Dal is the militant youth wing of the VHP.

20.   The *kshatriya* (warrior, king) is one of the four estates of ancient Indian society. The classic *varna* system ideally defines Hindu ritual and social rank. While used frequently as a reference point to establish rank, it should not be confused with empirical realities on the ground. The highest three *varna* (Brahmin, or priest; Kshatriya or warrior; and Vaishya, or commoner, cultivator) are called twice-born (*dvija*). The fourth *varna* is the Shudra (servile class). In this scheme, the "Untouch-

ables" (Harijan, Dalit) are considered below even the lowest of the Shudra, remaining outside of Hindu society proper (thus *avarna*). In Gujarat, because many communities aspiring to *kshatriya* status are not understood to come from the traditional aristocratic ruling groups, an instability haunts their aspirations to higher status.

21. For a more complete analysis of Modi's speech and its relation to the imagery of the preceding pogrom, see Ghassem-Fachandi (2006).

22. For some helpful discussions of meat, masculinity, and femininity in the context of Gandhi's nonviolence, see Erikson (1969); L. Gandhi (1996); Lal (2000); and Roy (2002).

23. *Musalman* is a term for "Muslim" commonly used in northern India.

REFERENCES

Andersen, Walter K., and Shridhar D. Damle. 1987. *The Brotherhood in Saffron. The Rashtriya Swayamsevak Sangh and Hindu Revivalism*. New Delhi: Vistaar Publications.

Anderson, Benedict. 1991. *Imagined Communities: Reflections on the Origin and Spread of Nationalism*. Rev. ed. London: Verso.

Appadurai, Arjun. 2006. *Fear of Small Numbers: An Essay on the Geography of Anger*. Durham: Duke University Press.

Basu, Amrita, and Atul Kohli, eds. 1998. *Community Conflicts and the State in India*. Delhi: Oxford University Press.

Basu, Helene. 2004. *Von Barden und Königen. Ethnologische Studien zur Göttin und zum Gedächtnis in Kacch (Indien)*. Frankfurt am Main: Europäischer Verlag der Wissenschaften.

Brass, Paul. 2003. *The Production of Hindu-Muslim Violence in Contemporary India*. Seattle: University of Washington Press.

Desai, Neera. 1978. *Social Change in Gujarat: A Study of Nineteenth Century Gujarati Society*. Bombay: Vora.

Douglas, Mary. 1966. *Purity and Danger: An Analysis of the Concepts of Pollution and Taboo*. London: Routledge and K. Paul.

Durkheim, Émile. 1995. *The Elementary Forms of the Religious Life*. Trans. Karen E. Fields. New York: Free Press.

Erikson, Erik H. 1969. *Gandhi's Truth: On the Origins of Militant Nonviolence*. New York: Norton.

Freud, Sigmund. [1930] 1994. "Das Unbehagen in der Kultur." In *Das Unbehagen in der Kultur und andere kulturtheoretische Schriften*. Frankfurt am Main: Fischer.

Gandhi, Leela. 1996. "Concerning Violence: The Limits and Circulations of Gandhian 'Ahimsa' or Passive Resistance." *Cultural Critique*, no. 35: 105–47.

Gandhi, Mohandas K. [1921] 1987. "My Meaning of Sanatana Hinduism." In *The Essence of Hinduism*, ed. V. B. Kheer. Ahmedabad: Navjivan Trust.

———. 1927. *An Autobiography: The Story of My Experiments with Truth.* Ahmedabad: Navjivan Trust.

Ghassem-Fachandi, Parvis. 2006. "Sacrifice, Ahimsa, and Vegetarianism: Pogrom at the Deep End of Non-Violence." Ph.D. diss., Cornell University.

Hansen, Thomas Blom. 1999. *The Saffron Wave: Democracy and Hindu Nationalism in Modern India.* Princeton: Princeton University Press.

Hardiman, David. 1987. *The Coming of the Devi: Adivasi Assertion in Western India.* Delhi: Oxford University Press.

———. 1988. "Class Base of Swaminarayan Sect." *Economic and Political Weekly,* no. 37: 1907–12.

Jaffrelot, Christophe. 1996. *The Hindu Nationalist Movement in India.* New York: Columbia University Press.

Kolnai, Aurel. [1929] 1974. "Der Ekel." In *Jahrbuch für Philosophie und phänomenologische Forschung,* ed. by Edmund Husserl. Vol. 10. Halle (Saale): Max Niemeyer.

Kristeva, Julia. 1982. *Powers of Horror: An Essay on Abjection.* Trans. Leon S. Roudiez. New York: Columbia University Press.

Lal, Vinay. 2000. "Nakedness, Nonviolence, and Brahmacharya: Gandhi's Experiments in Celibate Sexuality." *Journal of the History of Sexuality* 9(1/2): 105–36.

Mallison, Françoise. 1974. "La Secte Krichnaîte des *Svami-Narayani* au Gujarat." *Journal Asiatique* 262(3–4): 435–71.

Menninghaus, Winfried. [1999] 2002. *Ekel: Theorie und Geschichte einer starken Empfindung.* Frankfurt am Main: Suhrkamp.

Nandy, Ashis. 1980. *At the Edge of Psychology: Essays in Politics and Culture.* Delhi: Oxford University Press

Nussbaum, Martha. 2004. *Hiding from Humanity: Disgust, Shame, and the Law.* Princeton: Princeton University Press.

———. 2007. *The Clash Within: Democracy, Religious Violence, and India's Future.* Cambridge, MA: Harvard University Press, Belknap Press.

Parekh, Manilal C. 1980. *Shri Swami Narayana: A Gospel of Bhagavata-Dharma: or, God in Redemptive Action.* 3rd ed. Bombay: Bharatiya Vidya Bhavan.

Parikh, C. D. 1998. *Anya Pachhat Vargo-nu Kalyan* [Welfare of other backward classes in Gujarat state]. Ahmedabad: Navbharat Sahitya Mandir.

Pocock, David F. 1972. *Kanbi and Patidar: A Study of the Patidar Community of Gujarat.* Oxford: Clarendon Press.

————. 1973. *Mind, Body, Wealth. A Study of Belief and Practice in an Indian Village.* Oxford: Blackwell.

Pratham Mumbai Education Initiative. 2008. *Pratham Annual Report.* Mumbai: PMEI.

Rajagopal, Arvind. 1999. "Thinking through Emerging Markets: Brand Logics and the Cultural Forms of Political Society in India." *Social Text,* no. 60: 131–49.

Roy, Parama. 2002. "Meat-Eating, Masculinity, and Renunciation in India: A Gandhian Grammar of Diet." *Gender & History* 14(1): 62–91.

Shah, Ghanshyam. 1975. *Caste Association and Political Process in Gujarat. A Study of the Gujarat Kshatriya Sabha.* Bombay: Popular Prakashan.

Sheth, Pravin N., and Ramesh Menon. 1986. *Caste and Communal Time Bomb.* Ahmedabad: Hetvarsha Prakashan.

Singh, K. S., ed. 2002. "People of India: Gujarat." In *The Anthropological Survey of India.* Vol. 22, part 2. Mumbai: Popular Prakashan.

Smith, Barry, and Carolyn Korsmeyer, eds. 2004. *On Disgust.* Chicago: Open Court.

Smith, William Robertson. [1894] 2005. *Lectures on the Religion of the Semites.* London: Elibron Classics.

Srinivas, M. N. 1953. "Prospects of Sociological Research in Gujarat." *Journal of the Maharaja Sayajirao University of Baroda* 2(1): 21–35.

————. 1956. "A Note on Sanskritization and Westernization." *Far Eastern Quarterly* 15(4): 481–96.

————. 1962. *Caste in Modern India and Other Essays.* Bombay: Asia Publishing House.

Tambiah, Stanley J. 1996. *Leveling Crowds: Ethnonationalist Conflicts and Collective Violence in South Asia.* Berkeley: University of California Press.

Tambs-Lyche, Harald. 1992. *Power and Devotion: Religion and Society in Saurashtra.* Bergen, Norway: University of Bergen.

————. 1997. *Power, Profit, and Poetry: Traditional Society in Kathiawar, Western India.* New Delhi: Manohar.

Toomey, Paul M. 1992. "Mountain of Food, Mountain of Love: Ritual Inversion in the Annakuta Feast at Mount Govardhan." In *Gastronomic Ideas and Experiences of Hindus and Buddhists,* ed. R. S. Khare. Albany: State University of New York Press.

Van der Veer, Peter. 1996. *Religious Nationalism: Hindus and Muslims in India.* New Delhi: Oxford University Press.

Varshney, Ashutosh. 2002. *Ethnic Conflict and Civic Life: Hindus and Muslims in India.* New Haven: Yale University Press.

Williams, Raymond Brady. 2001. *An Introduction to Swaminarayan Hinduism.* Cambridge: Cambridge University Press.

Dictionaries

GED—*Gujarati-English Dictionary* (*Gujarati-Angreji Kosh*). Pandurang Ganesh Deshpande, comp. (Amdavad [Ahmedabad]: University Book Production Board, Gujarat State, 1974).

GUCD—*Gala's Universal Combined Dictionary.* L. R. Gala, comp. (Ahmedabad [Memnagar]: Navneet House, 2001).

FIVE

The Obligation to Receive

THE COUNTERTRANSFERENCE,
THE ETHNOGRAPHER, PROTESTANTS,
AND PROSELYTIZATION IN NORTH INDIA

Leo Coleman

It is not the office of a man to receive gifts. How dare you give them?
We wish to be self-sustained. The hand that feeds is in some danger of
being bitten. . . . He is a good man who can receive a gift well.

Ralph Waldo Emerson, "Gifts" (1844)

The practice of social and cultural anthropology has long been rooted in
an attempt to account for persons and social forms on the basis of
extended and, by the standards of most other social sciences, extraordi-
narily intimate encounters. Close involvement with others is not only
our method but in large part also our object; we seek to understand, generally speaking, the significant relations people make with each other.

From this basis we anthropologists speak of deep, participatory, long-
term collaborations with our research interlocutors as both an epistemological and ethical warrant for our work (the choice of "interlocutor" itself,
over "informant," signals a commitment to egalitarian and "dialogical"
modes of knowledge production). In reflexive moments we dwell on the
push and pull of our various research and professional responsibilities and
ask ourselves, anxiously, what we can give back to the participants in our

research, and how such giving can make our research stronger, deeper, richer, more closely attuned to the expectations and the lives of those studied. We say that we *work with*, *engage with*, and *collaborate with* people. But if participation and reciprocity in our research interactions is the highest normative demand, in ignoring other forms of emotional exchange in fieldwork we risk collapsing epistemology into ethics. It is not always possible to love the other; nor by loving, to know.[1]

Anthropologists have occasionally turned to psychoanalytic theory for insights into the impasses and travails of close involvement in emotional exchanges with others, in pursuit of knowledge, yet we have paid little attention to the deeply inegalitarian norms of the analytic encounter, and have often evaded the question of what it would, in fact, mean for ethnography to take seriously analogies from analytic practice—with its diagnoses, its patients, and its authoritative practitioners.[2] In this essay I provoke an exchange between one view of the countertransference in psychoanalytic work and anthropological theories of the gift, in pursuit of a heightened awareness of the unreciprocal emotional exchanges in which the ethnographer *must* engage in order to learn something. The analytic concept of countertransference appears particularly useful for thinking through the occasional need for the ethnographer to refuse to engage or participate with his or her interlocutors, in order to describe and interpret. I draw my specific notion of countertransference from the work of D. W. Winnicott, where it encompasses the analyst's emotional responses to the patient and what within the analysis can be done with them. This version of countertransference and the conception of the professional analytic work that accompanies it both appear useful for rethinking our models for ethnographic practice so that we can acknowledge and incorporate resistance, and the impasses reached in any relationship, as yet productive for knowing others.

I pursue these methodological reflections on countertransference and its utility in response to the insistent and unreflective demand that we constantly exchange with our research interlocutors—that we love them and seek to be loved in return. I present an ethnographic case of (my own) negative countertransference, and will, in closing, tailor the psychoanalytic materials for ethnography by integrating anthropological understandings of reciprocity and obligation into the existing psychoanalytical framework.

PSYCHOANALYSIS AND ETHNOGRAPHY

"To being with, the analyst is a certain kind of host." Thus Adam Phillips (1988: 11) sums up, aphoristically, the view of the British psychoanalyst D. W. Winnicott, who developed incisive and instructive models of the analytical work and of the emotional investments brought to that work by both patient and analyst, drawing on his broad experience in clinical work across an array of settings (most famously with children). In Winnicott's work the analyst is described both as a welcoming, nurturing listener, who "holds" the patient's symptoms and helps redirect them, and as a recipient and target of the contaminating, difficult, and potentially damaging uncathected emotional energies of his (often severely ill) patients. This dual view of the analytic work can be extended, I will argue, to certain ethnographic situations. Winnicott's recognition of the demands placed on the analyst and his heuristic simplification of the emotional landscape of the analytic encounter to dynamics of "love" and "hate" are both useful in my attempt to account for some of my own research encounters. Finally, Winnicott—as I will discuss at length below—introduces novel considerations of the analyst's "hate," and how it might be employed in both diagnosis and treatment.

In practice, the contexts of analysis and fieldwork are not only distinct but in some ways radically incommensurable. Ethnographers *go* to the field and are swallowed up by the live social contexts of our research, while patients *come* to the analyst and relinquish themselves to the asocial norms of the analytic space.[3] An ethnographer cannot adopt the stance of rigorous withholding that is classically demanded of the psychoanalyst; and more importantly, ethnography abjures any directionality in research toward a "cure" or a subjective transformation of the "informant."[4] We, rather, presume that the researcher him- or herself will be transformed by the fieldwork experience, though the limits of that transformation and the role it plays in our knowledge production are most often left vague and underspecified.

Yet psychoanalysis and ethnography converge in the epistemological doubling unique to the situation in which social relations (however attenuated) are both the means and the object of study. In each field, "methodology is a large part of its own subject matter" (Weiner 1999: 235), and theoretical insights come not primarily from the success or failure of the treatment or research (as is the case in social sciences more enamored of their own falsifiability), but rather from a reflection on method and an intrusion of methodological inquiry into the process of the work itself. "To call [psychoanalysis] a social science is to recognize that *its procedure makes use of the social relationships that are its subject matter.* . . . Like ethnography or linguistics, it uses its own subject of study as the medium of that study" (Weiner 1999: 239; emphasis in the original).

I aim to compare the ethnographic and psychoanalytic methods, in full awareness of the differences that pertain, not to collapse one into the other. I focus here on problems that have attracted much more attention from psychoanalysts than from anthropologists but that are shared by our two fields—the problems of the countertransference, its status as "objective" response to the demands of the other or as a factitious product of the researcher's own biography and psychic constitution, and the duty of the researcher to withhold and withdraw from emotional exchanges with his or her interlocutors in pursuit of knowledge. I hope to throw into relief the normative demand placed on fieldworkers for reciprocity and love in their intimate research relations, and seek to understand what this demand obscures.[5]

A CALL TO PARTICIPATION

My fieldwork in Delhi was largely conducted among intellectuals, activists, and middle-class elites as they developed new ways of relating to their government, pursued policy debates, and articulated grievances in the aftermath of the privatization of the electricity system there. I sought to understand changing notions of the public good and the shape of democracy in that country after a decade of economic reforms.

Most of my research in Delhi involved welcoming and open-ended interactions marked by generosity in the co-production of ethnographic and activist knowledge. But the circumstances in which—to my dismay and discomfort—I encountered rejection, wariness, or outright hostility, and more often various forms of solicitation to prove my interest in and loyalty to the aims of small and solidary groups of citizens, were frequent enough to require some reflection. While I met the demands of my interlocutors in those contexts, in order to gain access and learn something, I was also assailed by doubts about what might be seen as a censurable retreat into passive complicity and mute recording (though the immediate stakes were relatively low, they certainly might be high in another political context).

For instance, most of the groups I worked with had such names as "People's Action" or "People's Rule," and they spoke on behalf of the people in all their political action. And yet, these same groups established in practice quite narrow, class-specific criteria for participation in their meetings, in contrast to their embracing rhetoric of "the people." Many of the events I went to were held in venues where it was necessary to possess a great deal of symbolic capital, habits of status and distinction, just to gain entrance; comprehensive surveillance was exercised over the constitution of the public summoned together to attend these forums, sometimes with metal detectors at the door, at other times with predetermined lists of attendees. I was often subject to suspicious attention only partly allayed by my reassurances that I was not a journalist, that I was in fact a researcher (and why were they so afraid of journalists?), and sometimes, before or after such events, I was asked for significant sums of money to compensate for my presence there (requests that I invariably met). Many of my activist-interlocutors would not allow me to be a mere observer, to attend otherwise than as a supporter of their aims, an active witness, and a material contributor to their cause.

I was from time to time asked to lend my expertise to the ongoing political and policy debates, and occasionally found my contributions misappropriated and twisted to support political claims that traduced my own commitments and affiliations. More discomfiting, if less easy to pin down, was the diffuse expectation that I would participate in and lend my assent to a politics I did not agree with. In short, I didn't like some of the people I had to participate with as I observed them, and I didn't like their politics, but I had no way to express this aversion and even censored some of my fieldnotes, ambivalent about the status and validity of what I then saw as my wholly personal reactions.

By the end of my fieldwork, however, I had a better handle on my role in these observational contexts and in the interactions that transpired within them, because of a set of experiences I had elsewhere in India with religious proselytization. These latter ethnographic encounters, which I describe and analyze in detail here, occurred outside the locale and beyond the topics of my formal ethnographic research (though we might well pose the question of whether, for the ethnographer during fieldwork, there is any place "outside").

Amid my fieldwork and uncertain about the direction it was taking, I left Delhi briefly for a vacation in the foothills of the Himalayas. I returned to a resort town—a hill station—where I had previously stayed as a language student and, to fill my days, resumed courses at the language school there. Unexpectedly I found myself in a complicated relationship with two competing religious discourses, two attempts at proselytization, which ultimately made me rethink the role of the ethnographer confronted with challenges and demands from his or her interlocutors. On the one hand, one of my language teachers—an affable, if somewhat wounded, bachelor—at my express request began to educate me in his spiritual practices and worldview: as a Muslim, a Sufi, an opponent of witches and demons. On the other hand, I was thrust into sharing accommodations with a married, middle-aged pair of Christian missionaries, Americans, in whose company I found it easy at first to relax and enjoy myself as an American among Americans, and who soon began to offer me instructive narratives of the work of Jesus in their lives. In Delhi, ambivalence and resistance were present on both sides of the unequal exchange between myself as the ethnographer and my activist-interlocutors; reflecting on my role as a recipient of religious instruction in a different context helped me assess the significance, for ethnography, of such open-ended, uncomfortable, and difficult exchanges.[6]

A DESCRIPTION OF TWO FIELD ENCOUNTERS

After I had left Delhi, somewhat precipitously, and settled into the hill station where I had retreated for a vacation, I found myself leading the life stereotypically associated with "fieldwork." I was the only guest in an otherwise empty guesthouse, subject to the full force of the cook's and housekeeper's deferential and rather overwhelming hospitality. While the guesthouse didn't have an actual verandah, there was a large grassy terrace, where I took tea, overlooking the valley below and the large town spreading out along the distant plain. The staff and I enacted a farce nearly each day, when Anand, the cook, would offer to make "anything, anything" I wanted to eat, and he and his assistant Manish would listen patiently to my consideration of possible dining options, though we all knew that my choices were strictly limited by locally available produce and Anand's repertoire—still, as the keeper of his little mountain resort, he liked to pretend that a plenitude of cosmopolitan desires could be satisfied there.[7]

Twice a day, I hiked up to the language school for classes, which served mostly as a defined space for conversation on chosen topics. Trying to make the time useful, I steered the talk as much as possible to "ethnographic" topics: Indian character, local history, local custom, religion and ritual. This was comfortable, easy terrain for both my teachers and myself. We knew how to have a conversation that played out along familiar and well-tested lines of student and teacher, researcher and informant.[8] One of the teachers had, decades before, been a teacher and informant to much more famous anthropologists than I, and all the teachers were well accustomed to the students' demands for cultural know-how.

The school was originally founded as a place to train Methodist missionaries for work in India, and it is still attended by missionaries from the United States, Korea, and elsewhere for this purpose. It is now run by an Indian Christian foundation, but the staff are not uniformly Christian. I became friendly with one of the Muslim teachers, Ahmed, when I started asking questions about the *dargah*, or Sufi shrine, adjacent to the school. It is a small concrete structure, gaily painted, enclosing a stone outcropping that is said to be the tomb of a medieval Muslim saint who long ago wandered in these hills. The little shrine is quite new—it was built some twenty years ago by the Hindu head of the local army base, to whom the saint had appeared in a dream commanding him to glorify the grave.

When I asked about the shrine one day in class, Ahmed told me that he himself was a *mujavir,* a semi-official caretaker and worshipper at the dargah. More, it turned out that Ahmed was something of a *pir*—or saint—in training; his father was a powerful Sufi, and Ahmed himself had inherited some of his father's spiritual power. After several sessions in which I pursued conversations on this topic, Ahmed had me kneel in front of him in the classroom and placed his hands on my head, chanting under his breath as he slowly lifted his hands through my hair. He explained to me that he was transferring his power (*shakti*) into me, in order to make me strong (*mazboot*) and to protect me. As our meetings continued I asked further questions, and we began to take walks to out-of-the-way glens, on the other side of the mountaintop, to perform simi- lar rituals. I drew Ahmed out, asking him to teach me the various spiritual things he knew, and he didn't seem shy when it came to instructing me about magic and witches—or prostitutes.

In exchange for providing me with vocabulary for a variety of sexual situations, Ahmed wanted to know about my sex life in America, and this was another aspect of our conversations. Having completed reli- gious instruction in due solemnity, Ahmed then bragged about his con- quests, especially of the Korean Christian missionaries, and I, of necessity, invented a vigorous heterosexual life for myself to confide to Ahmed. Another teacher had told me that Ahmed had not long before suffered a humiliating divorce (I never got the details), but I was still sur- prised by the ferocity of his attitude toward women, his insistent cate- chizing of me in violent sexual jokes. But this was research, and contained by the limits of our class hours, so I went along and enjoyed the banter as best I could.

In my notes, I focused on the confirmation that Ahmed's religious practices and ideas provided of my prior reading and training in popu- lar Indian religiosity. Here was a Muslim, a devotee of a *pir,* who exulted in the fact that an elite Hindu had, by erecting the small concrete shrine, honored the tomb of his saint: a Sufi devotee apparently unconcerned by another's access to the source of his spiritual power, and who moreover incorporated me into his ritual life without attempting to indoctrinate me, without asking for assent to dogmas. He did not ask me to believe, merely to conform. He did not press for intellectual assent and conversion, for confirmation of the truth of his practice, but rather assumed that regardless of my intellectual stance, I would benefit from the rituals he knew how to practice.[9]

I had an interaction with Ahmed that was "research-worthy"—some conversations with him turned effortlessly into fieldnotes, lists of arcane terms, an ethnophysiology connected with witchcraft, and so on. I was calm, reserved, adequately curious, systematic, and undisturbed by Ahmed's instruction of me in the occult; as for the talk of women and heterosexual sex, I was mildly concerned by his misogyny (which I tried, in my fabricated stories, to counter) but not confronted with anything inassimilable to the research.

This space of orderly routine, relative mastery of my goals, and calm self-identification as fieldworker was interrupted by a very different kind of interaction, which split open my calm confidence and revealed some of the fissures inside. Maureen and John, two American missionaries from the Corn Belt, arrived at the guesthouse and moved into the room next to mine.

Maureen and John were also students at the language school, of longer standing than I. Middle-aged and very midwestern, they stuck out among the small group of generally younger students. But for the first couple of weeks of my residence there, I learned nothing about them other than what I gleaned through side glances. I knew only that they were Americans and some species of Christian. I kept my distance. Then I heard that they were dissatisfied with their current accommodations and they intended to move into my guesthouse. I had, of course, been living in solitary splendor for some time; I was bothered by the prospect of sharing with others my meals, my joking relationship with Anand and Manish, and my terrace.

On the day that Maureen and John arrived, I heard the two of them being shown into the vacant rooms along the terrace, and when I realized that they had settled on the room just adjacent to mine I decided to take some action, for our mutual benefit. I straightened my clothes and went out to greet them. I suggested, as kindly as I could, that it might be better if they took a room further down along the building, since the walls were thin, we could hear each other's every move, and so on. I remember emphasizing the fact that I was alone, and therefore quiet, while they were a couple, and would be talking and making noise. I feared they would have sex—but I did not say this.

Maureen bridled at my request, and her generous good cheer faded. She wanted sun, she said, and the room adjoining mine was the only remaining one not shaded by the hill that rose behind the house. I didn't press my point far, and retreated, frustrated and likewise resentful. Maureen had treated me with the intransigence of a mother being berated by an overweening son; she knew what she wanted and she intended to get it, and my objections, though they hurt her, were best ignored.

I avoided them that day and the next, staying in my room and taking my meals there—though I heard them coming and going, and my already disturbed sleep was further disturbed by their presence next door. Soon, however, I had to accept that my retreat had ended. I thus joined them one morning at breakfast. This was the first of some fifteen meals we would share over the course of the next two weeks, until I returned to Delhi.

Our interaction was mostly confined to these meals in the dining room: a low-ceilinged and dark room, often bitterly cold in those last months of the high-altitude winter. We sat bundled in extra layers as we ate—I wrapped in one of my *khadi* shawls, Maureen and John in puffy jackets and thermal knits. Those first few days we stuck to polite topics, sharing notes about the language teachers and about India. At every possible chance Maureen would proclaim her love for India and Indians and all things Indian. She spoke disparagingly of missionaries they had met in India who subsisted on cornflakes and Cream of Wheat, of a missionary family who had asked her to bring Bisquick and pasta and other packaged goods from America. She enthused over the food Anand made, and expressed disbelief of and scorn for others who "held themselves apart" from Indians, who lived behind high walls and in expat enclaves.

Her attitude was, perhaps, one of the things that thawed our relations at first. From this initial basis in a shared "interest" or investment in India—despite the difference of our investment and purpose—we began opening up to each other, offering more details of our lives. A space was established in which we could talk more freely.

Maureen and John belonged to what they described to me as a Word of Faith church. They had faith in Jesus' presence and efficacy in everyday life, the real existence of healing miracles, the promise of success to those who accepted Jesus. While both had been saved for some years, they had met each other relatively recently, at a mega-church in Tulsa, Oklahoma, where the religious movement to which they belong has its global headquarters. John had always lived in Tulsa; Maureen had moved there to join a renowned church, to go to Bible school, and to become a missionary. Shortly after she and John met and fell in love, they felt their Christian goals stifled by the bureaucracy of the large church they both belonged to, so they left that church to move to another, smaller congregation and, at about the same time, dedicated themselves to mission work. They were financing their mission themselves, and had incorporated themselves as a 501(c)(3) corporation (capable of receiving tax-deductible contributions).

Maureen and John were each fiercely independent people, individualists. Maureen rejected any notion of woman's subservience or ill-suitedness to God's work. John, I was told by Maureen, had had his own businesses for years; he didn't like to work for other people, for their gain. Maureen, for her part, had been in sales in Chicago until she was born again. They ran their mission work on very businesslike principles; they had incorporated themselves, they told me, so that people could donate directly to their efforts and would know exactly who was getting their money, rather than having donations funneled through a church or larger missionary organization. For Maureen, mission work was a form of salesmanship. She had a great product—Jesus—that she believed in wholeheartedly, and she was convinced of his efficacy in healing and transforming people. "I'm excited about Jesus," she said. "I'm excited to share his power with people."

Maureen and John had each been relatively successful people in this world; prosperity is not what they needed Jesus for.[10] Jesus' specific action in their life together was always defined as his healing work in saving them from depression and solitude, and making them a couple. John had been married before, while Maureen's midlife marriage with John was her first. Their marriage was proof of Jesus' saving and salving work in the world. Maureen was very open, if not specific, about her earlier life. She had been caught up in bad relationships, wrong ambitions, depression and pain. Jesus saved her from that. The single, magical act of accepting the truth of Jesus, of accepting him into their hearts, had transformed their lives, which had been beset by internal demons. But they had no illusions about the sanctity of all Christians.

Their pleasingly ironic view of the Christian community came out in their stories about why they had decided to switch churches. In justifying their decision, Maureen and John told me a long story about the way their relationship had been received by their first church. Once Maureen and John had decided to get married, the church had insisted that they participate in a premarital training group. They laughed at how clueless the younger couples in the group seemed, and at how useless the advice that they were given had been. They spoke of the stereotypes about relationships on which the counseling relied and the stilted videos that purveyed them. They described how they took on a distinct role in the group as a *real* model for the younger couples—a role almost subversive of the aims of the training. Their (then prospective) marriage, their older and wiser companionship, was a partnership—they shared the cleaning of their house in Oklahoma; John cooked at least half the time. The younger couples treated them with respect, and often thought that they were an old married couple who were there to lead the discussions. "But we were there, about to get married, just like them!" Maureen said.

But they didn't quite fit in, and they were both respected and excluded by this group of earnest young affianced couples. Maureen and John had volunteered to run the refreshment table at the premarital counseling sessions, but what had been a spontaneous, generous offer became their permanent job. Everyone let them continue this task rather than rotating the responsibility for refreshments; they were treated, it seemed, like staff rather than fellow initiates.

They did become friendly with one younger couple in the group. Maureen and John invited the couple to come over for dinner; they cooked and cleaned the house, and waited for their guests to arrive. But they never showed up, were not answering their phone. Maureen and John ended up eating alone. Finally, the next day, the young woman called Maureen and apologized. They had forgotten, had been on the road somewhere, hadn't remembered about the engagement until the next morning. Maureen arranged another date with her, but this time the couple canceled a day in advance of the planned dinner party. Maureen shrugged off the woman's excuses and apologies. She had not been treated well. There was an undercurrent of doubt and suspicion in the story. The story concluded without a real resolution, but it and other, similar stories were told repeatedly, as Maureen and John narrated and justified their decision to change churches, to find a less institutionalized and hierarchical community, and to be independent in their mission work.

Later, I read these stories a little bit differently. They were offered sincerely, unmarked, as stories. But they were also directed—probably in ways Maureen and John themselves were not entirely in control of—at me. Maureen and John were trying to reach out to me, establish their bona fides as people with whom I could talk. I was pleased with how progressive they were; I agreed with them and laughed with them as they mocked the marital training they had gone through, nodded solemnly as they spoke of the financial mismanagement of some churches' mission funds. And more, these were also cautionary tales, foreshadowing another theme: how important it was to be utterly sincere in one's acceptance of Jesus' messengers, whoever they may be, to accept his call when it came, and to allow his influence into every branch of one's life.

Our conversations were, as I said, in those first few meals, marked by a polite avoidance of conflict. John and Maureen asked me at the first dinner if I minded if they prayed before we began eating. I, of course, told them I didn't mind at all, that they should feel free to do as they would at home. I did not participate in their prayer. On the second night I waited for them to pray before dishing out the food, but they laughed when they saw I was waiting for them and said that they had already prayed before I arrived at the table. On the third night John again asked permission to pray, which I again gave—he seemed concerned that I not be forced to partake in their religiosity. That night and for the rest of our acquaintance Maureen, who usually conducted the prayer, included me in their prayers, repeating my name as she called on Jesus to protect me from disease and sorrow and to guide me and my work in fruitful directions.

Soon, I broached the topic of their mission work, what it was that they planned to do. Maureen had previously been a missionary in Peru—on a brief trip—and she contrasted her experience there with the possibilities of mission work in India. She had preached in the street in Peru, and she had been able to participate in big mass meetings in the central squares in towns. "But we can't preach in the streets here," she said. I asked why not. She hastened to assure me that there were no laws against conversion in India, but that the government wanted to protect people from being misled or misguided.

"The in-the-streets thing just doesn't work in India," she said. "People are too curious, and they might not understand what you were doing, they might agree to be converted and then go about their lives." This doubt about the sincerity of conversion was key, in terms both of their theology and of their relationship to the converted. John said, "You can't just accept Jesus and go about the rest of your life as if Jesus was not everything. Then there's no point." Conversion was understood by them as a cognitive and exclusive acceptance of Jesus, and this could not be accomplished by preaching in public—in India, at least. And, Maureen elaborated, it's dangerous for the converted—people are cast out by their families for becoming Christian. "You can't just inspire them to accept Jesus into their heart and then leave them," she said. Public witnessing doesn't work in India as a way of gaining converts, because "you can't be sure it's real" (that is, the conversion) and it's "not fair to them." The danger to the family relation was a heartfelt worry. Maureen said that her own family had had a hard time adjusting to her conversion. "They're Lutherans," she said. "They're believing people, but they were like, 'Why is she so excited about God?' Religion is a Sunday and Christmas thing for them." She continued, "That's why we have a lot of sympathy," articulating something I had myself been about to ask, "because we've both experienced a lot of exclusion in America—for being born again."

I wrote in my fieldnotes that I foresaw problems for them in that their thoroughgoing individualism and notion of singular identity as a Christian was potentially culturally incompatible with their "fieldsite." The individualism of Maureen and John's creed cannot allow the relativism and notion of a particulate self that is commonplace, if not in Indian society then at least in Indian sociology. I told them this as best I could, drawing on my reading as well as my experiences with Ahmed and elsewhere in India. I said that it was quite common in India to accept an allegiance to, say, a Muslim saint and maintain the rest of your normal social and ritual life, as a Hindu or a bureaucrat or what have you. Though they were polite in listening to me, they seemed to take this idea in particular as a challenge or an affront. After all, as a result of their acceptance of Jesus they had given up their professional lives, their home in Oklahoma, and come to India alone, determined to devote their lives to the evangelization of Indians.

I felt some responsibility to disillusion them about the ease with which they thought they might heal people's sorrows—I saw Maureen, especially, as something of a wild card, an unlicensed meddler in the emotional lives of others. She spoke often of the great love and faith people had given her, the thanks they had offered her, when she saved them. The satisfaction she gained from converting others was patent. I tried to act on my concern for them—I offered them gifts of knowledge and expertise. I gave them an article from *Frontline* about the Hindu nationalist party's campaigns against Christian missionization of "tribals." They were not unaware of these things—but they had their own fixed ideas about them, and they were incurious about my perspective. I had to insist through a whole meal that they might profit from reading the *Frontline* article, and was forced to press the magazine on them as they left the table that night. They never responded to my tutelage—at most, John would murmur that what I had said was interesting, and we would move on to other topics. Maureen would turn again to the theme of the solace Jesus can provide. "I know there is power there," she said at one such time. "I have seen amazing power in spiritual places, when people are cast down or depressed." Implicitly, with these claims she reached out to me for a response, an affirmation that I too was lost and that Christ would save me.

As I cautioned them to be careful of cultural and sociological difference (gently, I thought), I retreated to a position of authority, expertise, and—more importantly—relatively cold, emotionless facts, as a reaction against this emotional challenge posed to me by Maureen and John. But I was not emotionless in this move to objectivity. I time and again stilled the conversation, introducing an overtone of distress that cautioned us to pull back from whatever topic we had approached. One night, in one such moment of stillness, John turned to me and asked me what had made me interested in anthropology.

I started with platitudes, familiar and rehearsed, about having had a great teacher, being interested in the world, taking pleasure in meeting other people in unfamiliar places. They could follow me as far as this went, but I wasn't satisfied. I needed to tell them more, to convince them of my conviction. So I went on: I spoke of my passion for the discipline, which had grown the more I had been involved in it; I said that I liked the fact that unlike many other approaches to the world, anthropology took big questions seriously. Like religion—it is uniquely able to deal with religious experience without reducing it to something else, I said, to psychological or economic or biological needs and drives. I knew I was on dangerous ground, and I grew distressed. I was speaking of anthropology as a creed, as a truth that described and encompassed, provided a totalizing system for understanding the world, that reflected the unique and specific world without traducing it. That traded in certainties rather than in doubt. I quoted Lévi-Strauss's line about anthropology being one of the last true vocations.

As I spoke into the silence, I was very emotional, almost teary, and was shaking violently. I was desperate to extract something from them, anything that could pass as recognition. I was hardly able to hold a fork. It was cold in the dining room, but not cold enough to explain the shivers that seized me as I talked. In that moment, I had retreated to scholarly knowledge, secular authority, my status as an "anthropologist," and had gotten no closer to certainty. Or sincerity. I was trying to match the import of the terms they used in talking about conversion—truth, sufficiency—and trying to generate an emotional relationship to anthropology that would let it serve as a countersystem, that might convince *them*. I wanted to offer them a gift as powerful as Jesus, to neutralize the gift of grace they insistently pressed on me (I tried to offer this countergift regardless of the fact that I had not, as yet, accepted *their* gift). Obviously, I came up short, and I worried that I had bared some open wound, that I had revealed to Maureen a crevice she could exploit to prize me open, that my emotion had given the two of them a reason to bring me further into the circle of their prayers, and to ask me the question that Maureen said was the crux of their mission work: "Do you know that Jesus is real and wants to live in your heart?" The surrender—epistemic and emotional—that the question demanded was very close.

But they, for their own reasons, never asked me that question, and I mastered my reaction to Maureen and John. We continued to eat together for the last few days I was in the guesthouse, but we never again broached God topics, outside of the prayer they offered before every meal. Nor did we discuss anthropology or my work. Only, on the day I left, Maureen asked if they could pray for me, and I agreed. We stood in a circle, our heads bowed, Anand and Manish watching with some amusement, as Maureen loudly invoked the Lord. She asked the Lord to keep me safe, to protect me from illness, to give me good intelligence and application in my academic work. She blessed the encounter on the mountainside, all the things we had learned from each other. She thanked the Lord for loving us.

For my part, I participated mutely. I held Maureen's and John's hands, kept my head bowed, and when the prayer was over laid my hand over my heart and thanked them both heartily and sincerely. I gave myself over to the minimal requirements of politeness. Just as with my Sufi teacher or at a *dargah* or in a cathedral, I conformed to the sacred posture required of me without offering anything of myself. Only my presence.

EXCHANGE OF TRANSFERENCES

As I have related my encounter with Maureen and John to several other scholars, they have uniformly pointed out that this couple represent much that I am opposed to politically and intellectually in my native context in America and as an anthropologist. They represent red-state conservatism and a religiosity organized around belief and faith; their demand for assent and conversion participates in a "modern" and "Western" cultural notion of the subjective self as both bounded and autonomous and as the locus of agency and of (religious) transformation.[11] One friend even went so far as to say, "They are everything that you hate."

I was quick, perhaps defensively so, to counter these readings of the situation—I genuinely liked and enjoyed their company, I said; we laughed together, and shared among other things an easy reference to our midwestern roots. But I could not ignore the felt similarity between this encounter and the demands placed on me in my proper fieldsite. In Delhi, I was summoned to participation and cooperation by the activists with whom I worked, both in direct conversation and by the contexts in which I was involved with them: political meetings, strategy sessions, and quasi-public events like fund-raisers. Because of the expectations of such spaces, one's mere attendance is a sort of vote in favor of the aims of the political gathering. Both in Delhi and in the encounter with Maureen and John, *assent* was implicitly demanded, at the very least as a requirement of polite intercourse between speaking subjects in society.

However, John and Maureen were asking for something beyond polite participation or intellectual agreement (or argument) from me, as I realized only later—they were demanding conversion, though they never made their demand explicit. I offered them, in return, first my polite complicity, and then magazine articles and other, increasingly aggressive, tokens of my engagement with them. The impossibility of the situation emerged, finally, when they asked for my profession of faith (elliptically—that is, by asking me what made me want to be an anthropologist), and I inadvertently offered them a gift they could not accept. I offered them a countersystem, another creed. I failed to withhold the resentment and hatred that their demand precipitated, and store these emotions up for later interpretation; my reaction emerged into the space of our encounter (in my choice to use "religion" as one of the things that anthropology can explain), and disrupted our interaction. In that moment, as they listened mutely to my offering and I grew ever more distraught, I felt my hate in an unfocused and unmastered manner (I use "hate" here in the sense given it by Winnicott, discussed below). How could they demand this of me?[12] Finally, I tried to resolve the conflict by defining our conversations as a research space and adopting the same attitude I wore in other research situations—outward conformity and inward distance.

I was able to sustain this compromise only because I was leaving the guesthouse and the town where we shared our encounter, for this very distinction between outward behavior and inward self is one internal to the epistemology of Protestantism; the congruence between the two is a prerequisite for truth, and therefore Maureen and John were alert to attempts to separate them: "There's no point accepting Jesus and going about your life." Everything they said to me demanded authenticity of me, that I conceal the gap between my polite engagement and my private doubt, or rather that I reach a place where such a gap would collapse in the movement of belief. By contrast, the separation between doxa and praxis, between inward belief and outward behavior, between faith and action, is precisely what Ahmed, my Sufi teacher, and his nondualistic ritual practices allowed me—to accept his aid and succor in the always difficult project of life, without assenting to any final claim on the form that life would take in mine or another's circumstances.

We know that there are, in South Asia, complex, nondualistic theories of how the self becomes transformed by bodily disciplines and what we are tempted to call "outward" conformity (though this language doesn't do justice to the thought; see, e.g., Alter 1992, 2004). Neither yoga nor Buddhism demands instantaneous conversion and cognitive assent—indeed, it would be more accurate to say that they operate by eluding such assent. Ahmed did not demand of me a total, subjective, inward transformation, nor did he seek confirmation of my acceptance of his teachings in words (alone)—he demanded no reciprocation of his religious gifts, at least not in the same coin in which he offered them (though I did feel enjoined to reciprocate his sexual confessions).

As a preliminary conclusion, it seems that in my interactions with Ahmed and with Maureen and John, there were different structures of demand and expectation, different "regimes of truth." This cultural and epistemic difference, rather than a relative distance or distancing from emotional involvement on my part, was why I felt so comfortable maintaining a posture of acquiescence with Ahmed and not with my Protestant others. That is, I have tried to indicate that the differences in my relation to and responses to Ahmed, on the one hand, and Maureen and John, on the other, have a heuristic value for learning something about *them*. My relations with both were equally bounded by prior interpretation and investment on my part, of course, but it is important to recognize first that the differences in my responses to them do not point only to myself, in the privacy of my psyche. My own countertransferential reactions can be explored to indicate some of the investments brought to the encounters by the other participants.[13] This approach emphasizes a social or a cultural fact that shaped our two divergent interactions. Such an explanation is, precisely, a conclusion—it concludes interpretation and analysis—and my interest is to remain within the encounters and seek methodological insights.

An important part of the difference between these two interactions was a difference in the demands and expectations I put on myself. With Ahmed I could say I was "doing research," I was learning things, and therefore put aside my transferences, the unmasterable and unanalyzable traces of past relations that constitute so much of the self (as it is conceived in psychoanalysis); Maureen and John, on the other hand, provoked transference, and the provocation was mutual and unresolved. Our interactions collapsed into an *exchange of transferences*—from which we escaped only by my withdrawal—rather than achieving any actual dialogue.

I recognize the limits of these encounters and the boundaries of my rights of interpretation here—but it is precisely as a failure of appropriate interpretation that my encounter with Maureen and John has become diagnostic for me. As in my initial research experiences in Delhi, I failed to adequately interpret the interaction we were having and to discover the appropriate relation to them, a relation that would have allowed me to pursue the encounter and, also, to produce some ethnographic knowledge. I was not doing research in the guesthouse where we met, but my countertransferences—my sense of the burdens they were placing upon me, the challenge they offered—gain significance only through my heuristic exercise of treating our encounter as a research situation, applying the lessons of ethnographic practice to develop an understanding of what we both brought to it.

Yet the available anthropological literature on countertransference and psychological dimensions of fieldwork is not much guide to this mode of interpretation and employment of "countertransferences" within ethnographic interpretation. Emotional and unconscious reactions, we are told, are intrinsic elements of the ethnographic research situation, but a generally positivist and restorative outlook leads anthropological writers to exhort their professional colleagues to "know themselves," to control for countertransference, and to limit its appearance as data. Countertransference reactions are treated either as impediments to be overcome or, at best, as idiosyncratic facts of the researcher's personal biography that can either help or hinder research (see Hunt 1989). Katherine Pratt Ewing characterizes countertransference as a phenomenon that "prevents [the ethnographer] from seeing," or "makes it difficult [for her] to see beyond [her] own desires and fears" (2006: 108–9). The ethnographer undergoing countertransference "fails to maintain an independent perspective" (109). Ewing's metaphors of unimpeded sight and independent perspective—which run counter to her own overt commitments to dynamic and dialogical models of ethnography—reveal a residual positivism in our models of field research, a wish to "control for" the effects of our presence in the research situation and to move beyond the limitations of the emotionally embedded interactions that serve as our tool and our object—limitations, I might add, that we perhaps have not fully understood in themselves.

Gananath Obeyesekere (1990: 234) likewise treats the ethnographer's countertransferential reactions as arising from the ethnographer's "frustrations," as fundamentally imaginary, and as revealing more about the ethnographer and his subjectivity than about the intersubjective lines of tension, engagement, and disengagement in the encounter. Obeyesekere's reading has a warrant in classical psychoanalytical theory. Freud advised analysts to treat the patient's transferences as fundamentally irreal; and as for the *countertransferences,* to the extent that Freud considered them systematically, it was to advise that they be understood as, at best, symptoms and not feelings (see Wolstein 1988: 5). In dealing with the patient in the throes of the transference, Freud writes, you must "take care not to distract her from the love-transference, to frighten it away, or ruin it for the patient; but just as steadfastly you refrain from reciprocating. You hold on to the love-transference, but you treat it as something unreal." Freud admitted that this was a method of nonengagement with the emotional claims of the other for which "there is no pattern . . . in real life" (Freud 2002: 73).

However, Freud himself and other psychoanalytic thinkers later questioned the extent to which these identifications and reactions could be controlled for; a "totalistic" (Davidson 1986) view of the analytical situation developed, eventually leading psychoanalysts—among them, Jacques Lacan (1977: 123–35, 231) and D. W. Winnicott—to throw into doubt the analytical usefulness of the very term countertransference and to think instead of the analyst's (and, *mutatis mutandis,* the patient's) "total response" to the other in the analytical situation (Winnicott [1960] 1988: 268). For Winnicott in particular, this move grew out of reflection on the "role of the analyst" and an understanding that for analysis to move forward, the unconscious must "have a conscious equivalent and become a living process involving people" both within and without analysis (265). In addition, his inquiries into countertransference and its functions were animated by a desire to differentiate the work of the analyst to meet the needs of different patients; specifically, he insisted that analytic practice must vary between normally neurotic patients and those "psychotic" patients who claimed more from the analyst, presented more challenges and more difficult analytic problems. In the latter cases, the analyst's greater intrusion in the analytic space might be warranted, in the service of the developmental project of the patient. Again, the boundaries between ethnographic and psychoanalytic practice must be acknowledged and respected, yet the kind of methodological inquiry that Winnicott conducted might be useful here: less, perhaps, for his insight into the positioning and involvement of the analyst within the analytic space than for his recognition that both diagnosis and treatment—interpretation—can be hindered or even stalled when the analyst is presented with unassimilable claims, and when he is not easily aware of his own frustration, fear, and hate.[14]

"HATE IN THE COUNTER-TRANSFERENCE"

Winnicott's understanding of the claims on the analyst, of the complexity of the demands put on him by his patients, led to essays marked by a lively subjectivity, a constant tacking back and forth between the symptoms of his patients and his responses to them—his own symptoms, one might say. He documented in his clinical essays his own experimentation within the analytical space; and his open-ended and experimental approach—which might well be likened to the enforced improvisation of most ethnographic situations—often spills into his prose as well. But what dominated his practice, and kept his essays from sinking into specious general speculation based on uncontrolled subjectivity, was a rigorous sense of the limits of the analyst's involvement, his self-subjection to a professional posture: what we might, in our idiom, call canons of professional ethics, and what Winnicott inconsistently called "the professional attitude" ([1960] 1988: 264).

These features are all evident in his remarkable essay "Hate in the Counter-transference" (1949). In this article, Winnicott dismisses as analytically useless one level of countertransferences—those resulting from an ill-examined set of personal motivations, unmastered reactions belonging only to the analyst—and recommends further training analysis for analysts in this condition. A second level of countertransferences is also quickly dispensed with—those that are merely idiosyncrasies of the analyst, which do not interfere with the analysis and "make his analytic work . . . different in quality from that of any other analyst" (Winnicott 1949: 68). From these two types of countertransference, Winnicott distinguishes what he calls the "objective counter-transference," the "analyst's love and hate in reaction to the actual personality and behavior of the patient, based on objective observation" (69). As a commonplace example, he offers this observation: "A patient of mine, a very bad obsessional, was almost loathsome to me for some years. I felt bad about this until the analysis turned a corner . . . and then I realized that his unlikeableness had been an active symptom, unconsciously determined" (69).

Hate emerges first into the analytical situation, Winnicott says, and is intrinsic to it, because of the demands the patient puts on the analyst, because of the insistence that the analyst relate to the patient's symptom and at the same time produce an understanding that will eliminate it.[15] Certain types of patients, he says—psychotic as opposed to "normally" neurotic patients—demand more from the analyst, produce more frustration, and are more hateful. Assessment of this hatred is useful both in diagnosis and in pursuit of a cure: "Hate *that is justified* in the present setting has to be sorted out and kept in storage and available for eventual interpretation" (Winnicott 1949: 69). In these cases, the analyst must "be prepared to bear strain without expecting the patient to know anything about what he is doing, perhaps over a long period of time. To do this, he must be easily aware of his own fear and hate" (71).

Winnicott's model of the analytic work here derives from his developmental theory, his understanding of the emergence of the personality in the relation between infant and mother. The analyst confronted with a demanding, psychotic patient is *"in the position of the mother of an infant unborn or newly born"* (Winnicott 1949: 71; emphasis in the original). In the period immediately following the infant's birth, the mother is used "ruthlessly" by the baby, and she, quite normally, hates him. For she is frustrated. "He excites her but frustrates her—she mustn't eat him or trade in sex with him" (73; see also Phillips 1988: 89–90). But, like the analyst, the mother must be in control of her fear and hate, and must not put too great a strain on the infant's capacity for understanding by giving direct expression to her hatred. She must hold it (and him); she must hold back from various kinds of interchange and exchange.

There are two parts, therefore, to the claim about the mother's and the analyst's hate: (1) it is real, and (2) it must be withheld. To rephrase the latter point, the demands of the infant or the patient must be withstood, in order for another stage to be reached. If mother and analyst are both enjoined to hold, and to withhold, that injunction is in the service of the "developmental project" of the infant or the patient.

But sometimes, in analysis and interaction, the hatred needs to be given expression. Winnicott's strongest analytical example is of an "truant" boy, of whom he and his wife took charge after the boy had run away from the hostel—a home for children displaced during World War

II—where Winnicott had been involved in caring for him.[16] Winnicott saw that assuring this boy of their love would do nothing to help him, and indeed the boy continued to act out in their care. Strategically and carefully, Winnicott allowed himself to give expression to the frustration this boy produced in him, devising structured punishments and telling the boy when he misbehaved that "what had happened had made me hate him" (1949: 72). Winnicott does this in order to facilitate the maturation and emotional development of the boy. "It is notoriously inadequate to take such a child into one's home and to love him," he writes. "What happens is that after a while a child so adopted gains hope, and then he starts to test out the environment he has found, and to seek proof of his guardians' ability to hate objectively. It seems that he can believe in being loved only after reaching being hated" (71).

For psychoanalysts, the thought that the analyst must manage his or her reactions to the patient, must withhold and retreat at times, is unsurprising. Winnicott's contribution lies, in part, in his recognition that "hate," or negative countertransference, constitutes as important a part of the emotional dynamic of analysis as the more canonically approved "love." The idea of employing the countertransferential reactions within the analysis is yet more novel, for it requires treating the emotional reactions of the analyst (whether positive or negative) not as fundamentally irreal, factitious products of an artificial social relation, but as real products of real interactions that might be the basis for further exploration of the personality of the patient, and ultimately treatment and cure. Countertransference becomes, in Winnicott's work, a kind of analytic action, a way of making interpretations and pushing the analysis forward, not—as it is classically defined—as an illegitimate *re*-action to private representations.

Winnicott's model of the hate in the analytical encounter and his sometimes idiosyncratic sense of its possible use in diagnosis and treatment present a host of challenges to anthropological appropriation, and I am not proposing that it can be taken over wholesale. Anthropologists, like mothers, may have an especially difficult time recognizing and managing our own justified hatred; the occasions when we find our field interlocutors "loathsome" may present particularly difficult moments for us—as would be indicated by the general tendency to emphasize the "irreal" or "countertransferential" nature of our negative emotional reactions. In one regard, this is all to the good. Unlike the analyst (and still more unlike the proselytizer), we do not enter into our research relations with the hope of precipitating a transformation in the other, or effecting a cure.

Yet the times when we are put in the service of another's aims, subjected to his or her demands, are more common in ethnography than we might like to admit. The hate this provokes is not allowed to enter into our professional self-awareness, our estimation of whom we are researching. Like the analyst, we have a set of professional compensations that permit us to withstand the demands of our interlocutors and resist introducing disruptive personal reactions: "I am discovering things," we might tell ourselves; or "I get immediate rewards through identification" with the others around me. Or, in extremis, we might resort to "I get paid" (the quoted phrases here are from Winnicott's list of the psychoanalyst's compensations [1949: 69]). However, our compensations and our reliance on them in our methodological reflections may serve only to obscure conflicts that could, if attended to, provide the materials for deeper ethnographic interpretations—interpretations that would take into account the objective hate (and love) and find its sources in the social contexts of our research.

The broader lesson to draw for ethnography, at this point in the development of the discipline, is that we might gain something by examining withdrawal, distance, and even hate as forces shaping the field encounter, rather than simply asking how we can get closer to our interlocutors, engage more authentically and more intimately with them. We have no interest in changing or transforming the other, but we might, by acknowledging our own hate and frustration, be able to develop greater insight into the nature of other subjectivities. When presented with recalcitrant epistemologies, combative interlocutors, and practices that present political challenges and provoke ethical reflection, we might do well not to "push through" our discomfort, opposition, and hate, employing it instead within the processes of interaction and interpretation.

EVANGELICAL CHRISTIANITY AND
THE OBJECTIVE HATE

A sort of conversion hysteria—to pun on Freud's most famous cases—on the part of the ethnographer is a recurrent theme in ethnographic works dealing with American evangelical Christianity. Evangelical Christians seem to evoke among anthropologists more identity anxiety, greater fear of epistemic contamination, and a more highly felt danger of "going native" than other others do. In their ethnographic works on evangelicalism, both Susan Harding (2000) and Vincent Crapanzano (2000) discuss, reflexively, their own discomfort and frustration as they were proselytized by their interlocutors. Yet, in different ways, they both expel this emotional reaction and treat it as exogenous to the purpose of their research, in ways that indicate the limits of a reflexivity that tries to neutralize or circumvent the ethnographer's felt resistance and hate.

Susan Harding's *Book of Jerry Falwell* (2000) is structured around a complex transferential relationship negotiated along the fraught boundary between the evangelicals' faithful witnessing and demand for conversion and the anthropologist's ambivalent response, her search for epistemic certainty. Harding focuses on fundamentalist language as performative and perlocutionary act, asking why it *works*—and employs her own seduction by it as proof that it does indeed, despite the best rationalist defenses, work. But she stages her argument as an ethnographic adventure among a marginal people, poorly represented in "modernist" understandings, who need the care and attention of the anthropologist in order to rescue them from the status of "repugnant cultural other" to which dominant elites relegate them. In an earlier essay, Harding (1991) writes that she personally opposes the projects of fundamentalist Christianity in American political life, but she bars any consideration of this opposition, this intellectualized hatred, within the process of research and relegates it instead to the realm of politics. She advocates love for and loving attention to the Christian's language in order to produce "better representations" of this antagonistic other, who might then be more effectively opposed on the political field (1991: 392–93).

Vincent Crapanzano (2000) similarly returns often to scenes of prose-lytization, and describes his discomfort as he was witnessed by funda-mentalist seminarians during research for his book on literalism in American life. Crapanzano's choice of this research project and his style of writing are more nakedly partisan than Harding allows herself to be, but he likewise displaces his discomfort and felt hate, though in the opposite direction. When confronted by argumentative Christians with countersystems to his own linguistic and hermeneutic commitments, he insists on his own authority as a hermeneut and claims that evangelical "literalism" doesn't rise to the standard of a "real" hermeneutics or a valid linguistics. That Crapanzano invests so deeply, throughout the book, in the defense of his own hermeneutical expertise, and shows him-self defending these commitments as "truths" against the epistemic attacks of his antagonists (e.g., 2000: 54), indicates that he is overmas-tered by his own sense of the interpretive proprieties in his attempt to describe interpretive cultures that are very close, and yet oppositional, to his own. He ultimately fails to provide us with any insight into how and why evangelical Christians make the arguments they do, and instead only insists, endlessly, that their arguments cannot be a faithful reading of a true linguistics.

On the one hand, then, Crapanzano, in the throes of unresolved coun-tertransference, draws a picture of the fundamentalist as a benighted lit-eralist exegete whose intransigence and unwillingness to accept the superiority of Crapanzano's arguments reveal the inferiority of evangeli-cal thought. He constantly attests, resentfully, to his interlocutors' insis-tence on turning the conversation to a conversion-oriented rhetoric and away from the technical points of hermeneutics and linguistic theory where he wishes to keep it (where he can win). On the other hand, Hard-ing presents her understanding of the efficacy and seductiveness of fun-damentalist language as the primary insight, while deliberately refusing to bring together the interpretive and political levels of her project, to ask questions about the social and political consequences of Christian social forms. That is, she creates a zone of privative anthropological engage-ment, which provides no ultimate escape, no avenue for her hatred or indeed her interpretations, other than an endlessly deferred political future. Both Crapanzano and Harding, in their different ways, remain at the scene of encounter, endlessly exchanging with their interlocutors.[17]

RECEPTIVITY WITHOUT RECIPROCITY

Any encounter is necessarily, to greater or lesser degrees, composed of an exchange of transferences. The lesson to be learned from Winnicott's methodological exploration into hate in the countertransference is how to recognize, store up, and employ in interpretation the *objective* hate (and love); how to use the emotional materials emergent from the encounter itself so that it may move forward—sometimes only in field-notes and ethnographic interpretation, but nonetheless forward—so that something more than the encounter itself can be accounted for in the ethnographic text: something of the subjectivity of the other can also appear there.

Winnicott reminded psychoanalysts that countertransference was not all bad, all factitious, with this caveat: what keeps the analytic encounter from collapsing into an exchange of transferences "is the analyst's profes-sional attitude, his technique, *the work he does with his mind*" ([1960] 1988: 265; emphasis in the original). Or, as Freud put it, "you [must] steadfastly refrain from reciprocating" (2002: 73).[18] The ethnographic "abstinence" cannot, of course, entail refraining from material aid to our interlocutors, activist work in the field, simple friendliness and concern.[19] All of these are and must be present—they constitute a part of *our* professional com-pensations. But there is an element of our work that forces us to withstand the aggression of others' demands and desires, to withhold ourselves, to withdraw. I would like to suggest that just as Winnicott revised Freud's demand that the analyst analyze in *total* abstinence, we might also refor-mulate Freud's injunction to better suit our sense of the dynamics of exchange and obligation—not, for ethnographers, a steadfast refusal to reciprocate, but rather a stringent obligation to receive.

As one standard ethnographic trope would have it, I was a guest in India, a recipient of hospitality. But when a guest is asked to participate in—even enact—rituals, to address the presiding deities of a cosmos to which she does not belong, which has no prior or immediate claim on her, the roles begin to shift, and the work of the ethnographer is inadequately captured by that metaphor. In the latter circumstance one becomes in a sense a host—a host of contaminating, exogenous ideas or matter. And the host is more obligated to her guest than the guest is to the host, obligated neither to eat nor to destroy the guest, nor to trade in sex with her (Winnicott 1949: 73; see above).[20]

There was a surprising salience of reciprocity and hospitality in all my conversations with John and Maureen. Our interaction began with my request to them not to take the room next to mine. I asked them to keep their distance, I tried to foreclose the possibility that we might become intimate. Maureen clearly resented this attempt, and returned often to the theme of hospitality, recognition, reciprocity. Indians are so hospitable, so generous, she said. They told me the several stories discussed above of invitations extended and refused, ungracious treatment they had received at their old church. I felt myself chided by these stories; I certainly was failing to accommodate and integrate their demands. I was not receiving them and their faithful efforts to reach out to me, but was parrying their offers with challenges and countergifts. Eventually I withdrew into the privacy of interpretation, the privacy of the ethnographic text.[21] I now understand that my challenges and attempts to reciprocate, as well as my interpretive withdrawal, were expressions of my "hatred," my negative countertransference—but this was not something my ethnographic habitus, my ethnographic training, had prepared me to experience; and my unmastered countertransferential hate hindered any interpretation that would acknowledge the objectivity of that hate.

In seeking to understand my encounters with Maureen and John without evading the countertransferential aspects of the situation, the contrast with the calm and efficient interactions I had with Ahmed are of primary importance—not only for the insight into differently structured religious demands that I have been able to develop above, but also because my interactions with Ahmed serve as a sort of "normal" and ethically neutral fieldwork situation, one in which demands and claims are laid to rest by a candid instrumentality on both sides. I sought knowledge, and he got paid. That is, the encounter with Ahmed was bounded, on my part, by the compensations similar to those that allow the analyst to reserve, conceal, even dissipate his hatred. "I am learning things," primarily; but Winnicott lists another important compensatory mechanism: "Moreover, as an analyst I have ways of expressing hate. Hate is expressed by the existence of the end of the 'hour'" (1949: 69–70). Both Ahmed and I benefited from the circumscriptions on our interaction within the "hour" of our language classes. Moreover, I was only playing at doing research, and Ahmed too was no doubt amusing himself and trying to diminish the boredom of his long days at the language school. We tacitly permitted ourselves to pursue fantasies in the space of our conversations, to speak of imaginary things we had never done, to express hatreds and desires not otherwise allowed us.

Jonathan Parry (1986), in his reevaluation of Mauss's argument about "the spirit of the gift" and the social obligation of reciprocity, shows that Hindu *danadharma* (the religious duty-of-the-gift), the "normative Hindu law," includes many categories of gift for which return is neither expected nor desired, gifts that embody a part of the person—his sins, his waste—and that must be decisively and permanently alienated. Elsewhere, Parry (1989, 1994) deals with the predicament of those who receive these polluting and poisonous gifts, and indeed the incorporation of substance via gifts presents a problem for both indigenous and anthropological reflection in and on India.

After reading Winnicott, and reflecting on this narrow and bounded space of encounter in the mountains, I might propose that the anthropologist, too, is in the position of a subject obliged to receive poisonous and dangerous gifts. Unlike in the Indian texts examined by Parry, it would not be a notion of coded substance or pollution that would animate the anxiety of receiving the gift for us. Rather, our methodological anxiety springs from a normative ideal of reciprocity in fieldwork, which at times accords poorly with the actual task of the ethnographer. Our ascetic ethic of fieldwork forces us to receive ("never decline an invitation," as the old fieldwork adage runs), tells us that we ought to be respectful and receptive, but also enjoins us to withhold reciprocity. This second aspect of the fieldwork ethic, however, is largely unrecognized and is in manifold ways defended against, not least in the recent ethnography where it emerges as a problem, via its symptomatic manifestations as anxious queries about what we can "give back."

We can read—as, indeed, Parry does—Mauss's essay on the gift as a long meditation on the conflicts activated by incomplete or truncated exchange cycles, though this interpretation emerges only in a deconstructive reading. As Parry notes, "Cases in which the gift is not reciprocated are virtually excluded from Mauss's purview by the way in which he has defined his problem in terms of the archaeology of contractual obligation" (1986: 457). In commercial society, various compensations are elaborated that obscure the fundamental conflicts generated by one-way prestations—not least the ideal of the "free gift"—and we have little conception of the obligation to receive, the position of the subject who accepts without being *allowed* to give back. And not only we, but also others, have failed to iron out the conflicts inherent in this position; Parry points out that the obligation to receive is the one obligation most recalcitrant to close specification or resolution even in the Hindu texts where he finds its traces (1986: 462).

Winnicott seems to have understood something of the nature of this obligation, and of the frustrations generated by the professional necessity to receive and withhold in interaction with his patients. Unlike Winnicott, who has the shield of his professionalism and the telos of a cure to help justify his withdrawal from the patient, the action of withholding his interpretations, and his emotional engagement until they can be used appropriately (either in the analysis or after the analysis is concluded), anthropologists have no rigorously formulated justification for our stance of receptivity without reciprocity. It might help to conceptualize our work as being like that of the analyst, with its frustrations and its compensations. First of all, we might say, the ethnographer is a kind of host.

NOTES

I am grateful to John Borneman and Abdellah Hammoudi for the invitation to present an earlier version of this essay on a panel they organized for the

2006 Annual Meeting of the American Anthropological Association, and for their continued close readings of this text as it has been reshaped for inclusion in the present volume. I have benefited greatly from the comments and advice of Talia Dan-Cohen, Parvis Ghassem-Fachandi, Isabelle Clark-Decès, James Boon, and the reviewers for University of California Press. The Wenner-Gren Foundation generously funded part of my fieldwork in Delhi in 2005–06. The Princeton Institute for International and Regional Studies funded my initial research trips to India, during which I was first introduced to the faculty of the language school I write about here. I of course bear sole responsibility for errors and all sins of omission and commission.

1. But see Borneman (chapter 9, this volume), who attempts to retain the polyvalence and ambiguous moral charge of the term *collaboration* as a way of understanding fieldwork in its complexity; cf. Marcus (1998).

2. Obviously, the question of the ethnographer's authority was not a problem for earlier attempts to bring together ethnographic and psychoanalytic methods, though it has been at the center of methodological reflection since *Writing Culture* (Clifford and Marcus 1986). Devereux (1967) offers a particularly useful early comparison of ethnography and psychoanalysis, which reminds us that in the human sciences no firm demarcation can be made between observer and observed. His work examines countertransference and objectivity in particular detail, and suggests that we integrate the emotional reactions of the observer into analysis of social life in order to achieve a "real, and not fictitious, objectivity" (quoted in Davidson 1986: 277). Devereux's work and Davidson's (1986) review of Devereux's and others' approaches to countertransference in ethnography were both key resources in the early stages of this project.

3. I am grateful to John Borneman for helping me to refine this distinction.

4. Spivak has cautioned that in appropriations of psychoanalytic theory, "to dissimulate the space of the 'cure' disqualifies any methodological analogy taken from transference" (1999: 206). Spivak further points out that literary-critical and theoretical appropriations of psychoanalysis make the "arena of practice" in which psychoanalytic work is embedded "disappear," and hence evade that aspect of *work* that "persistently norms the presuppositions of psychoanalysis in responsible action" (1999: 107). In both ethnography and psychoanalysis an encounter is at stake, and both disciplines have been "persistently normed" by the ethical demands of the other; therefore, analogizing from psychoanalytic practice to ethnographic practice is different from a similar procedure in literary studies.

5. Moore (chapter 6, this volume), writing from long and sustained ethnographic engagement in Tanzania, opens similar questions about the perils and possibilities of both engagement and withdrawal in ethnographic relationships, and she alludes in closing to the role of frustration and even "hate" in the task of ethnographic knowledge-making. Moore's insights help condition some of my "wilder" analogies and analyses, drawn from my own unmastered countertransference, and remind us in a Winnicottian vein that the first task of the ethnographer must be "to be prepared to bear strain . . . perhaps over a long period of time. To do this, he must be easily aware of his own fear and hate" (Winnicott 1949: 71).

6. One could further explore the difference between the "religious" and the "secular" nature of the interactions I am studying. But there are greater similarities between the claims of my Christian interlocutors and those of my secular, activist informants than between the two obviously "religious" encounters discussed later in this essay.

7. Names of people I encountered in the field have been changed.

8. Though the roles are by no means parallel, there I was both student and researcher, and my teachers were also "informants." The importance of such roles and their negotiations in the field are among the several complications that distinguish the analytical from the ethnographic space.

9. It occurs to me that this believe/conform distinction also applies to Ahmed's relation to my sexuality, as he neither inquired nor cared if my desire might not be toward women—as long as I "acted right," our interaction need not be disrupted. This kind of assumption of heterosexuality was not, by any means, universally the case among men I interacted with in India. But then, Ahmed seemed to have no interest in either converting or seducing me.

10. Coleman (2004) cautions that academic analyses of prosperity gospel movements have focused too much on the material rewards they promise their adherents. His essay opens a wider analysis of the "charismatic gift," which can grasp the totality of goods that adherents of these movements seek from their participation. I discovered Simon Coleman's work on Word of Faith movements in Sweden when final revisions on the present essay were nearing completion (see also Coleman 2000).

11. Coleman says the material transactions that constitute the Faith Christian community "can be fruitfully assessed from a perspective focusing on constructions of the born-again person which challenge Western concepts of the bounded, autonomous social actor" (2004: 424). How-

ever, he restricts his analysis to the construction of a "enclaved sphere of exchange" in which Christian participants are able to view themselves as "active agents reaching out into the world by monetary and spiritual means" (437). That is, he reinstates in his analysis the very discriminations between "inner" and "outer," "subject" and "object" that he hopes to show are not operative in Faith Christianity. I agree that anthropologists are well positioned to move beyond methodological individualism, but ethnographically Maureen and John were individualists: they rejected hybridity and porousness in their religious subjectivity in a way that contrasts starkly with the attitude of my Sufi interlocutor Ahmed.

12. Maureen and John, of course, would say that they were merely offering me a gift; but as Emerson wrote, "It is not the office of a man to receive gifts. How dare you give them?" (1940: 403). As anthropologists have long recognized, no gift is free or freely given: rather, it always expresses a demand and involves an obligation (though not necessarily an obligation to offer a gift in return).

13. It is worth noting that my "hate" in the encounter with Maureen and John, just as much as my "love" in the encounter with Ahmed, was conditioned not only by countertransference as classically defined— traces of past relationships inappropriately applied in the present—but by my *prior knowledge* of religious subjectivities and their differences in Indian Sufism and American evangelical Protestantism. That is, the "work I do with my mind" (to adapt Winnicott's phrase [(1960) 1988: 265]), my professional engagement in the field, is what licenses my recognition of my hate and my love, and saves the narrative of my countertransference from being mere autobiography.

14. In his survey of psychoanalytic concepts of countertransference, Wolstein attempts to recast the analytic encounter as a cooperative space of mutual recognition and self-discovery. He tells us that with the acknowledgment of countertransferences as an essential part of the analytic work, psychoanalysts and patients "began to experience one another as coparticipants in a shared field of inquiry—both, now, capable of participant-observation—[and] they found they could do it from both sides of the field. . . . [T]hey became both participant-observers and observed participants with one another" (1988: 11). It is precisely this sort of mutuality that I found barred in certain of my field encounters, above all with Maureen and John. In place of the mere alternation between "participant observer" and "observed participant" offered by Wolstein, Winnicott's work provides a model of the analytic situation that is relational but nonreciprocal. I have chosen to emphasize, as

did Winnicott, the professional responsibilities of the analyst, the "counter" in the countertransference, and his recognition that analytic exchange is one constantly marked by conflict, deferral, and resistance rather than by easy coexistence. This recognition is the spur for my interest in analogizing from his work to ethnography.

15.   For psychoanalysts, interpretation is both analytic task and part of the treatment; this is yet another area of difference between ethnography and analysis that merits further inquiry.

16.   That Winnicott and his wife took the boy into their home, thereby for a time taking total responsibility for his upbringing, is at the very least unconventional psychoanalytic practice. Winnicott has been criticized for his departures—often undertaken willy-nilly—from the analytical norm, and he himself demonstrates some anxiety in presenting this case.

17.   In other essays, especially his reflections on transference in work with white South Africans, Crapanzano does address concerns similar to those I am bringing up here (see Crapanzano 1984).

18.   The Standard Edition renders this phrase "resolutely withhold any response to it [the transference-love]" (Freud 1958: 166). For reasons that should be clear, I have preferred the more recent Penguin translation.

19.   Katherine Pratt Ewing (2006: 108) has a salutary suspicion that activist work is detrimental to clear negotiation of the fieldwork situation.

20.   See Simmel (1971) on the stranger, and on the paradoxes of hospitality in ancient literature.

21.   A retreat to the ethnographic text is totally different from Harding's *privative* withdrawal, which forbids interpretation rather than encouraging it.

REFERENCES

Alter, Joseph. 1992. *The Wrestler's Body: Identity and Ideology in North India.* Berkeley: University of California Press.

———. 2004. *Yoga in Modern India: The Body between Science and Philosophy.* Princeton: Princeton University Press.

Clifford, James, and George E. Marcus, eds. 1986. *Writing Culture: The Poetics and Politics of Ethnography.* Berkeley: University of California Press.

Coleman, Simon. 2000. *Globalisation of Charismatic Christianity: Spreading the Gospel of Prosperity.* Cambridge: Cambridge University Press.

———. 2004. "The Charismatic Gift." *Journal of the Royal Anthropological Institute,* n.s., 10: 421–42.

Crapanzano, Vincent. 1984. "Kevin: On the Transfer of Emotions." *American Anthropologist* 96(4): 866–85.

———. 2000. *Serving the Word: Literalism in America from the Pulpit to the Bench.* New York: New Press.

Davidson, Ronald H. 1986. "Transference and Countertransference Phenomena: The Problem of the Observer in the Behavioral Sciences." *Journal of Psychoanalytical Anthropology* 9(3): 269–83.

Devereux, George. 1967. *From Anxiety to Method in the Behavioral Sciences.* The Hague: Mouton.

Emerson, Ralph Waldo. 1940. *The Complete Essays and Other Writings of Ralph Waldo Emerson.* Ed. Brooks Atkinson. New York: Modern Library.

Ewing, Katherine Pratt. 2006. "Revealing and Concealing: Interpersonal Dynamics and the Negotiation of Identity in the Interview." *Ethos* 34(1): 89–122.

Freud, Sigmund. 1958. "Observations on Transference-Love." In *The Standard Edition of the Complete Psychological Works of Sigmund Freud.* Trans. under the editorship of James Strachey, assisted by Anna Freud, with Alix Strachey and Alan Tyson. Vol. 12. London: Hogarth.

———. 2002. "Observations on Love in Transference." In *Wild Analysis.* Ed. Adam Phillips. Trans. Alan Bance. New York: Penguin.

Harding, Susan Friend. 1991. "Representing Fundamentalism: The Problem of the Repugnant Cultural Other." *Social Research* 58(2): 373–93.

———. 2000. *The Book of Jerry Falwell: Fundamentalist Language and Politics.* Princeton: Princeton University Press.

Hunt, Jennifer C. 1989. *Psychoanalytic Aspects of Fieldwork.* Newbury Park, CA: Sage.

Lacan, Jacques. 1978. *The Four Fundamental Concepts of Psycho-analysis.* Ed. Jacques-Alain Miller. Trans. Alan Sheridan. New York: Norton.

Marcus, George. 1998. "The Uses of Complicity in the Changing Mise-en-Scène of Anthropological Fieldwork." In *Ethnography through Thick and Thin.* Princeton: Princeton University Press.

Obeyesekere, Gananath. 1990. *The Work of Culture: Symbolic Transformation in Psychoanalysis and Anthropology.* Chicago: University of Chicago Press.

Parry, Jonathan. 1986. "The Gift, the Indian Gift, and the 'Indian Gift.'" *Man,* n.s., 21(3): 453–73.

———. 1989. "The End of the Body." In *Fragments for a History of the Human Body,* ed. Michel Feher, with Ramona Naddaff and N. Nadia Tazi. New York: Zone; Cambridge, MA: distributed by MIT Press.

———. 1994. *Death in Banaras.* Cambridge: Cambridge University Press.

Phillips, Adam. 1988. *Winnicott.* Cambridge, MA: Harvard University Press.

Simmel, Georg. 1971. "The Stranger." In *On Individuality and Social Forms: Selected Writings*. Ed. Donald N. Levine. Chicago: University of Chicago Press.

Spivak, Gayatri Chakravorty. 1999. *A Critique of Postcolonial Reason: Toward a History of the Vanishing Present*. Cambridge, MA: Harvard University Press.

Weiner, James. 1999. "Psychoanalysis and Anthropology: On the Temporality of Analysis." In *Anthropological Theory Today*, ed. Henrietta L. Moore. Cambridge: Polity Press.

Winnicott, D. W. 1949. "Hate in the Counter-transference." *International Journal of Psycho-analysis* 30: 69–74.

———. [1960] 1988. "Counter-transference." In *Essential Papers on Countertransference*, ed. Benjamin Wolstein. New York: New York University Press. [Originally published in *British Journal of Medical Psychology* 33: 17–21.]

Wolstein, Benjamin. 1988. Introduction to *Essential Papers on Countertransference*, ed. Benjamin Wolstein. New York: New York University Press.

SIX Encounter and Suspicion in Tanzania

Sally Falk Moore

My fieldwork in Tanzania extended over many years, from 1968 to 1993. It was intermittent: a few months at a time, and then an interval of months, or a year or two, and then another visit. The reflexive remarks that follow are retrospective and selective. There are too many stories to tell.

The first summer I was accompanied by my husband and two teenage daughters; they refused to be left behind. The advantage: I could "show" my family to my Chagga acquaintances and demonstrate that I was an ordinary human being in an extraordinary situation. They understood that in my "real life," I was a teacher. When I went to Kilimanjaro on later trips, it was sometimes with my husband, sometimes alone.

We lived in a very shabby old hotel on Kilimanjaro, in Marangu, just at the end of the only paved road leading from the town of Moshi, 25 miles away. I had breakfast and dinner there. The hotel kitchen packed me a hardboiled egg and some fruit and bread for lunch. I would eat it wherever I happened to be and share it with whomever. It was a basic form of Chagga politeness to share. Even very small children are taught this fundamental principle. From them I accepted mushy half-chewed bits of banana as their mothers watched. After a time, the kitchen began to produce more than one egg, and more than one slice of bread for my lunch packet. During this period of fieldwork, I had no worries.

But my mood was not consistent. Over the years, I went from completely comfortable and confident to uneasy to frightened, and back. What is clear is that the objective information I collected about the Chagga and published about that period in Tanzanian history stands (Moore 1986). I disdained reflexivity in writing, because I considered it my job to observe and report on Chagga affairs, not to document my own experience. I wanted what I had to say to be something others could confirm. In addition, my ability to include the ingredients needed to create a more personal narrative was greatly restricted by the political implications of publishing such materials. For one thing, I wanted to be able to return to Tanzania, and I did not want my comments to include material that might lead to being refused research permission. For another, I did not want anything I had to say to be used to harm anyone. I met my quota of dunderheads in the bureaucracy who claimed moral superiority as they spouted the clichés of the new socialism, and I met plenty of property owners ready to cheat their closest relatives, but I had no intention of writing about any of them in ways that would make them identifiable.

I thought that because I was a white American, and hence politically suspect, anything not directly relevant to an impersonal objectivist account should be deleted. The worry that something might imperil my research permission was never-ending. I thought that to keep one's head down and make oneself as inconspicuous as possible was the way to go, though there is no way that a white person can be inconspicuous in an African country. Enough time has passed so that I can now write about my experience without the concerns I had in the past.

There is something inherently weird about many a fieldwork situation. Intruding on the lives and affairs of communities of strangers, even when they are cheerfully willing to have one do so, is not a normal way of making friends. The Chagga understood very well that I was collecting information about their way of life for scholarly purposes. They also understood that this activity had a professional rationale, that it would somehow further my career. They were not shy about asking me who was paying for me to be there.

What I did not anticipate was the extent to which I became privy to activities that were disapproved of, or had been made illegal, by the new socialist regime of Julius Nyerere and his government. Most of these activities were entirely commonplace in the communities with which I had contact. Even the local members of officialdom were unperturbed by them. I was much more shocked than they were.

Take, for example, the matter of *masiro*. The newly introduced philosophy of landholding prohibited the local custom of lending a plot of land with the expectation of having it returned one day. *Masiro* was a ritual gift presented annually to anyone from whom one had "borrowed" a plot of land. This was a way of recognizing that the original owner had title—that is, had continuing rights in the land. Indeed, the original owner could reclaim the plot if he had the means to compensate the occupier for any improvements that had been made. The government had abolished all title, saying that all land belonged to "all the people." It followed that the payment of *masiro* was illegal because it acknowledged the existence of ownership, as distinct from the use, of a plot.

Of course people went on paying *masiro* secretly and thus memorialized a whole web of contingent rights in land that the state not only did not recognize but prohibited. Any *masiro* paying constituted a political insult to the land law project of the new regime. I did not tell anyone about the instances of which I knew. That would have turned these matters into public issues. I was more than discreet—if anything, self-effacing. And I was pleased with the result of my silent complicity. I felt that I was trusted. That was my conception of my local place until the political winds changed in the middle and late 1970s.

I should add that in the eyes of some of the African scholars I met at the University of Dar es Salaam, I was suspect from the beginning, for very different reasons. Not only was I an American, but I was identified with the Chagga and their reputation for insufficient enthusiasm for the regime. The Chagga had their reasons. For one thing, they had been dealt a terrible blow by the national educational policy. The Chagga had long been very keen on getting an education for their children. In the colonial days, when school had to be paid for, they made considerable sacrifices to put at least one child into the system. With the advent of President Nyerere and socialism, elementary school became universal and free, a change that made the Chagga very happy. But the bad news was that their access to higher education was virtually cut off. The proportion of educated Chagga in schools and in public positions was considered too large. To rectify this imbalance for the next generation, places in upper schools were reserved for children from ethnic groups that were under-represented on the national scene. Excluding the Chagga from eligibility for higher education was the result of a form of ethnic affirmative action. Understandably, the Chagga resented this policy. They tried to start some independent schools but were refused permission.

At the University of Dar es Salaam, the excitement about Nyerere and his program was so great among those committed to African socialism that even this understandable resentment was not forgiven. After all, the policy was for the good of the state. And when I reported some goings-on on Kilimanjaro that did not conform to their conception of the situation, they responded by saying, "Oh well, that is just the Chagga; what else can you expect?"

My research was sponsored by successive deans of the Law School at the University of Dar es Salaam. I was known to be an anthropologist, but my law degree was what won respect. Anthropology was anathema, viewed as having been the handmaiden of colonialism. I was fortunate to obtain official permission to study the social context and history of law on Kilimanjaro. Very few Americans were admitted. Even the Peace Corps was expelled.

The Chagga of Kilimanjaro were well known, and their adaptation to the new laws that came with socialism was patently worth exploring. Much earlier in the century (in the 1920s, to be exact), they had organized one of the first African-run cooperative societies on the continent. For decades they sold their crop of coffee into the world market through this cooperative, and gradually integrated into a partially monetized economy. I was impressed with the co-op's success, and by the fact that it was run not by outsiders but by Africans themselves.

Before I started my fieldwork, I assumed that their long experience with the cooperative would make the Chagga especially welcoming of a socialist head of state. I was wrong. "They do not need to teach us *ujamaa*. We already have *ujamaa*," they said. "Ujamaa" was the term used for socialism. They meant that the *ukoo* or patrilineal lineage (often localized) and the neighborhood—that is, the sub-village—were the foci of cooperation, and they felt they did not need the Party, the Tanzanian African National Union (TANU), to reorganize them into cooperative communities.

To prepare myself for fieldwork, I had read what was available in the library about the Chagga, and I wondered at the absence of a full monograph about them by an anthropologist. Two anthropologists had done studies on Kilimanjaro. One was Michael Von Clemm, whose dissertation at Oxford was closed to all readers because he feared it contained material that might be damaging to some Chagga individuals. The second was a man named I. Kaplan, who published very little on his experiences. He had apparently promised to send the Chagga chief Marealle a copy of his dissertation when it was finished. Marealle sighed when he told me about Kaplan, "Now it has been seventeen years, and I have heard nothing."

What there was in the way of information available to me was a very large tome on the subject of Chagga law by a remarkable German missionary. It described material from the precolonial nineteenth century to 1916 (Gutmann 1926). There were also the writings of travelers: a book by the British colonial officer Sir Charles Dundas (1924) and a very useful history of the rivalries between various Chagga chiefdoms by Kathleen Stahl (1964). Reading Gutmann in California in preparation for my first trip, I thought that his descriptions of Chagga traditions were of a world that had surely vanished completely. I was expecting that the Chagga would have discarded the whole of their exotic past and opted for a socialist philosophy, literacy in Swahili, a cash economy, and Christianity. I was wrong.

Chagga modernity was selective. Since the principal way in which the Chagga obtained the plots of land on which they depended for a living

was through kinship, through inheritance, many of the traditional customs attached to kinship remained. And in spite of their being nominally
Christian, substantial otherworldly beliefs were not abandoned. In their
view, the ancestral dead could easily affect the lives of the living.

Why did this people not attract the attention of anthropologists? Was
it that they were not primitive enough to be of interest? In the 1960s it
was still the fashion in some quarters of anthropology to seek out for
study the least modernized people, who might represent the *real* Africa,
the original state of being, not some transformed product of exposure to
colonial ways. When I told Meyer Fortes about my plan to go to Kilimanjaro, he said, with evident disdain for my choice, "I bet they all wear
pants." I took seriously the "modern" prosperous vision of the Chagga
that was imparted by the Yale anthropologist George Murdock. Murdock had visited Tanzania, and he described in glowing terms the modern building in Moshi town that housed the cooperative headquarters.
He was impressed. But the building spoke to the prosperity of the cooperative. It did not tell much about the residents of the mountain.

I was determined to learn about their situation. But before I get on
with describing my fieldwork labors, I want to introduce the reader to
some unsettling stories that represent the general atmosphere in which I
lived and worked. What went on around me, particularly in the 1970s,
was quite disturbing, suggesting that beneath the peaceful life in the
countryside was an underlying disorder that might seep, perhaps even
burst, into my life. The ideals of African socialism generated immense
enthusiasm in Tanzania and overseas. But in the end, despite continuous
reiteration of the ideology, the policies and practices of the government
did not deliver what was promised.

EPISODE 1

One day in the seventies, when I was in Dar es Salaam, I went out to the
university to see the young man who had recently been appointed director of development studies. We were already friends. I had met Justin
Maeda in the United States when he was a Ph.D. student at Yale in the

Department of Political Science. He was a Mchagga (*Mchagga,* singular for Chagga person; *Wachagga,* plural for Chagga people; *Chagga,* the term without prefixes used in English to designate the people), a very serious, hardworking fellow who had, through a Lutheran connection, gone to Sweden, learned Swedish, and obtained an undergraduate degree from a Swedish university. (How's learning Swedish to show a zest for education!) For a time, he became a teacher in a Dar es Salaam political education college, an educational unit organized by the government for the instruction of those, such as the principals of schools and others in responsible positions, who needed a short course in the values of African socialism. Getting that job was a real show of political favor.

In 1975–76, when we met, I was teaching at Yale, and I had already been to Kilimanjaro a number of times. The chair of the Department of Political Science asked me if I would help him with his thesis. I agreed to read each chapter as he produced them, and gave him general advice. He was writing up case studies of villages he had visited, which had been reorganized to fit the *ujamaa* model—the socialist model of what a village should be. One village had succeeded economically, while others had not. When he wrote his first draft, his purpose was clearly to please the government, to tell them that the *ujamaa* model was a glorious experiment. His prose read like a political brochure. It was an appalling replication of government speeches and texts, no doubt rather like what he had been teaching at the government political college. Yale's political scientists were not pleased.

However, the footnotes and the tables of numbers made it plain that the successful village had been a success before it became an *ujamaa* village, and that the others, having had no such luck, were in various degrees failures. I persuaded him that he should be more candid, move the data that were in the footnotes into the text, and eliminate some of the propaganda. I told him that he was young—political change would probably come in his time, and the propaganda in his thesis might not have a long shelf life. Be that as it may, I told him that he should write about what he actually saw and not make political commentary, that he had good data which should be his focus. He should believe in his thesis.

He revised it accordingly and got his degree. Needless to say, with a Ph.D. from Yale, in a country that had very few people with graduate degrees, his career in Tanzania was assured. He soon found himself the director of development studies at the University of Dar. I had, by that time, begun to understand something of the Tanzanian strategy about development. In the governmental reform that came with socialism, development agencies were created to match every existing department of government. Rather than dismantling existing ministries and incurring the hostility of everyone who worked for them, the reformers left them more or less intact while a parallel "government" was more generously funded in the form of development programs. The task of the Institute of Development Studies was to survey the country's development projects, compare them, and report to the government on whether they were carrying out the directives of the state, and with what success. It was a substantial enlargement of my friend's Ph.D. project.

When I saw him in his office, he was very welcoming, and I was very glad to see him. We exchanged family news. I told him what I was up to on the mountain. And he told me about his department. But toward the end of our conversation he had something surprising to say. He advised me that if I ran into trouble, I should flee and take refuge with his brother who lived in a rural area near Arusha, not far from Kilimanjaro. He gave me details about how to get in touch with this man whom I had never met. I was astonished by the implicit warning. There had been no intimations of such trouble on previous visits. But I was glad to know he and his family would be ready to provide help, should it become necessary. I left the campus and went back to town. I was suddenly worried. What threatening possibilities did he have in mind? What could happen?

EPISODE 2

Unfortunately, I cannot remember the exact date when I saw soldiers accosting young girls in Moshi town. I know that it was in the 1970s. The soldiers appeared to be tearing at the girls' clothes, ripping the hems of their skirts. I could not imagine what they were doing. I found out what was going on later, when one of the soldiers approached me. He said I should be arrested because my skirt was too short. He told me that there was a campaign to make women dress more modestly. Short sleeves, a décolletage—these were considered immoral. I had heard that this campaign had originated with the Muslims on the coast, but now it seemed to be official policy. My offense was that my skirt did not cover my knees.

Up in the countryside where I lived and worked, the soldiers were never seen, so I did not take the reports of a campaign seriously. Nor did anyone else. I had never been approached before. But in the town the soldiers got on with the work of making women conform. Apart from confronting young girls, the real fun for the soldiers was to capture a tourist, anyone who was white.

I took refuge in a shop where I could buy a newspaper, but the soldiers followed me. By chance, I was planning to leave Tanzania a few days later and I was in Moshi only to make some last-minute arrangements. I told them I was not staying and would they please leave me in peace. They did.

When I got back to the hotel by bus to finish packing, I was told about some people who had not been so lucky. A white couple were stopped and pulled out of their vehicle by some of the soldiers on the morality campaign. Their hemlines were inspected and the tightness of trousers assessed: their clothes were deemed immoral. They were both arrested, their car was impounded, and they were told to leave the country.

Of course, a few years later, the next time I returned to Tanzania, there was no short skirt campaign. That any of this had happened was barely remembered. I went on about my ethnographic business (in a longer skirt) without any trouble.

EPISODE 3

From the start, I was living, as mentioned before, high in the banana belt in a seedy old hotel at the end of the macadam road that comes up the mountain from Moshi town. The hotel was surrounded by the homesteads and gardens of the Chagga. It was not possible to rent one of these small houses in the villages because Nyerere denounced landlordism as a wicked capitalist way to make a living. Rather than offend, I settled for the inelegant hotel, which was often empty.

As part of the final decolonization effort, it was Tanzania's policy to Africanize all organizations. Thus the old German lady who owned and ran the hotel on Kilimanjaro was told to look for an African whom she could make the manager of her hotel. There had been various attempts to get her into trouble so that the hotel could be confiscated and taken over by envious others with Party connections. Because she was a Tanzanian citizen, her possession of it was entirely legal at the time; those who tried to wrest it from her control were not successful, despite their strenuous efforts.

Among the tourists who arrived one day was another old German lady. Few German tourists ever came, so the company was particularly welcome. The owner and the guest chattered away and seemed to like one another. The visitor had come to the mountain because she wanted to affix a plaque on a rock somewhere on the mountain in memory of her father, Hans Meyer. He was said to be the first European to have climbed Mount Kilimanjaro, having made his explorations in the 1880s and 1890s. He established that the ice fields of Kibo, one of the peaks, were already shrinking rapidly. Global warming has done the rest. I am told that now much of the snow and ice have vanished.

Meyer's daughter had an African driver who had brought her to the hotel and had previously taken her touring in the country. She liked the driver and she proposed him as the perfect candidate for the job of hotel manager. He had been to secondary school; he spoke English; he was courteous and entirely presentable. He was not a Mchagga, but she said that did not matter. The hotel owner was pleased to have her "manager" problem solved.

The young man was hired and given one of the small cottages that were attached to the hotel as a place to stay. All the other hotel help were Wachagga and lived with their families rather than on the premises. An elderly, somewhat dilapidated fellow known as "the *askari*" (the soldier) sat (and slept sitting up) at the entrance door at night, but otherwise the hotel was without help between dinner and breakfast. In short order, the Perfect Candidate was made the nominal manager of the hotel. The German visitor had her plaque screwed into a rock somewhere and left.

Well, the Perfect Candidate soon gave the old German owner reason to get rid of him. He began pimping. He installed girls in his room. All day long, men came and went. I was asked if I had seen anything. I had not, but others had. There was no doubt about what was going on. The old lady had to be delicate in making accusations against an African, as the people who wanted to get her into trouble so they could take over the hotel were always watching. She met this setback in much the way she had met all previous misfortunes that I knew about. She would come into the main reception room, arms akimbo, waving her hands and saying, "Cinema, cinema!" (pronounced *seenay-ma*). She alleged that there was so much drama in her life that she did not need any artificial entertainment, television or film—bourgeois luxuries that were beyond her reach in any case. At that time, the hotel had electricity, provided by a generator, for only a few hours in the evening. There was just enough dim light to play solitaire. (Now there is electricity all the time.)

I do not know how she pulled it off, because it happened while I was away, but the German owner did manage to get rid of her delinquent manager. The next time I visited, there was a different manager—the first in a series. Some years later, the owner threw up her hands, gave the hotel to the Catholic Church, and left to retire in Germany.

These vignettes will not tell you anything worth knowing about the Chagga, except that they are like other people, but they do tell you something about the general atmosphere. Much that that went on was unexpected, and some of it was threatening enough to make one nervous. There were many more incidents worthy of the cry "Cinema, cinema!"

SOME DIMENSIONS OF "THE FIELD"

In 1967 the Chagga numbered nearly half a million. For the most part, the mountain was populated by owners of small gardens who grew coffee and bananas, and sheltered the occasional cow, goat, or chicken. Scattered among these small-scale farmers were a number of educated professionals who did not depend on the coffee for a living but had off-farm jobs of one kind or another. I arrived on the mountain humbled by the conceptual and geographical scope of so large a field project, but pleased by the fact that it did not deal with the tribal, homogeneous, bounded unit that was the classic object of anthropological interest.

Kilimanjaro was not a conventional milieu for anthropological research, and law was not a conventional theme. I had chosen to work there for a number of reasons. One was that thanks to the missionaries, it had long been a Christian area. I thought that a woman there would find fewer impediments to gaining access to courts and people, male and female, than would be the case in one of the Muslim communities on the coast. I also thought, because of the long-standing existence of their coffee cooperative, that the Chagga might be especially receptive to the socialist message. I was right about access, but wrong about their attitude.

The Chagga had started the cooperative in the 1920s with the enthusiastic support of a British colonial officer, Sir Charles Dundas, who believed in the cooperative movement and introduced the idea. He was said to have ridden his horse all over the mountain, distributing coffee seedlings wherever he went. The co-op was run by Chagga, and they fought hard to keep it that way when the British administration later tried to take it over. There were some ups and downs in the history of the KNCU (the Kilimanjaro Native Cooperative Union), but by the time of independence it was functioning quite efficiently, selling Kilimanjaro coffee into the world market. The government of Nyerere reorganized the cooperatives of Tanzania several times, but for the locals, the ordinary business of selling the coffee from their gardens continued.

Contrary to what I had supposed, the Chagga perceived no link between the cooperative movement and the socialism of the Tanzanian nation. In fact, in the period running up to independence, the Chagga and their leaders had been very slow to join TANU. Their comments to me about socialism were wry, to say the least. "Nyerere says we should get *ujamaa* [African socialism], but we already have *ujamaa*. We cooperate." "The government tries to help us. We used to get coffee insecticide from the Indian merchants. They were thieves and they charged a lot. Now the government has fixed a low price on coffee insecticide. That is good. [pause . . .] But now there is no insecticide! [laughter . . .]" It had found its way into the black market. So, they told me there was a black market and I knew that it was, by definition, illegal. This was the first of many mundane illegalities of which I became aware.

I had other glimpses of their attitude toward the new government. For example, I saw how the villagers received official visits. One day the district commissioner visited the area. Schoolchildren were waving green leafy branches all along the route taken by his limousine. He waved regally in return. Should one attribute significance to the fact that except for teachers, there were no adult participants in the celebration and greeting? Was this nonappearance a passive protest? After independence, membership in the Party was a nominal requirement, but no one outside of the leadership felt terribly moved to do more than was required. Membership was universal and obligatory, and membership cards were given to everyone. The visits of dignitaries also placed burdens on hotels, which were expected to give every major visitor and his entourage a feast awash in beer. The hotel was obliged to foot the expense, and to make it known that it was an honor to serve such important people. The resentment was confided to me afterward.

The official attitude toward the United States was negative, while China was the idealized foreign country. And although this official stance did not determine the behavior of most individuals toward me, far out in the countryside, there were odd exceptions. Here is one: when I decided to try to find out whether most men married "the girl next door," whether affinal networks were localized, I had a surprise. I went to a Lutheran church, met the pastor, and politely told him the purpose of my visit: I wanted to know if he had any marriage records that would tell me which sub-village the spouses came from. At first he said I could not see the records. Then he asked me whether I was from the CIA.

Obviously more conversation was needed to persuade him that I was not a spy. I have no idea what he thought the Central Intelligence Agency would do with the marriage records of this little village, or indeed how he knew of the CIA. Anyway, I told him more about my life, that I was a teacher and that my studies had nothing to do with the American government. And after a while he softened, becoming willing to show me his marriage records and ready to tell me at length about the "cases" of offenses against the teachings of the church that came before him. Principally these seem to have been about adultery.

In the town of Moshi, and in Dar es Salaam, I expected that my research permission would give me official access to institutions and to written records. My study was sponsored by the Law School at the University of Dar es Salaam, and after I showed my credentials to innumerable bureaucrats, the files were usually opened. But a small organization like a local church was another matter. The pastor had no way to check my credentials, and no criteria for judging the authenticity of the letters I showed him. If he gave me the access I wanted, he was risking a reprimand from the local Party officials for overstepping the rules. Such access depended on my own ability to approach people tactfully and generate friendships, and of course to make it known that I would pay for their time if I needed their help regularly. In the early years, all of that seemed unproblematic.

Thus it was startling in the mid-1970s to begin to encounter expressions of hostility. Several previous trips had established me as an acceptable person in many households, and as a close friend of my regular assistants, but strangers were another story. One of the first signs was a trivial event that occurred as I walked down toward the river at the bottom of the hill on which I lived. There was a teacher's college on the way. In accordance with local custom, I greeted all the people I met on my path—often students on a break from their classes—with "Jambo," and usually the greeting was reciprocated. But one day, the reply from a young man was "Jambo shetani," or "Hello, devil." I just walked on, but I was a little unsettled.

Another day some children stopped me on the road and wanted to touch my skin and hair. That was OK. Others had done this before. But then they followed me on my way and started to chant insults—that I might be a witch, that I might have witchcraft materials in my bag and the like. I was surprised. Eventually they tired of the game, and we went our separate ways. When I told my favorite assistant, Hawkins, about this, he said that there had been a lot of propaganda on the radio about strangers: the Chagga were instructed to tell the authorities if they ever saw a stranger in their villages, warned that these people were dangerous—they might be spies or witches—and that their presence should be reported at once. Clearly there was nothing personal about this, but that did not make it pleasant, and I began to feel that I could not charm all strangers, that something had happened to the friendly ambience of Kilimanjaro.

On the smallest scale, I did everything I could to avoid giving offense. Having been warned that I might be robbed on the roads where I often walked alone, I did not wish to appear wealthy. I did not wear a watch, though I sometimes concealed one in my bag. I did not wear any jewelry, save a plastic bracelet of the kind that could be bought in any Chagga market. When asked for money by local people I met as I walked, I could honestly reply that I had none with me. In conversation, I would avoid comparisons between the American way of life and the African way. I would answer what I was asked as openly and honestly as I could, and I looked for opportunities to show that I wanted to learn from my African friends. I caused much merriment when I said I wanted to learn how to carry things on my head as Chagga women did. They found my clumsiness hilarious. All my ignorance about how to plant and how to grow things delighted them, to say nothing of my errors in Swahili, and my tendency to get lost on the winding paths between the banana gardens. They would laugh at me with evident pleasure. I found the laughter good-natured and was pleased by the benign attention. But surely they knew as well as I did that I had come by plane, that the cost of my getting there was more than the annual income of most farm families. And perhaps more irritating, I was free to come and go. They had to stay on Kilimanjaro. I had more choice. I was a worldling, and they were stuck.

When I went to local political meetings to see how the socialist project was going in the village, I was welcomed. I remember one such outdoor meeting during a period of drought. The rains were overdue and people were worried. During the meeting the rain began—first a drizzle, then a really heavy downpour. People jumped for joy, hugged me, and very nicely said, "Mama, you have brought the rain. Thank you, Mama." Not that they really believed that, but their behavior certainly was a counterfoil for the occasional nastiness of others.

The minutes of Party meetings were kept quite regularly. They were inextricably embedded in Party mythology. For one thing, the agenda of such meetings was supposed to be produced by The People, *quite spontaneously.* The People were to accept Party help, if "needed," in translating their wants into bureaucratic form, but the ideas were supposed to emerge from local discussion. I obtained minutes of meetings from a variety of villages, and, as I suppose I should have expected, the major topics taken up were identical, whatever the village. The Party leaders inserted their official conception of things into the expressed opinions of The People. Did the higher-ups believe in all of this unanimity? How aware were they that they were deceiving themselves? This was obviously not a topic I could discuss with Party officials, and I withheld comment. Clearly, this practice reflected the Party's tendency to make records that would confirm its view of the "peasantry" and its needs.

The Chagga in general seemed to accept such Party action as simply the way things were. And naturally, the local Party men were themselves all Chagga. Some prestige seemed to attach to their office, which may have enabled them occasionally to obtain special favors. In former times, the relation of the ordinary farmers to persons in authority involved connections with the chiefs and their many deputies. One of the first acts of the independent government, to which one would have expected some reaction, was to abolish chiefship. It appeared as if the socialist ideal of political equality could be realized instantly. The Chagga people with whom I discussed this seemed to think that their former chiefs were freeloaders, and that it was not a bad idea to unseat them. But the truth is that the old duffers were still addressed as "ex-chiefu" and shown respect. Some of the old chiefs lived in the largest and most modern houses. I suppose there was some worry among the residents of the chiefdom that they might somehow come back into office. In any event, some were rich by local standards, and their networks were extensive and still sometimes powerful. They might do one a favor.

I stayed away from the chiefs until many years into the field project, lest being identified with them would impair my attempt to display political neutrality. Toward the end of my visits I came to know Petro Itosi Marealle, who had briefly been one of the most important chiefs among the Chagga. Rather than leave so powerful a man on the mountain to ruminate about the new government, or perhaps to organize an opposition, Nyerere gave Marealle a series of important administrative appointments that required his presence in Dar es Salaam. There he could be watched and kept busy.

The old chief was a very sophisticated man. He had written a book about Chagga culture (Marealle 1947), and soon thereafter had met Nyerere in London while Nyerere was doing an M.A. at the University of Edinburgh. When Nyerere came to Moshi in 1956, Marealle invited him to visit at home. Marealle had also had experience in the United Kingdom, visiting Oxford in 1961.

Marealle eventually retired from his independence-period government jobs in Dar es Salaam, and during one of my later field visits he took up residence in his house on the mountain. He often came to the Kibo hotel in the late afternoon to have a beer there and to buy a few bottles to take home for his three wives. By that time I was no longer worried about how people would react if I were seen talking with him. At his invitation, I went to see him at his house and he showed me old photos and files of correspondence, which included some notes from Malinowski.

Petro Itosi Marealle was always very happy to boast of ways he had gotten around the rules of the government. He had a Japanese car on which he had paid no duty, because his son had sent it to him from Japan in the figurative diplomatic pouch. The son, an ex-military officer of high rank, was sent to China for a time, and then to Japan, and then to London, in a state of temporary exile because Nyerere thought he had been part of a coup plot by a group of military officers. It sounded like a very benign alternative to jail. This son returned to Kilimanjaro in 1995, at about the time that Tanzania decided to have multiparty elections. He was thinking of putting his hat in the political ring, so confident was he that he was politically forgiven.

In addition to the house in Marangu on Kilimanjaro, foxy old Petro Itosi also had a house in Dar es Salaam. Having more than one house was strictly forbidden. This second house was occupied by a diplomat, and what was in fact a rental was concealed under the form of a sale whose price was being paid in installments. He discussed this with me with a twinkle in his eye. He had pulled off another fast one.

Petro Itosi's daughter-in-law was not as secure as he was. Another Party rule was that no one was allowed to possess more than one piece of land, which could be no larger than the possessor could work. While the chief's family could obviously afford to hire a person to work in the gardens that surrounded their house, I often saw his daughter-in-law laboring there. She was afraid that one of the locals might complain to the Party about their landholding, putting it at risk. So, she quite ostentatiously worked the land and made sure that I saw her doing so. I suppose that her aim was to make certain that she had an influential witness.

Everyone knew what the rules were about landholding, because the Party gave a great deal of publicity to the abolition of title. All title was taken by the state, and in theory the title to all land belonged to The People. So what did real people have after this change was put into force? They had possession. And the right to possession could be bought and sold. A special land court was established, which was supposed to handle the confusions that might have arisen from these new laws. However, most Chagga villages simply made do with their own customary understandings about these matters, and carried on as before. For most people, the issue of multiple plots did not come up; or, if it did, they managed to assign the extra plot to a female relative without male issue, with the secret understanding that the plot was still the donor's, and would eventually revert to him.

As for how ordinary people coped with the new institutions, I was puzzled about their ability to figure out what the rules were. When I learned that there were unofficial "bush lawyers" who helped people in their dealings with officials and with the courts, I wanted to meet one. My assistant, Hawkins, duly produced a very lively middle-aged bush lawyer who told me about some of the cases in which he had been involved. The most interesting thing I learned about him was that he was illiterate, yet knew what documents people needed in the courts. For example, if a woman wanted to collect damages for a beating she had received from her husband, the bush lawyer would tell her she needed a note from the hospital detailing her injuries. He was known as a person who knew what papers were required and what to do with them. He coped with his illiteracy by having a young assistant who could read. After some time had passed in our conversation, seamlessly, almost parenthetically, he started to tell me about a lengthy controversy in which he himself was involved. He hoped that I could help him. I inferred that he had wanted to meet me not only because he knew I would give him a little gift at the end of our interview but because being a lawyer myself, I might be able to help him reopen his case. The account went on for a long time, and was full of detail. I could not help him, but I had to listen as he expanded on his problem.

Listening to what people wanted me to know, rather than what I was trying to find out, was a large part of the fieldwork encounter. From discussions of the family troubles of my many contacts to information about the pastor's congregation to details of the bush lawyer's own "case," the conversations stretched on interminably. The bush lawyer hoped that if I thought over his case, I might change my mind. He talked on. I wished him well. In the end, he gave up, and made the gesture that I learned was conventional. He tapped his lower lip again and again, meaning "feed me." The request for pay.

MAPMAKING, LAND TENURE, AND CHAGGA CRUELTIES TO KIN

In the beginning of my fieldwork, as I launched myself into the research, I started by inquiring where the nearest court was. I asked permission to observe a session and it was cheerfully granted. I sat on one of the benches in the back and listened. When the proceedings were over, I approached the magistrate to ask him whether he knew anyone who could sit with me and explain what I did not understand. He said he had just the man, Hawkins Ndesanjo, who lived in his village about 6 miles away. We settled on a modest salary (after I found out what a white-collar job paid) and he fitted himself into my schedule, and into my project. Sometimes he accompanied me to one court or another, sometimes I sent him on his own to copy some documents or make some inquiries.

Finding people to help me to learn what I needed to know was not difficult. Shortly thereafter, in another "village" (an administrative designation for a territory that might have as many as 20,000 inhabitants) I found a schoolteacher who had some free time, and she, too, became involved in my work. I later consulted a Catholic priest at the mission station in Kilema, and he referred me to an elderly gentleman named Stanislaus Mosha, who had lots of time, lots of information, and, like everyone else, lots of relatives. I particularly wanted my assistants to be persons who did not know each other, and who came from a variety of villages to ensure that the information I obtained would be a set of independent views. I wanted to test what one asserted against the statements of another. For most of them, their willingness to work for me continued over the years.

People were friendly, not shy, and ready to smile. In fact they wanted to tell me much more than I asked about. They soon told me many stories about their kin and neighbors. One story led to another. I collected genealogies and tried to get my new friends to make approximate maps of the areas nearest where they lived. This turned out to be the greatest methodological find of my entire time on Kilimanjaro. In the end we produced a master map of about three hundred adjacent families, representing a number of patrilineages in a sub-village of Mwika. I saw at once that some of the former chiefly lineage lived on the more desirable sites near the main road, but scattered their relatives throughout the chiefdom. Others lived in kinship clusters when they could, but leaped at any empty plot that became available.

At the same time as the mapmaking, I began a systematic census of the residents in each household, recording not just their numbers but the answers to many questions about each resident: age, education, relationship to the owner, person from whom he had acquired the land, lineage of the spouse, whether the individual had ever been involved in any legal disputes, whether any members of the family were absent, and other nosy things. The demographic information was public, and no one hesitated to give it to Hawkins or to me. I am less sure about whether the question about disputes was answered honestly, but some people used it as the occasion to talk about how they had been wronged.

The census was an eye-opener, since decades of history were embedded in that geography. Almost all the land was inherited and held in trust for descendants, entailed. The entailment was a customary moral imperative. This simple device, mapping, eventually told me obliquely that there were far too many descendants, that subdividing would not work for the next generation, and that therefore more land disputes were surely in the offing. If further subdivided, the plots would be too small to feed a family, and there was no unoccupied land into which family members could expand.

As I followed out-migration to the cities, it did not at first occur to me to ask much about the absent members of the households. Originally I thought that leaving was just an occasional thing, a reflection of individual choice. But later my mapping and census taking showed that the trend was widespread. I was standing in the midst of a demographic change of some magnitude. This must have influenced the way people felt about their situation, making some of them feel very insecure. In one lineage whose affairs I followed in detail between 1968 and 1993, of the fifty-three adult members of the younger generation, twenty-seven had gone to live in the cities. The land shortage was affecting family life in a radical way. And the population increase showed no signs of relenting. Everyone had many, many children, in some cases from several marriages.

The collection of quantitative material about the location of households was work that could be done in my absence. At the same time I collected other documentary records: case records from the courts, yearly records from the cooperative, and other materials. As well, intense personal contact with some informants over many months—in the case of Hawkins and his kin, over years—told me about the emotional strains that lay embedded in the land facts. For example, there was a man in Hawkins's lineage who went into debt, deeply into debt. He drank; he bought things; he spent money he did not have; he was reputed to be irresponsible. His brothers came forward and paid what he owed. I thought this was a piece of fraternal generosity, of the lineage solidarity so often spoken of in the work of other anthropologists working in Africa. It appeared to me to be an example of what Goran Hyden had called "the economy of affection" (1980). In fact, Hyden attributed the failure of socialism in Tanzania to the primacy of the economy of affection: according to him, socialism could not catch on with the "peasants" because of their commitment to family ties.

It turned out that I was wrong in thinking that the brothers paid the debtor's obligations out of affection. What the more prosperous brothers wanted was that he should sink more deeply into trouble so that they could then lay claim to his land. They wanted to take it over cheaply, as if the land itself were surety for the debt that was owed. Because of the strong sense of lineage entailment, brothers were supposed to have right of first refusal whenever there was a land sale. In this case, the brothers competed with each other and approached the debtor separately and secretly. They applied a great deal of pressure on him not to sell to an outsider, a non-kinsman, complete with moralizing admonitions. This debtor became enraged at his brothers and found their contempt for him unbearable. As a result, he did sell his land to an outsider to spite his brothers, and settled his debts to them from the proceeds. I asked one of his kinsmen whether he got a better price from the outsider than he would have from his brothers, and I was told that money was not a factor in his decision: it was anger that drove him to choose an outside buyer.

As was true of most of the interesting accounts of kin cruelties, I could not verify the motives of those involved in detail. However, the behavior of his brothers was not unusual. The frequency of such slaps in the face, dealt particularly by the more fortunate to poor relatives, made it clear to me that Chagga lineages were often very punitive to their kin. I felt sorry for the poor fellow but I could not show it. I had to display indifference, the way Hawkins did. I wondered whether the issue was simply his willingness to sell to an outsider, or if the kinsmen had disliked him for years. Were there other, older concerns at play? I could not find out. I was told that he was and had always been a bad sort, and that was the end of the conversation. I tried to discover where he would go, what he would do. No answer was forthcoming.

Some of the methods by which kinsmen showed that they despised one of their number were long lasting. They might, for example, exclude a member from all family rituals and celebrations as a punishment for some violation of their standards of fraternal performance. A particular instance comes to mind. In a Mwika lineage that I knew well, one poor fellow begged for a goat from his cousin, saying he was going to use it in a ritual slaughter by a *mganga* (customary healer) hired to make his sick son well. But once he obtained the goat, he sold it in the market and kept the proceeds. All hell broke loose. His kinsmen deemed him a liar and an immoral, cheating person, and for years thereafter he was not invited to participate in his brothers' slaughterings or in kinship beer parties. Exclusion and other internal forms of avoidance were considered absolutely justified. I held my tongue, but I was shocked by the durability of these rejections.

How did the new socialist government affect this land-short, kin-based scene? The Kilimanjaro branch of TANU was, on independence, reorganized to include everyone. Local ten-house cells constituted the base of the Party. The head of each ten-house cell was called "the *balozi*," and all events in the cell of interest were to be reported to him. He was to keep records in which he was to note births and deaths, antigovernment activity, meetings, lawbreaking, land transfers, and the like. On paper it sounded revolutionary, but in practice it was not. At the lowest level, the new "socialist" administrative changes consisted largely of renaming what was already there. At higher levels, the new government defined a flow of information upward, and sent orders downward, through a Party administrative structure that had not existed earlier. Government functions and innovations were carried out by a hierarchy of "development committees" and development officials who worked closely with the TANU organization.

The Chagga learned much about formal organization from the bureaucracies of the socialist period, and they transferred some of these models to lineage organization. For example, in the late 1980s the leader of one lineage, a senior elder, died after a long illness. He had made many sacrifices to his ancestors, but succumbed nonetheless. His successor was chosen in 1990. Using the vocabulary of Party organization, the new head called himself the "lineage chairman." He was a dynamic fellow and had a bright idea about how to aggrandize his position. He wanted to fuse his lineage branch with another, geographically close branch that had long been autonomous, making him more powerful and locally more important.

For years, the creation of formal organizations other than the Party was discouraged, indeed prohibited; the government continually worried that any group might cook up antigovernment plots. Even big meetings of kinsmen were forbidden unless permission had been obtained in advance. But by the 1980s the socialist orthodoxy had faded and freedom of assembly began to be possible again. The lineage chairman succeeded in persuading both branches to agree to the consolidation. He was very businesslike: after listing all the household heads in a notebook, he then proposed that every member household contribute a small sum of money for a collective fund. He had learned this lesson from the socialist reorganizations. He opened a bank account (the first he had ever had) and deposited the money, which he designated to be spent on vocational apprenticeships for young people in the lineage who had not passed the exams for secondary school. These young school-leavers could become bricklayers, carpenters, or tailors or find some other way to be trained to make a living in the cities.

The membership agreed, and the plan was soon under way. There was one dissenter, however, a man who had been the head of the second branch of the lineage and thus lost all authority when the two branches were amalgamated. He wanted to keep the two branches separate, so that he would continue to be head of something. He boycotted all the chairman's meetings, and refused to contribute to the common fund. The chairman sent him a stiff letter saying that he was banished from all the beer parties, rituals, or celebrations that might be held in either branch. He replied that the ancestors would not have approved of the consolidation and that his rival was violating the fraternal bonds of the ancestors.

The dissenter bore up for a year in his state of exclusion, but eventually he sought reinstatement in the amalgamated lineage. The chairman assented, under certain conditions. The rebellious kinsman should prepare a beer party for the whole lineage, admit his guilt, and apologize. He did as he was told, and bygones became bygones. Nevertheless, the contradictory nature of the new structure should be noted. The chairman was enlarging and strengthening the ties between the lineage branches, but at the same time his use of their funds to support careers was encouraging out-migration of the young.

In all this, the central government made manifest some of its views of the land shortage problem in ways that mixed the inviting and mildly threatening. It encouraged volunteers to found new communities in the wilderness areas of southern Tanzania, but wanted proof only of the success of its programs. Hence when the initial excitement of the pioneering program waned, and some disappointed volunteers returned, any criticism of the program was taken as evidence of antigovernment sentiment.

Allied with China, and deeply suspicious of anything American, the Tanzanian state often asserted its determination to be self-reliant and exhorted its citizens to follow its model. Certainly Tanzania wanted to shake loose from old British ties, and feared that international development loans would have political, not just economic, costs. But Tanzania could not always maintain self-reliance. When, early in the years after independence, the government was threatened with a coup, I was told that it was saved by the British navy sitting in the harbor of Dar es Salaam.

Vigorously Africanist in its orientation, the government made Swahili, not English, the national language. Local tribal languages would continue as the domestic language of many households, but Swahili was the language of public action, and the language of the schools. On Kilimanjaro the domestic language was Kichagga, the language in schools Swahili. Yet English remained in use in key institutions, such as the University of Dar es Salaam. The authorities could take English out of the discourse of the police, but they could not take it out of the books that were in the libraries.

Meanwhile, family life went on rather as before. In the central belt, each little smallholding of land continued to grow its coffee and its bananas. The women all bought and sold vegetables at the same local markets. Most people lived in mud and wattle houses with thatched roofs, the wealthier in mud brick houses with tin roofs. In general there was no household electricity and little running water. Normally, women would fetch water from the local pump, filling huge cans that they carried back on their heads.

A number of institutions that were supposed to be maintained or to change for the better simply deteriorated. I observed the deterioration in such diverse objects as the colonial gardens of the president's house in Dar es Salaam and the buildings of the white stucco university situated outside of Dar. The records of local cases from the law courts around the country were collected and said to be officially archived at the university. But when I went to the room where they were housed, I saw that the records were scattered on the floor, with only a few on the shelves. After tackling some of this mess myself, I spoke about it to various people, from faculty members to custodians. Their universal response was "Picking things up is not my job."

THE BIGGEST SHOCK

One day, in the fall of 1979, when I came back to the hotel from a busy day of seeing people, I was given a message that a certain person in Moshi, a Mrs. M., wanted to see me at once. I asked if anyone knew who she was and was told that she was a security person, and that I had better go. I went to Moshi the next day and she said in an accusatory tone, "I have heard about you. We have been watching you. Yesterday you went to the market and you stayed there a long time. You watched everything." She went on, "I am asked, 'Why is this stranger here among us. What is she doing?'" Yes, I answered, I was there. I am trying to understand how the market works, how the women arrive at a price for each item being sold.

She was plainly not satisfied. She told me that my work must be supervised. For a start, I would have to submit a written list of all the questions I intended to ask of anyone, and to indicate who would be asked them. Then, if the list were approved, I could go on with my research. I was very uneasy. She continued, "You should be glad about this. It shows they are being politically responsible. You are in trouble. But this is not a racial matter. Tanzanians do not care what race you are. It is not hostility. They are taking political responsibility. Please be careful."

Dismayed, I got on the bus, went back to my room, and started to compose a list of ambiguous questions. I thought that if my inquiries were general enough and innocuous enough, she could hardly object. And probably this security officer was mainly interested in justifying her position. On the optimistic side, I thought that if I complied with the request to write a list she would be happy and let me go. I was wrong. I also thought, more pessimistically, that I was being trapped into making a move that would get me into trouble. I handcopied the list, since there was no copying machine to be had anywhere near. I duly went to Moshi the next day. The security lady would not see me that day, and I left my questions with her secretary. Things looked bad. Eventually she returned a list of questions, but they were not mine and they had been so altered that I did not know how to proceed.

The next day I tried to feel normal and less afraid. I decided not to ask anybody any questions but to go to the court that was near where I lived, the one where the magistrate had been friendly and found me a research assistant. I would look at the files of case records, as I often did. When I got there I found that the courtroom was empty. The little room where the case records were kept was locked, and nearby stood a young man I did not know. He said, "Perhaps you should do something with development, not with us. I must inform my superiors about what you have been doing. You are not to go in there [the room with the records] any more."

Dumbfounded, I asked him by what authority he was keeping me out. He replied that the orders came from a high official. I told him I would have to contact my friends in Dar es Salaam to clear up this "mistake." He said it was useless.

I went back to my room and resolved to go to Moshi the next day to arrange to get an air reservation to leave. I was able to make the arrangements. I did not go back to the court. And I knew that to go to Dar to see people who might reverse these orders would take considerable time and might produce nothing. Who knew what was going on inside the Party, and what risks were involved. I remembered what my friend the director of development studies had said about the possibility of trouble. I left in November 1979, a month earlier than I had intended.

What is clear is that the Party regulars, at least at relatively low levels, conceived of socialism as a total system. It was, for them, rather like Durkheim's idea of mechanical solidarity. Anyone who came from a place that by definition was structured by other principles was a threat. As an American, I did not have to do anything: just my presence— indeed, my existence—was dangerous to the total system. I had labored hard to win the trust of the Chagga, the people whose lives I tried to understand, and person-to-person I had succeeded. But there was no way I could win the trust of the small-time bureaucrats in the Party offices. I would wait them out.

When I returned in 1993, everything about the tightened Party discipline of the late 1970s had almost vanished from official memory. With the Tanzanian economy in shambles, Nyerere had stepped down from the presidency in 1985; he was succeeded by Ali Hassan Mwinyi, a man from Zanzibar and a Muslim. The World Bank and the International Monetary Fund pressured the government to change to an open market economy, and Mwinyi implemented the change. Nyerere, in a talk at the London School of Economics delivered a few years after his retirement, said about Tanzania's socialism, "We failed."

As for me, in the 1980s, I did research in West Africa. When I went back to Tanzania in 1993, my research application was processed and approved by the University of Dar es Salaam without a murmur of disapproval. The Law School was welcoming. In Moshi the Party bureaucracy signed everything without incident. The security lady had disappeared. I went up-mountain and met with my old assistants. There, apart from the absence of the old German lady, the death of Petro Itosi Marealle, and the fact that the Catholic Church had somehow transferred the hotel to one of Marealle's relatives, it was as if nothing had changed.

CODA: UNCERTAINTY IN THE FIELDWORK SITUATION, INDETERMINACY IN THE CULTURE

I started fieldwork in my 40s. I had begun my professional life much earlier as a lawyer. I was an associate attorney in a Wall Street law firm for a year, and then, for six months, I aided in the preparation of one of the prosecution cases at the Nuremberg trials. Subsequently switching professional focus, I studied anthropology. At the same time I went into three years of psychoanalysis. This prolonged period of careful, emotionally laden introspection undoubtedly increased my self-awareness and, indirectly, prepared me for fieldwork and the internal restraints I had to exercise. After the analytic period I married and had children and began my teaching career. All this experience preceded my fieldwork in Africa. Going to Africa was not to be an adventure to discover myself: I wanted to learn about the effect on the countryside of the Tanzanian socialist experiment (installed at independence from British colonial rule) and to meet and talk with many individual Chagga about their lives and concerns.

In the course of my work in Africa, many things happened to me, and around me, but many of these happenings did not have to do directly with the Chagga. I resisted writing a personal narrative, keeping self-reflection quite separate from my fieldwork reports. The content of such an account might have had local political repercussions, a possibility that was worrying. And whose business was it that I felt this or that? I did not want to expose my own doubts and dilemmas to the profession, let alone to the political watchers. I did not want to make myself the center of my ethnographic descriptions. I did not want to dilute my account of the Chagga with stuff that was mostly about Sally Moore. I had read ethnographies in which one learned more about the anthropologist than about the people being studied. I did not want to write what is now called "auto-ethnography."

And I wanted to be as sure as I could be that what I was reporting about the Chagga was true. I was wary of typifying from limited evidence. My many return journeys to work in different so-called villages were undertaken in part to make certain that I could distinguish the unique happenstance from the general state of affairs (the land shortage, for example). The people were diverse: educationally, religiously, economically, occupationally, and otherwise. This was no uniform culture in the colonial sense of the imagined homogeneous "tribe." There is no space here to discuss the colonial and postcolonial periods, which were not uniform in any way: a proper account would have to include the many variations, individual and social, that were evident. Though too many existing descriptions treat these as flat and unitary and exaggerate the impacts of policy, I will have to leave a full correction for another time.

I spoke Swahili, though not as fluently as I would have liked, but I did not speak Kichagga. On occasion, Chagga among themselves often switched back and forth. Some Chagga spoke English, which helped me very much. There were cultural commonalities among the people I came to know, practices and ideas that were very different from my own, but even in this there was much variation. Some people were more "traditional" in their ways and some were more "modern." As one of my assistants said to me as we passed a man working on his garden plot, "See that man. See what he is doing. In the old days he would not be doing that work. It would be *aibu*, shameful for a man to do woman's work." What is an anthropologist to do with such a piece of information? Was this just my assistant's idea? Was it a generally held view of the relations between the sexes? How recently had men begun to do such work?

On the part of the Chagga, there were many degrees of commitment to ethnic custom, of literacy, of devotion to the teachings of the church (Catholic or Lutheran), of attention to African socialism, of worry about witchcraft. All of these institutions had tenets, and rules, and enforcements of conformity—each one circumvented at one time or another. In the beginning of fieldwork, to make sociological or cultural sense of all this diversity and multiplicity of practice and thought was difficult, to say the least. In addition, in writing about what I saw and heard and read I had to be mindful of the political implications of what I might say. Needless to say, today I no longer feel as constrained, but at the time I had to watch my step.

Long-term fieldwork is never long enough to capture everything. It is not as if the field is a finite, bounded entity about which one learns more and more, coming ever closer to the goal of completion. There is no such thing as completion. First of all, the "whole" is never visible or measurable. Perhaps (pace Heisenberg) there ought to be a fundamental uncertainty principle attached to fieldwork. Moreover, things are changing all the time. One can interact only with a part of a society at a time. And while a given domain is in view, events emerge elsewhere, often out of sight, that may affect what one is looking at. One is never finished. One simply stops. In the beginning the sense of incompleteness emerges like a self-accusation, but that feeling attenuates when revisits have filled the file drawers with solid and not-so-solid data.

Like all cultures, Chagga culture is capacious. In its system of values, it accommodates the traditional healer as well as the hospital. It presumes that the inheritance of a banana garden is the best path to economic well-being. Yet for some enterprising individuals, the culture is also open to innovative investment and technical work as an alternative way to make a living. Not only do cultures have regularities and norms, but they also have open zones of indeterminacy. People make choices. They use the zones of indeterminacy creatively, a fact that greatly complicates fieldwork (for a theoretical discussion of indeterminacy, see Moore 1975: 210–35).

Meanwhile, change takes many forms, and long-term research makes one very much aware of the shifts. Adult children go off to the city to find work. The structure of the family changes. A man cannot count on being surrounded by his children as he ages. More women embrace family planning. The price of coffee changes. The government changes. And so it goes, as Kurt Vonnegut would say.

It all spells uncertainty for any anthropologist trying to get a durable fix on the ethnographic scene. Association with particular informants over the long term may approximate friendship. I felt very warmly toward these people, and they were clearly glad to have me back every time. But with some there were money problems, or unreliability was the difficulty. These troubles can turn dealing with assistants into unpleasant transactions.

And the number of less significant disappointments is legion. I cannot begin to count the occasions when I made an arrangement to meet someone who did not show up. I walked many miles each day to make contact. The villages in which I did most of my work were 4 to 6 miles distant from my hotel, in Kilema and in Mwika. In a milieu without telephones, there is no expectation that anyone will announce a change of plan. There is no way to do it. And afterward, one has to smile and pretend that the letdown did not matter. It always mattered to me. If excuses were made, I could never tell whether they were lies. And perhaps worst of all, I felt I could never show anger. I hated this, but making a nice face was the price of getting on with the work. And in the long run, and the run was long, I think it paid off.

To the extent that reflexivity means being preoccupied with oneself, brooding over the disappointments and insults, celebrating oneself when the going is good, it is usually not worth writing about. But to the extent that reflexivity means self-awareness in the curious situation called "fieldwork," such self-consciousness is absolutely necessary. It is a complement to observing and talking with the very people one has traveled such a great psychological and physical distance to meet.

REFERENCES

Dundas, Charles. 1924. *Kilimanjaro and Its People*. London: Witherby.
Gutmann, Bruno. 1926. *Das Recht der Dschagga*. Munich: Beck.
Hyden, Goran. 1980. *Beyond Ujamaa in Tanzania*. Berkeley: University of California Press.
Marealle, Petro Itosi. 1947. *Maisha ya Mchagga hapa Duniani na Ahera*. Marangu: n.p. [Reprinted in 2002 by Mkuki na Nyota Publishers, Dar es Salaam.]
Moore, Sally Falk. 1975. "Epilogue: Uncertainties in Situations; Indeterminacies in Culture." In *Symbol and Politics in Communal Ideology*, ed. Sally Falk Moore and Barbara G. Myerhoff. Ithaca: Cornell University Press.
———. 1986. *Social Facts and Fabrications: "Customary" Law on Kilimanjaro, 1880–1980*. Cambridge: Cambridge University Press.
Stahl, Kathleen. 1964. *The History of the Chagga People of Kilimanjaro*. The Hague: Mouton.

SEVEN

Encounters with the Mother Tongue

SPEECH, TRANSLATION, AND INTERLOCUTION
IN POST–COLD WAR GERMAN REPATRIATION

Stefan Senders

> I used to speak dialect, but then I had to speak Russian. They forced
> us. I hated it and I never learned to speak it well. Now I am learning
> *Hochdeutsch* and I can't speak that either. I have no mother tongue!

Irma, 89-year-old *Aussiedler*

In the mid-1990s I was in Berlin, Germany, doing research on *Aussiedler,*
or "ethnic German" repatriates. The Berlin Wall had fallen in November
1989, but there was already a widespread feeling of frustration concerning the newly conjoined Germanies. Many in both east and west wondered aloud whether things might be better if the wall were still
standing. In the former East Germany, and in Berlin in particular, violence against foreigners had increased; there had been murders, and tensions had increased to the point that the federal border police had been
called in to provide security on the Berlin subways. It was an uncomfortable time, particularly for the most vulnerable populations, including
the city's many Turks, the many Bosnian refugees who had been forced
by war to flee their homes, and the Aussiedler—repatriated *Volksdeutsche*
who claim German citizenship and identity, but who, because of their

many years in the Soviet Union, didn't easily fit the part. "They're not really German," people said. "They don't even speak German."

In the context of repatriation, the ability to speak German is one of the principal signs of German identity and integration. Language competence, because it is seen as a prerequisite for entry into the German economy, is viewed as a key to Aussiedler integration. Nonetheless, at the time of my research, the majority of Aussiedler did not speak German well and many barely spoke it at all. Many Aussiedler do eventually learn to speak German, but they rarely "master" it (*die Sprache beherrschen*); instead, as they say, they are mastered by it (*beherrscht werden*). Most recent Aussiedler speak Russian, and can only muster a stilted and bookish German. For the Aussiedler I worked with, language—speaking, in particular—was a source of great discomfort. Because they could not speak German well or fluently, every word was a reminder of their failure to be the "Germans" they claimed and hoped to be. Speech became both a source and sign of trauma, undermining and attacking their identities.

Because the German government has long been aware that many Aussiedler struggle with German, it has provided subsidized and quasi-mandatory language training for incoming repatriates. They have been offered special classes in "German for mother-tongue speakers," apart from the ubiquitous "German for foreigners." The training is more than just linguistic; the classes serve a disciplinary function, modifying Aussiedler's behavior and making them more acceptable, more German.

To be German, of course, requires more than minimal linguistic competence and a willingness to act German. German citizenship law is widely stereotyped as being entirely based on the principle of *jus sanguinis,* or the law of blood or descent. But the law, rooted more in the exigencies of cold war politics than in a romantic ideology of blood, is more nuanced than that. Alongside descent it draws on anthropological and psychological notions of culture and identification in determining identity: Aussiedler are required to have a subjective identification with German culture, and to have suffered for it.

A key term in this ideology of reproduction is *Muttersprache* or, in English, "mother tongue." The concept of *mother tongue* has historically taken two forms: one could be classified as totemic, and is focused on reproduction at the level of the nation or *Volk*. In Germany this mother tongue is *Hochdeutsch,* or "High German," and it is Germany's national and bureaucratic language. The other form of mother tongue is more closely associated not with language as a system but with speech as act and experience. *Mother tongue* in this sense is a way of describing *how* one speaks—"I speak German as a mother tongue," or "She speaks English as a mother tongue"—and it refers both to the subjective state of individual speakers and to their ability to *express themselves.* Speaking, as a sign of sensuous identification and mimesis, serves as an indicator of belonging; when it fails, it becomes a source of disidentification and trauma.

The two forms of mother tongue—as system and as subjective experience of practice—are closely related, and in interaction they buttress one another. Without speakers, without nationals, a mother tongue as national-totemic language is meaningless. The whole idea of "national language" assumes a metonymic relation of speakers to nation. The speaker symbolically embodies the whole, and the spoken word comes to stand as "a refraction of the immanent national essence" (Herzfeld 1992: 111). Can it also be said that without a mother tongue, no speaker, no speaking subject, can be imagined? What is it to be without a mother tongue?

In this essay I explore the role of speech, translation, and interlocution in the context of post–cold war German repatriation. In addition, I inquire into what knowledge of these issues might be produced—uniquely—by fieldwork encounters. The concept and history of *Muttersprache,* for example, appears to be ideally suited to library research; what supplement could fieldwork add? Here I argue that the encounter brings the concept into a new epistemological arena, that of risk, a move that offers new insights available only through encounter-based inquiry.

EPISODE 1: SPEAKING

For Aussiedler, the absence of the mother tongue reshapes speaking into an admission and experience of lack, failure, and impasse. To speak, then, is to fail in self-consummation, while to adopt silence is to refuse identity and its privileges, to seek refuge in interiority, to survive by playing dead. To speak without the mother tongue enacts a dreadful separation between the speaker and her desire, her self.

On one occasion, Alexander, a young Aussiedler from Kazakhstan, asked me if I would come to his apartment to join him for a meal with his mother, Klara, and her former German teacher, Kristina.[1] Alex had been extremely anxious for a week or so before the dinner, and he thought that my being there would make things go a bit easier. I was to meet him at the apartment on a Friday afternoon around three-thirty.

Alex was in the living room when I arrived, and Klara came out of the kitchen and met me inside the door. A young woman, probably no older than 40, thin, she wore her blond hair piled up in a bun. She was dressed completely in black—black polyester blouse, black pants—and her pants were tight; I could see where she had taken in the seams to fit them more snugly. Her teeth, many of which were capped in gold, were brilliant.

Klara and I had known each other for a while, and she seemed happy and relieved to see me. She hugged me tightly and kissed me. Then she put her hand lightly to my cheek and held it there for a long moment, resting. Suddenly she was moving again. Putting her arm around my waist, she held me close to her hip as she led me down the hall into the living room.

The room was small and densely furnished with a TV, a couch, two chairs, a bookshelf, and two clocks, one of which, made to resemble a huge stainless-steel wristwatch, hung on the wall. Alex and Klara both asked me to sit down, and Klara disappeared into the kitchen. Alex opened two beers. The two of us sat on the couch drinking, hardly speaking. Alex was visibly nervous, and he seemed too worried to say anything.

On top of the TV the digital clock clicked over to 4:00, the time the guests were expected, and then 4:01, one minute late, and Alex looked at me hopefully: "Perhaps they won't come." Klara came in from the hall with plate after plate of food. There was enough for ten: thick cuts of fat bacon, greasy chicken, pork-and-onion dumplings, bread, two bottles of brandy, cans of beer, a bottle of *Sekt*. She set it all out on the small low table. "Perhaps," she said, "we'll have to eat it all ourselves! That would be great!" The doorbell rang. Klara swore. We all got up to answer the door.

Kristina came in first, followed by her husband Rolf, and then her daughter Gudrun. Klara greeted them warmly and we shook hands all around. Kristina was almost bellowing, and she praised the neighbor-hood (which was really run-down) and the apartment. Then she turned to me, exclaiming how happy she was to meet "more of the family."

We made our way slowly down the hall into the living room, and we sat down on the couch and the chairs around the table. Kristina handed Klara a bottle of aperitif she had brought as a gift. Klara turned immedi-ately to open it, but Kristina stopped her with a strong whisper and a wave of the hand. We all sat, looking at the food. Klara disappeared for a moment and then returned, bringing with her three more bottles of *Sekt* and more beer. She opened the both bottles of brandy and began eyeing the aperitif. Kristina looked horrified. We began to eat.

As the dinner went on Klara became increasingly nervous. In the first fifteen minutes of the meal she had started to speak but had stopped to correct herself more than a dozen times, and after that she sat silent. "You see," she said finally, "I can't speak properly. I make so many mistakes. I can't . . ." Alex interrupted to correct her, and Kristina joined in, taking up her familiar role as teacher. She began by correcting Klara's grammar, then she suggested alternative vocabulary, and finally she turned to the dinner itself. "When you invite people, in Germany, over to visit at four o'clock," she explained, "they don't expect a big meal! They expect cof-fee and cake! And they *never* expect so much to drink!" Alex and Klara might have been ashamed, but they protested, with some humor, that "Aussiedler always drink a lot. It's Russian."

After an hour had passed, Klara had turned on the TV next to the table. Gudrun, a teenager, had gotten into a low-key fight with her father over her drinking. Alex had spent most of the meal quietly watching Gudrun, and Kristina had found out to her surprise that I was not a Russian but an American writing about Aussiedler. She had a lot to say about them, and she always talked about "Aussiedler" in the third per-son, despite the presence of both Alex and Klara right there with us. She went on and on. I nodded and smiled, wishing I were somewhere else.

Klara stood and quietly went to bed. Alex said little. Kristina talked. Finally, perhaps moved in part by Gudrun's mounting frustration, she and her family left, shouting colloquial and incomprehensible good-byes as they descended the stairs. The dinner had been more of a humiliation than a celebration.

As I rode the train back to my apartment, I thought about Klara's sudden loss of voice and final suffering retreat from the scene. She, unlike Alex, had grown up speaking dialect German at home. Although the language she preferred to use was Russian, she could still speak German quite well, even if it sounded like neither television German nor Berlin German. Her neighbor, she told me, had at first assumed she had come from the German countryside, not from the former Soviet Union. Alex told me that Klara could speak German "only when she doesn't think about it." Despite her communicative competence, Klara felt afraid to speak freely in front of her teacher, and she rapidly reverted to the role of child-student, retreating first into silence and then into injured absence. Alex, too, regressed when his desire for Gudrun (he obsessed about her for weeks afterward) was shown to be nothing more than fantasy.

I couldn't avoid thinking about my own participation in Klara's disappearance and suffering. I had simply gone along with Kristina in her disciplinary project. I was able, allowed, to speak—with all my slips and infelicities—because I made no claim to the language. I was a visitor from far away, speaking as a foreigner. Klara and Alex were "home," and yet every word denied that they belonged. I had become, unwittingly (as in so much of what I did in the field), a participant in the large-scale process of identity management and regulation.

For Klara and Alex, the whole event was supposed to have been an opportunity to *become* themselves in a way they had not yet succeeded in doing. Klara had hoped that speaking would be a confirmation of her repatriation, and that it would signal the satisfactory completion of her identity; instead, it dissolved those hopes. It should have been a display of competence, an extension of a *host's* hospitality, and thus an expression of ownership and mastery. The supposed identity-work of language failed, and its failure meant exclusion from a future world she desired and a return to the past she did not, that of the "Russians." For Alex, the dinner, ideally, should have been a point of entry into circuits of German sexuality and potential reproduction; he wanted to get together with Gudrun, to become someone who *could* get together with Gudrun. But finally he was unable to overcome the silencing pressure of disciplinary discourse.

For my part, I started to get a sense of what it meant for me to *speak*, and what it could mean to stay silent. I could see that I had played the role of collaborator and interlocutor, mediating and translating among discourses—official, legal, disciplinary, disciplined, resistant—and I began to get a better understanding of the role of language and translation in the repatriation process.

EPISODE 2: TRANSLATION

For Aussiedler, and for the officials who regulate their entry into Germany, the work of "translation" is critical. One couple I worked with described for me what they had gone through in the application process. Irma and Rheinholt had applied for Aussiedler status while they were living in Kyrgyzstan, and although they were granted preliminary acceptance, their final status was to be confirmed through tests administered in Germany. Upon their arrival in Friedland, the largest Aussiedler reception camp in Germany, Rheinholt was asked a few questions and required to write his name. Because he could barely speak German and could write only in the Cyrillic alphabet, he was helpless, and Irma, who could speak and write a few words of German but who is "ethnically" Russian, was not allowed to say anything.

The official who conducted the interview, they told me, was "polite" and allowed them to pass, but some months later Rheinholt received a postcard calling him to the Marienfelde Transit Camp in Berlin for an interview. There he was questioned in depth: Had he been attending a German-language course? What German traditions had he maintained? What German holidays did he know? Rheinholt couldn't understand the questions at first, so an interpreter was brought in, but as Irma put it, "neither of them could understand the other." Undaunted, the official asked whether he had ever visited the German National-Theater in the capital of Kazakhstan, Alma-Ata. Rheinholt replied that he had lived not in Kazakhstan but in Kyrgyzstan, more than 300 kilometers from Alma-Ata. "Maybe," he later told me, "maybe the official was confused . . . or maybe he didn't understand it when I said I hadn't visited the theater.

But he wrote it down the wrong way, that I *had* visited the theater. Then he checked up. And he wrote that I had lied to him. It was so mixed up!"

Officials, too, find translation difficult and disconcerting. One way they determine whether Aussiedler are authentically German is by checking documentation—both official, such as the *Volksliste* used by the Nazis during World War II to identify ethnic Germans, and unofficial, such as family Bibles or personal letters. But the documents, while regarded as "objective signs," often resist simple translation. To take one example: in the process of repatriation, names are seen as representative of identity, but when officials examine records of Aussiedler names and name changes, even these documents lead officials to feel "insecure" (*führt zur Verunsicherung der Standesbeampten*) as they shift in both form and meaning over time—"It can happen that when an official checks into an Aussiedler's birth records the names of the parents are written in their Polish form. Later the bureaucrat may get a notarized copy of the family book (*Familienbuch*) in which the names of every person involved, including the non-German relatives of a spouse, are recorded in German form and script" (Gaaz 1989: 165).

Even when officials work directly with repatriates, the work of translation is fraught. Frau F., a supervisor at the Marienfelde Transit Camp, where Aussiedler are processed when they come to Berlin, described her work to me as "difficult," because the prototypical applicant, which she categorized as a "refugee," is a blank, having escaped with nothing but his "naked life." His history, therefore, requires excavation, interpretation, and translation. She explained:

> Often one asks the younger ones: Did the tradition carry on? Were they always close to the German, or did they go off in the country where they lived? . . . So one has to ask . . . how was it in your place? How big was it? Na . . . 300 inhabitants. Did you have a German institution? No. Well, was there anything? Ja . . . 20 kilometers away. Then you say . . . now can I go 20 kilometers every Sunday to church? . . . In Russia that was so far . . . there was no transportation . . . and when there was a car everybody jumped aboard. . . . It's also a question of what you can expect. But there are others who say, "We have tended to it among ourselves" [*Wir haben es unter uns gepflegt*]. They had an old man who was *Bible-fest*, for example, who got the others together and held a Bible study.

In the absence of mobility, the presence of "an old man holding fast to the Bible" offers the possibility of a link to tradition—embodied in the word. But Frau F. also needs to distinguish the word *heard* from the word as *trace of experience*. Has the applicant "only heard" of a custom, or has he experienced it personally? To experience tradition is, in Frau F.'s words, *immer aufrecht zu erhalten*, to "keep it up."

Frau F. routinely asks applicants about their labor histories, and she finds in the idea of *work* a concept she can comprehend. "One said," she recounted, "'I was director of the savings and loan.' And I imagined, as a Berliner, a huge building with lots and lots of people . . . and there you really are *somebody* as the 'director of the savings and loan.' But it turned out that he had the main postal job in a tiny town. . . . Practically a one-man business!"

In the act of translation, Frau F.'s imagination at once intrudes on and is essential to the examination process; to evaluate applicants' claims, she needs to identify with them—"and there you really are somebody"—itself a process that alienates them—"And I imagined, *as a Berliner . . .*"

EPISODE 3: LEGAL TRANSLATION

All of this talk about talk and translation is important for Aussiedler, as it is critical to their being accepted, legally, in Germany. In the past, German courts assumed that Aussiedler would speak German as a mother tongue; but in the 1990s, those assumptions began to change. In one case, for example, two siblings entered Germany from the former Soviet Union with the expectation of being granted Aussiedler status. But they were, at least on the first try, rejected; one of the critical pieces of evidence for the rejection was their inability to speak German as a mother tongue.

The court, however, ruled after an appeal that Germans from the former Soviet Union could not be expected to have mastery of German, and the decision went on to provide a detailed history of the Germans in the Soviet Union—a story of loss, dispossession, deportation, death, repression, and final redemption in repatriation. This narrative, the judges argued, was more important in determining authentic identity claims than language. Identity should be seen as a matter of "consciousness," "identification," and "experience," and they pointed in particular to enduring consequences of linguistic and cultural repression. The upshot was that the inability to speak German, as a sign of repression, is in itself a sign of "German" identity (see Senders 2002).

To an extent, the ruling was politically motivated, but more importantly, it represented a turn away from the romantic ideologies of language and descent, and toward a narrative-based identity. Aussiedler were encouraged to understand their identities in terms of historical narrative rather than of immediate and embodied experience. At the same time, while it diminished the legal importance of linguistic fluency for repatriates, it did little to change the assumption that speaking, not what is said, should emanate from being.

The strategy adopted by the court, beyond making sense politically, was preeminently *therapeutic*. The goal, in therapeutic terms, was to bring the analysand to the capacity for self-narration, to the capacity to "narrate to the Other his own history in its continuity" (Žižek 1989: 133). As one German official put it, the history must be propagated "so that Aussiedler can understand their own cultural tradition and know how they fit into the totality of German culture" (quoted in Schwab 1992: 5). The recitation of history is here a fundamentally therapeutic approach to a problem defined by trauma, repression, and lack.

Government representatives and politicians repeat the authorized stories, printing them in brochures and newspaper articles, books and lectures—and the stories are simple and remarkably uniform. They tell of the Germans moving into Russia at the behest of Catherine the Great and setting up vibrant communities on the Volga. Over time the Germans are stripped of privilege and status, and finally they are transported to Siberia and Kazakhstan by Stalin. There they have waited, suffering, for the opportunity to "return" to Germany, where they might again live "as Germans among Germans."

The stories deftly tell their way around any sense of Aussiedler's investment in their lives. They skip over Aussiedler's work, their learning, their loves—and they concentrate on their role as "Germans abroad," waiting to come "home" to embody their rightful identities. In order to become the "Germans" they supposedly already are, Aussiedler must submit to the negation of their experiences. In order even to articulate their desire to repatriate, they must be willing to formulate their desire in a language that is not their own, and that they cannot control.

INTERLOCUTION AND CASTRATION

From a therapeutic perspective, one task of analysis is to bring the analysand to the acceptance of traumatic loss—"to consent to symbolic castration as a price to be paid for access to his desire" (Žižek 1989: 133). If the analysand refuses to accept loss, the fulfillment of desire is precluded. Here, for Aussiedler, such refusal is marked primarily by the retreat into silence, into being "mastered by" language. The impasse can become pathological, resulting in somatization and dissociation.[2] Aussiedler I met groped for stories that were correct enough, and true enough. When the stories failed, when language proved inadequate, the stories were replaced by expressions of the senses and the body—smells and tastes, shivers, spit, and, more than anything else, tears.

Early in my research, I had begun interviewing families living in a hostel in the center of the former West Berlin. I found people suspicious at first. Two theories dominated: the first was that I was selling bogus insurance, and that I would try to con them out of what little they had; the second was that I was a government agent sent to assess the veracity of their claims to German identity. Both fantasies were relatively easy to dispel (I wasn't selling anything, and my obvious foreignness made it unlikely that I was working for the government) and our conversations quickly warmed up; moving past the expected citations of official histories, their discourse became more difficult to contain within the limits of "conversation." Often talk gave way to tears, sometimes for hours at a time, and at times it was displaced by calls for touching—"feel my arm . . . feel the goose bumps on my arm . . ." On other occasions, it fragmented into polyglot performance, as when a woman and her daughter sat close to me, reading poetry into my ears—Russian in one ear, German in the other—with neither expecting me to understand. Sometimes the conversations simply dissolved into anger.

One evening I had been sitting with Emma and Maharita for a long time, and the women, mother and daughter, had spent much of it crying. They were telling stories of their repatriation, stories of deportation and mistreatment. As we talked, and as the women wept, Waldamar, Emma's son-in-law, came into the room and sat silently against the wall. He made no move to join us but just sat and listened. I had never met him before, but when I tried to make some kind of signal that I wanted to introduce myself, he did not respond. He just sat there, not looking at me, not looking at the women. I tried again but got no response. The apartment seemed small, and I felt uncomfortably hot.

Waldamar's silence seemed aggressive, and I could hardly listen to the women because I kept worrying about him. At the same time, there seemed to be nothing I could ask or say that would not bring on a flood of tears from the women. Emma and Maharita had been crying on and off for more than two hours. I still wanted to know more about their stories, but I felt guilty for sweeping into their lives to bring up painful memories, to bring tears and anger. I had a headache, the room smelled bad, and I wanted to leave.

Then Waldamar spoke. What exactly did I want to know, he asked. Did I want to hear about their lives in Russia? I tried to explain that I wanted to hear and understand their stories, and to understand what it meant to them to come to Germany and live as Aussiedler. Waldamar got up, walked across the room to the bedside and picked up a wooden chair. He planted the chair directly in front of me, its back facing me, and straddled it. His face was no more than a foot from mine.

He began to talk, and to shout. He was spitting, and his sentences were coming in fragments. "For fifteen, twenty years of work and life," he shouted, "we received around 4,000,000 rubles. Four thousand marks! What is that? [He spits into his hand.] It's nothing!" He would have been a rich man, he tells me, if only he could have brought it all with him. What he received as social assistance in Germany for one month was more than his life's work had been worth. He repeats himself, no less loudly, and I wonder if I can stand to sit there any longer. The two women are crying. I suggest that perhaps we should stop. But no, they want to go on. "It's important," they say.

Our "conversation" stopped only when finally, late in the night, I stood to leave, forcing an end. I went to my apartment feeling sick and guilty. I felt guilty for just having been there asking questions, and for bringing up feelings that were so obviously painful. The anger brought back bodily memories of my own childhood and of my father's unpredictable anger. I remembered viscerally my complete inability to respond, to reason, and to speak. And the crying, which seemed inseparable from the stories, left me shaken. I felt that my research was failing. There was just too much excess, and not enough "material."

Our "interview" had turned into a catalog of apparent failures. Maharita and Emma had in large part given up language and been driven to, or sought refuge in, tears. Waldamar, for his part, found expression only in shouting and spitting. I had lost any security I might have had: I could certainly not claim the status of a distant or observing knower; and even given my "participation," I found myself reenacting old conflicts from other relationships entirely. All of this—tears and anger, goose bumps and aching silence—entered our relationships when our language was failing, and once it entered I quickly came to the limits of my own language: I had no adequate response, and no way of resting comfortably. I had, moreover, no way of incorporating the experience within what I had naively assumed would be "interviews" in which I would hear "narratives" and "stories" that I could then analyze with "narrative analysis." It was, in other words, a signal of my own inadequacy, and of the inadequacy of the theoretical tools I had at my disposal.

I eventually came to see tears and anger as some of the few means of expression by which Aussiedler could escape the pressure of institutionalized history, and by which they could recover some of what had been lost in their repatriation. Because language itself was the unrelenting sign of their symbolic castration, to escape it, if even for a moment of tears and anger, allowed them to experience a self-identification without lack.

Their tears and anger also brought me to the very edge of my own language. It is likely that I would not have known what to say or how to say it even in my own "mother tongue," but in German, a language I had learned only as an adult, I had neither the right words nor the subtlety of inflection to respond. I was merely hoping to maintain my balance. At the same time, it also was clear to me that my presence, as irritating as it was, offered the Aussiedler I was with a safe opportunity to practice. We went to language school together, and we often laughed at each other's graceless expressions.

In retrospect, I have come to understand these experiences as central to my ethnographic work, even though at the time I considered them failures. My intense discomfort forced me to listen for expressions I did not want to hear, and to consider the ways my own past shaped my ability to encounter others. I think of this kind of destabilization as part of what makes ethnographic work and knowledge unique.

Ethnography pushed me, as knower, ever closer to my limits, and it put my project, and me, at risk. I had, I suppose, come to the field with an exaggerated sense of the strength of "method," a means by which I would perceive the world and express those perceptions without having to give up much of anything. I had hoped that I could come to understand what I saw and experienced without having to acknowledge my own inadequacies. What I found instead was that neither anthropological method nor long-internalized coping strategies were much good; to take just one example, I found myself still working through my reactions to my father's, and my own, anger.

Such experiences were often painful, but they offered the possibility of new relationships based on risk and submission—to the limits of the self, of *technē,* and of language, and to the Other. These possibilities are only hinted at in the terms *participation* or *performance,* and they did not surface in my own anthropological training. But vulnerability of this sort may be what enables ethnographic knowledge-making to become transformative rather than merely extractive. The process transforms, undoes, the knower and the known, creating instead a space of interlocution that opens to mutual understanding.

I was trained as an anthropologist at a time when rhetorical and narrative analysis was particularly powerful. As a student I was inspired by the writing culture debate, and I spent much time working on understanding ethnographic tropes, narrative strategies, and rhetorical moves. At the time, it seemed possible that much of what anthropology had to say could be derived from (and denied by) the analysis of texts.

If the ostensive purpose of anthropological theorizing is to get beyond both native self-description and "common-sense understanding" (see Taylor 1985: 124)—that is, to make an Other more comprehensible—from what vantage can that knowledge come? The "textualist" paradigm suggests that rhetorical technique might solve problems of power and domination. There might be, somewhere, some new way to write or edit ethnography such that it would move us closer to equality, farther from ethnocentrism, and closer to accountable representations. But these desires seem no more likely to be fulfilled than the Aussiedler's longing for self-realization through a language they do not possess. In a sense, the fantasies run in parallel: Aussiedler long for a mother tongue in which they can be present as complete and dominant speakers; anthropologists long for a language and method that will enable access to the Other unmarked by domination, and that will produce for them "understanding."

Charles Taylor (1985) has argued that anthropology has been stuck between two epistemic poles. On the one hand, the Other is seen as the sole source of her own understanding—this he calls the "incorrigibility thesis"; and on the other hand, the Other should be understood in the knower's own terms—this he calls the "interpretive thesis."

The incorrigibility thesis fails for a number of reasons: it offers little in the way of real illumination, as it assumes that self-understanding is accurate and sufficient; it precludes the possibility of any communication of knowledge; and it begs a whole raft of questions concerning membership and legitimacy. Taylor offers the incorrigibility thesis as a theoretical end point, a pole, but it is fairly well represented in the world. Debates concerning "native ethnography" and the legitimacy of "outsiders'" interpretations of cultural phenomena are common enough, and they are based on the assumption of incorrigibility.

The interpretive thesis is presently regnant in anthropology, but its problems—domination, ethnocentrism, misrepresentation, and so on—are well-known and many. The interpretive thesis is particularly important for those outside anthropology who would "interpret" culture, such as marketers, focus group consultants, and journalists. It enables us, and them, to work relatively easily with our assumptions about the Other.

There is a third possibility, however: what Taylor calls "a language of perspicuous contrast. This would be a language in which we could formulate both their way of life and ours as alternative possibilities in relation to some human constants at work in both. It would be a language in which the possible human variations would be so formulated that both our form of life and theirs could be perspicuously described as alternative such variations" (Taylor 1985: 124). Taylor's proposal moves beyond the blunt and naive realism of a data-driven approach modeled on the natural sciences, and it allows that social phenomena require an epistemology based on understanding. Yet his suggestion of a simple juxtapositional "language" seems to me inadequate.

Taylor, to my mind, never makes sufficiently clear what this language would be, nor does he show how it might overcome the limitations of current modes of representation. He does suggest that whatever understanding is produced in this new language should undermine the hierarchical structure of anthropological knowledge, that the anthropologist should be as much under examination as the Other, and that the terms of analysis should not be allowed to avoid scrutiny. The point, he argues, is that "understanding another society can make us challenge our self-definitions. It can force us to this, because we cannot get an adequate explanatory account of them until we understand their self-definitions, and these may be different enough from ours to force us to extend our language of human possibilities" (Taylor 1985: 131).

In its simplest formulation, the proposal is for double translation: our language into theirs, theirs into ours, potentially producing what John Borneman and Abdellah Hammoudi (in their introduction) have called "double-edged critiques" that undermine any easy distinction between knower and known, aiming to illuminate the communicative possibilities we share (see Borneman, chapter 9 in this volume). Such a double translation, Taylor suggests, would demonstrate the contingency of both languages. But it strikes me that the "language of perspicuous contrast" need not be a programmatic solution based on "translation," a term that assumes the substance and stability of an original utterance—a mother tongue. Instead, such a language would better be seen as not language at all; rather, at issue is shared experience and participation based not on the translation of texts but on submission, encounter, and the acceptance of mutual risk. Such encounters destabilize both the researcher and the researched, creating contexts in which each depends on, demands of, and cares for the other.

.   .   .   .   .

One afternoon I was on the subway with Alex, Lisa, and Lisa's sister. We were headed east toward Marzhan, where they lived in a hostel they shared with Bosnian refugees. We had just come from our language school, where we had been laughing and talking playfully, but now they all were silent. When I spoke, none of them responded—until we were off the train. Then they told me: they wouldn't talk on the train because it was too dangerous. One slip and they could be identified as foreigners and targeted, perhaps even killed. We arrived at the hostel and we passed the afternoon and much of the night talking, eating, and drinking. It was late when I got up to leave and head out to the subway. As I left, Lisa's sister took my arm and pulled me close to her: "Don't say anything," she said. "Just don't say anything and they won't know. Your voice will give you away."

NOTES

Special thanks are due the Aussiedler who shared their time and stories with me, and John Borneman, Ann Russ, Antonia Saxon, and one anonymous reviewer, all of whom have offered insights and criticism that have helped me improve this essay. The remaining faults are mine.

1.   Throughout this essay, names have been changed.
2.   Symptoms I heard of included stuttering, eating disorders, self-isolation, excessive envy, aggressiveness, stomachaches, headaches, sleep disorders, and bedwetting.

REFERENCES

Gaaz, Berthold. 1989. "Fremdenländische Namensform und deutsches Personalstatut: Zur Namensführung der Aussiedler." *Das Standesamt* 6(7): 165.

Herzfeld, Michael. 1992. *The Social Production of Indifference: Exploring the Symbolic Roots of Western Bureaucracy.* New York: Berg.

Schwab, Sigfried. 1992. "Aussiedler—nach deutschland heimgekehrt?" *Informationsdienst zum Lastenausgleich* 1: 5.

Senders, Stefan. 2002. "Jus Sanguinis or Jus Mimesis? Rethinking 'Ethnic German' Repatriation." In *Coming Home to Germany? The Integration of Ethnic Germans from Central and Eastern Europe in the Federal Republic since 1945,* ed. David Rock and Stefan Wolff. New York: Berghahn Books.

Taylor, Charles. 1985. *Philosophical Papers.* Vol. 2, *Philosophy and the Human Sciences.* Cambridge: Cambridge University Press.

Žižek, Slavoj. 1989. *The Sublime Object of Ideology.* London: Verso.

EIGHT

Institutional Encounters

IDENTIFICATION AND ANONYMITY IN RUSSIAN ADDICTION TREATMENT (AND ETHNOGRAPHY)

Eugene Raikhel

BACK FROM THE FIELD

Several months after my return from the field, I was reading online newspaper articles in the basement of NYU's Bobst Library when I came across an extraordinary story. Sergei Tikhomirov, the director of St. Petersburg's Municipal Addiction Hospital, where I had conducted much of my fieldwork, had been arrested and charged with having ordered the murder of a fellow administrator—the deputy director in charge of finances. This woman had been killed by a small bomb planted in the doorway to her apartment. The director had reported that a similar remote-controlled device was placed—but did not detonate—near his apartment; it was later deemed a ruse, planted to deflect suspicions from him. Police reports suggested that while the specific motives for the murder were unclear, illicit money flows in the hospital were somehow involved.[1]

My initial shock at reading the article stemmed both from the fact that the violence had taken place between physicians (contract killings are still common in many spheres of business in Russia, but much less so in medicine) and from my own proximity to that violence. Though my acquaintance with the victim was limited to seeing her around the hospital, I had met with Tikhomirov the previous spring when he signed off on my project—and the murder had taken place only days after I left the city. To put it mildly, the hospital had not turned out to be the kind of fieldsite I had first expected.

While preparing to depart for St. Petersburg, I had been told by my graduate advisors to conduct my fieldwork with care. I had chosen to focus my research on transformations in Russian addiction medicine, known locally as "narcology," a topic which would require that I spend significant amounts of time in institutional settings—clinics, hospitals, rehabilitation centers, and the like. The danger, it was suggested to me, was that such fieldwork might prove "too easy." The idea was not simply that a certain level of arduousness is necessary for fieldwork to be experienced as a "rite of passage." The concern was that the very things that made conducting research in such a setting potentially attractive—the spatial, temporal, and social structure and stability that institutions supposedly lend to one's otherwise open-ended days—would be too familiar to me, too much like the rhythms of my life at home. I would be lulled into an ethnographic complacency, unreflectingly accept the underlying assumptions of my interlocutors, and thereby lose the productive level of cognitive distance (and dissonance) needed to maintain the visibility of difference.[2]

Learning of the murder tragically confirmed my sense that the Municipal Addiction Hospital was far from an institutional space of predictable bureaucratic regularity. As I reconsidered what it had meant to conduct fieldwork in a clinical setting where such a deadly commercial battle could take place, I returned to the broader methodological, epistemological, and ethical questions posed by clinical ethnography. In addition to the hospital, I had worked extensively in another St. Petersburg institution—the House of Recovery, a 12-step-program-based rehabilitation center for alcoholics. Had my fieldwork in these two clinical spaces differed fundamentally from research I had conducted outside of institutions? Moreover, what had I learned through this work and how had I learned it? Is what John Borneman and Abdellah Hammoudi call (in the introduction to this volume) "encounter-based fieldwork" possible in institutional or clinical settings? And finally, what experiences of mine were unique to contemporary Russia and what widespread in clinical and institutional settings (increasingly common as ethnographic fieldsites) throughout the world?

In this essay, I attempt to address these questions by comparing typical experiences and practices of identification and anonymity in the state-run Addiction Hospital and the House of Recovery. "Identification" can refer both to the determination or recognition of "what a thing or a person is" ("identification of" or "self-identification as") and to "the becoming or making oneself one with another, in feeling, interest, or action."[3] Here, I play on both meanings and their relationship with one another. I begin with the Addiction Hospital, describing the institution and my work there, and then shift to the House of Recovery. In each case, I examine how my possibilities for self-identification were opened up or foreclosed by ascriptions of identity made by my interlocutors, and how such opening up or foreclosure in turn shaped our mutual potential for identification *with* one another. Finally, I discuss anonymity, different types of which were central both to the House's 12-step program and to a service provided at the Addiction Hospital, known as "anonymous treatment." The essay concludes with a brief consideration of identification and anonymity within ethnographic practices.

INSTITUTIONS: THE HOSPITAL

The main building of St. Petersburg's Municipal Addiction Hospital is situated on a tree-lined street of nineteenth-century buildings on Vasilievsky Island. The area was one of the first parts of the city to be laid out; the succession of parallel numbered streets, called "lines," suggests

the Enlightenment ideals of order that Peter I and his city planners sought
to impose as they constructed St. Petersburg in the eighteenth century
(Lincoln 2001: 24). With the recent upsurge in the real estate market, this
district in the historical center of the city has regained its status as a desirable place to live. While some of the old housing stock still contains
Soviet-era communal apartments, other buildings have been converted
(back) into elite homes for the wealthy and for new professionals. St.
Petersburg University lies several streets to the east of the hospital; on its
other side, an avenue has been recently converted into a pedestrian walk-
way lined with boutiques, cafés, beer halls, and the occasional sushi bar.

In the midst of so much recent change, the cracked and dirty walls of
the Addiction Hospital initially struck me as signs of deterioration or sta-
sis. Like many of the city's prerevolutionary structures, the building
bears visible marks of its transformation from private residence for the
elite to municipal hospital. Just inside, past the landing, a large metal
gate stretches across what was presumably once the main vestibule; an
attendant sits in an adjoining booth, controlling traffic into and out of the
clinical section of the hospital. Most of the wards are accessible only by
way of the building's muddy, pitted, and overgrown courtyard where,
during the summer months, patients and nurses stand by entrances to
staircases, smoking and chatting. In the nineteenth and early twentieth
centuries, these "black entrances" and stairwells opening onto court-
yards were meant for use by servants: they are narrow and spare—concrete stairs with unornamented metal railings. Above the doorway to
one ward hangs a faded sign—designed to light up—with the words
"Quiet: Hypnosis in Progress."

From the mid-1970s until the late '80s the Addiction Hospital served as
the hub of a municipal and regional treatment network for alcoholism
and addiction in (what was then) Leningrad. The network, which had
taken shape in the wake of several Soviet campaigns against "drunkenness and alcoholism," included not only institutions (like the hospital)
under the aegis of the Ministry of Health but also explicitly penal ones
run by the Ministry of Internal Affairs (Beliaev and Lezhepetsova 1977;
Babayan and Gonopolsky 1985; Segal 1990). These different institutions
were instantiations of varying disciplinary and professional ideologies

about the nature, etiology, and appropriate treatments of alcoholism. On one end of the spectrum were the narcological dispensaries for outpatient treatment established in each of Leningrad's administrative districts (*raiony*); on the other were labor colony–like institutions intended for those "chronic alcoholics who resist treatment for drunkenness, and additionally disrupt labor discipline, social order [*obshchestvennyi poriadok*], or the rules of socialist communal life [*obshchezhitiia*]" (Tkachevskii 1974: 38).[4] The dispensaries can be seen as representing an ideal of outpatient care espoused by early Soviet social hygienists, and the labor colonies the punitive ideal of the police and judicial systems; the Addiction Hospital was situated somewhere between these two extremes, receiving patients for inpatient treatment from the dispensaries, and occasionally sending them off to the colonies. With its "compulsory treatment" (*prinuditel'noe lechenie*), prolonged inpatient stays, and heavy use of medication, the hospital represented the predispositions and priorities of psychiatry—the parent discipline of Soviet addiction medicine.[5]

Though this system of addiction treatment had been deeply transformed by the time I first visited in 2003, the Addiction Hospital still retained many of its institutional characteristics from the Soviet period. During a preliminary research trip, I made contact with several physicians at the hospital: a geologist friend of the family put me in touch with Aleksei Vladimirovich,[6] a medical researcher who had served as a physician on several geological field trips to Crimea. Though trained as a narcologist, since the mid-1990s Aleksei Vladimirovich had been working as a researcher in a neurological institute and moonlighting as a lecturer on neurophysiology. However, he knew several narcologists working at the hospital, and took me along to visit a ward run by his former classmate Irina Valentinovna, a warm and personable woman in her early 40s. While the trouble experienced by Aleksei Vladimirovich in understanding why my research project required me to speak to physicians and patients ("Can't you just get information about narcology from books and articles?") suggested a set of epistemological assumptions very different from my own, Irina Valentinovna was more open to the idea of fieldwork. "In reality, things don't work the way you'd think they do if you only read texts," she agreed, setting out a tray of cookies and chocolates.

Shortly after the fall of the Soviet Union (and close on the heels of the final Soviet anti-alcohol campaign), Irina Valentinovna explained, the Russian Federation had moved to dismantle the explicitly punitive elements of the narcological system. The last of the labor colonies for alcoholics were shut down in 1994 (although they had essentially ceased to function during the late 1980s), she continued, the same year that new legislation did away with involuntary hospitalization for noncriminal alcoholics (see White 1996; Entin et al. 1997; Gilinskii and Zobnev 1998). Throughout the 1990s and 2000s, physicians at the hospital had struggled to manage the increasing numbers of alcoholic patients (many were now homeless, which had been rare during the Soviet period) as well as a precipitous rise of the use of injected heroin (along with a concomitant spread of HIV infection) (Kozlov et al. 2006). These efforts were frustrated by drastic budgetary cutbacks stemming from the dismantling of the Soviet-administered economy generally and the restructuring of the health care sector in particular (Twigg 1998; Balabanova, Falkingham, and McKee 2003). While basic treatment remained free of charge, the hospital had begun to offer various for-fee services (these included improved accommodations and food). Nevertheless, Irina Valentinovna continued, with its 600 beds, the hospital was practically the only state-sponsored facility in the city offering inpatient treatment for alcoholism and drug addiction.

When I returned to St. Petersburg that autumn I again contacted Aleksei Vladimirovich. This time he put me in touch with Grigorii Mikhailovich, a former medical school professor who was now a mid-level administrator at the hospital. Grigorii Mikhailovich allowed me to begin speaking to physicians at the hospital, but explained that in order to interview patients my project would need to be approved by the hospital's director, Sergei Tikhomirov. With evident unease at the prospect of an American researcher working in the hospital, he seemed anxious to pass off responsibility for me to his superior.

The process of obtaining permission to speak with patients dragged on for months. It seemed that every time I called him, Grigorii Mikhailovich delayed my next visit to the hospital—once a conference had come up unexpectedly, the following week everyone was busy filing their annual reports—yet each time he asked me to call back in several days, assuring me that a meeting with Tikhomirov was imminent. For two weeks his cell phone was dead: as he later explained, the service (funded by the hospital) had been turned off for nonpayment. I wondered whether any of this was deliberate stalling on Grigorii Mikhailovich's part. Had I failed to set our relationship in the right direction by not bringing him a gift, or was he reluctant to bring my project to the director's attention for his own reasons?

Upon returning to St. Petersburg from a brief trip home to New York, I received word from Tikhomirov's office that my proposal had been forwarded to the city's Department of Public Health and that I was to write up a "research contract" (*dogovor o sotrudnichestve*) stipulating my own responsibilities, as well as those of the hospital, during the course of research. Having dutifully drafted the contract and shepherded it through the offices of several municipal administrators, I returned to the Addiction Hospital to receive Tikhomirov's signature. He was a small bearded man with a squint who seemed to spend most of his time deskbound. After signing the document, he pointed to a clause stating that I would "present myself to patients as a graduate student in social anthropology." "Let me give you a piece of advice," he said. "When you speak to the patients, it's better to tell them you're a psychologist. They're used to speaking to people like that."

IDENTIFICATIONS: THE THERAPIST

When I had first begun fieldwork on my dissertation project, my expectations about how people would identify me—as well as the methodological issues that this identification would entail—were based both on my previous experiences as an adult in St. Petersburg (a brief fieldwork trip as an undergraduate and several month-long stints of language study) and on my readings in the ethnographic literature. As I had been born in the city, then called Leningrad, and emigrated to the United States with my parents at age 4, I was perceived by people who knew about my background as an émigré—a well-established and long-standing social category in Russia. Like all ambiguous and hybrid categorizations, this one could be interpreted in different ways by interlocutors and presented in different ways by myself, at some times emphasizing affinity between us (I was "returning home") and at other times accenting distance (I was "an American"). Language inflected my personal story as another ambiguous marker for identification. Despite my often shaky grammar, my Russian has little enough accent for me to pass unnoticed as a "foreigner" in many everyday conversations. This ability could, however, lead to moments of abrupt discord in conversations, particularly when my interlocutor's assumption of speaking to a fluent "native" suddenly ran aground on my lack of local knowledge.[7]

Yet this project was different from my previous visits; I had never worked in a clinical setting in Russia, and I knew that my fieldsites, my chosen topic of alcoholism, and my interest in speaking with both physicians and patients would present a new set of challenges. Given my lack of medical training or experience with research in this environment, I expected to be unambiguously viewed as an outsider by physicians. However, I also wanted some entrance into the lifeworlds of patients: at the very least, I hoped to learn of their clinical experiences. I had been encouraged in graduate school to try to "follow patients home" into their domestic lives, and at the time I still thought that such an effort might succeed. Moreover, I knew that my first introductions to both patients and physicians (and the ways I would be identified by them) could either facilitate or foreclose possibilities for ethnographically rich encounters.

The problem of how to identify oneself or of what "role" to assume has been particularly acute for ethnographers working in clinical settings, in part because these institutions seem to allow for so few possible ways of being. For instance, Sjaak van der Geest and Kaja Finkler have argued that fieldworkers spending extensive lengths of time on hospital wards have essentially three options in adopting a role: medical practitioner (doctor or nurse), visitor, or patient (2004: 1998). The first and last of these, while seemingly offering institutionally validated positions from which to participate and observe, are difficult to assume completely. To be a practitioner, one needs specialized medical training (increasingly common among medical anthropologists, but hardly an appropriate prerequisite for fieldwork); to be a patient, one must be ill or feign illness.[8] Many ethnographers assume that their disciplinary practices and their institutional association—typically a project must be formally approved by a clinic's administrators—will mark them in the eyes of patients as associated with the staff. Some fieldworkers have inhabited this association ambivalently, negotiating the methodological and ethical difficulties it poses (Rhodes 1991: 3), while others have found that the connection with practitioners fits their purposes and have sought to accentuate it (by wearing white coats and so on). On the other hand, some researchers interested in the experiences of patients—especially in settings such as psychiatric hospitals or clinics, where patients' agency is particularly circumscribed compared with that of the staff—have made efforts to temper their identification with practitioners by such means as "avoiding sociable contact with the staff" (Goffman 1962: iv), assuming patients' clothing and physical comportment, and taking medication (Estroff 1981: 20–34).

A handful of researchers have gone so far as to feign illness or its symptoms, most often in studies of mental illness (Goldman, Bohr, and Steinberg 1970; Rosenhan 1973; but also see van der Geest and Sarkodie 1998). Many of these studies were carried out by psychologists, whose discipline has developed a set of assumptions and practices regarding the deception of subjects that are very different from those of anthropology (Lederman 2006: 484). In some cases, the strategy of posing as ill has been adopted less as a means of establishing trust among other patients than as a way of testing the claims of labeling theory. For instance, in a well-known study carried out by the psychologist David Rosenhan during the early 1970s, researchers faking symptoms of psychosis not only were admitted as patients to psychiatric hospitals throughout the United States, but once on the ward they were able to openly take fieldnotes without arousing the suspicions of staff members, who interpreted this action as pathological "writing behavior" (Rosenhan 1973: 253).[9] Rosenhan's argument was that identifications of behavioral pathology are produced by physicians and patients in particular social contexts, rather than inhering fully in the bodies, minds, or actions of patients, and his method was central to making this argument. As I describe later in this essay, not only are the possibilities for such characterizations of oneself—as mentally ill or addicted—heavily contingent on local (and institutionally specific) ideas about the nature of an illness (its etiology, symptoms, visibility and so on), but the ethnographer can also unintentionally become the object of such identifications.

The risks of perceived connection to clinic staff have been especially important for ethnographers working in post-socialist settings, as in any place where medical professionals are closely associated with the authority of the state (Rivkin-Fish 2005; Skultans 2005). Soviet physicians were public servants; in addition, the institutional bases for their professional autonomy (professional associations) had been undermined as early as the 1920s by the Communist Party (Field 1991). It has often been noted that the Physician's Oath of the Soviet Union affirmed a doctor's responsibility not only to his or her patients but also to "the principles of communist morality" and "the Soviet state" (Bloch and Chodoff 1991: 519). As Michele Rivkin-Fish has argued, this potential for being identified with the state threatened physicians' "legitimacy as healers" (2005: 26), leading many to employ various means of social exchange to personalize their relationships with certain patients and to distance themselves from associations with bureaucratic authority. Such associations were arguably even stronger in the case of medical specialties such as narcology and psychiatry, whose clinical authority during the Soviet period had been heavily bolstered by legal provisions for compulsory treatment (narcologists sometimes called on the police to bring noncompliant patients in for visits), as well as their close relationships to the penal-juridical systems (Connor 1972; Tkachevskii 1974). Given that the most effective ways of dispelling the distrust engendered among patients by such perceived links to the state are informal practices of sociality and exchange, ethnographers working in post-socialist clinical settings have often been wary of the formality imposed by the consent forms that their home institutions require (Skultans 2005: 496–98).[10]

Thus, when the hospital director suggested that I identify myself to patients as a "psychologist," I grew quite concerned. For the director, such an identification was just a pragmatic methodological shortcut; he explained that introducing myself this way would expedite my interviews by giving the patients a frame of reference with which they were familiar. To be fair, some of the assumptions implicit in his proposal struck me as reasonable. For instance, it was clear that introducing myself as an anthropologist might not strike the right note, given some of the ideas circulating locally about anthropology. (One of the hospital administrators told me that upon learning of my disciplinary background he had wondered whether I planned to measure the circumference of patients' heads.) However, "psychologist" hardly seemed an improvement. While I certainly hoped that patients would somehow benefit from my listening to their stories, I was worried that they might misconstrue our conversations as formal therapy and thus assume I was a staff member. At the time, I thought there were several reasons for such a concern about misrecognition, including the range of conversations construed by local addiction doctors as "psychotherapy" and the fact that people who carried out group therapy or social work were sometimes categorized as "sociologists."

As I began to visit the hospital regularly, it became clear that though my concerns about patients' misrecognition of our encounters were misplaced, the best I could do to avoid being associated with clinical authority was to mitigate physicians' representations of me. In most cases Grigorii Mikhailovich acted as an intermediary, putting me in touch with the physicians in charge of particular wards. Most were uneasy with the idea of my spending time informally on the ward; instead, they allowed me to speak to patients individually in consultation rooms. Some went even further and insisted on selecting patients for me to speak with. One had the habit of approaching patients in the ward's hallway and asking loudly: "Sasha! Do you want to help advance international science? Just answer a few questions from our American colleague!"[11]

Of course, even within these relatively constrained circumstances, there was room for much difference in the framing of our interactions. Some patients were withdrawn, answered questions tersely, and resisted my attempts to open up a broader conversation about their lives. It is important to remember that we were often discussing subjects—their diagnosis as alcohol dependent or the circumstances leading to their stay at the hospital—that were, for many, difficult to speak about. My interlocutors were primarily men, and while male drunkenness is (still) often conceived in heroic terms in contemporary Russia, a diagnosis of alcoholism continues to carry a heavy stigma.

Not surprisingly, then, it was often (though not always) most difficult to have extensive and engaging conversations with the rare middle-class patients whose lives remained relatively undisrupted by their drinking or drug use. For instance, my fieldnotes include a rather short and abruptly ended interview with Ivan, a businessman who explained that he had been pushed into alcohol dependence because all of his business meetings (many of them, he told me, with *mafiya* figures) had to be conducted over vodka. On the other hand, many of the hospital's patients had spent significant portions of their lives in prison and assumed toward me a posture that was at once formally deferential and firmly unforthcoming. Other patients—particularly those who had been taught to narrate their life stories as "drunk-a-logs" in the local 12-step rehabilitation program described below—were eager to relate the details of their lives. A few explicitly presented their stories to me as object lessons in moral failure or the dangers of the bottle. I had little certainty that many of these men appreciated the chance to tell their stories, and I had no doubt that they did not construe our conversations as psychotherapy.

Rather, it was the physicians who were much more likely to allude to our encounters as beneficial. For instance, after several hours of conversation about the burdens of paperwork and stifling bureaucracy, the lack of sufficient material resources, the frustration caused by recalcitrant patients, and her general sense of futility caused by her inability to significantly affect the course of most addictions, a physician in the acute ward of the hospital exclaimed, "It's nice to be able to speak to someone about this. No one listens to *our* complaints." At other moments I was treated less as a listening ear and more as a colleague, a fellow "expert" (albeit in a very different discipline). Such identifications were, of course, never particularly stable—the narcologists remained keenly aware that I would represent them and their specialty—but they were sufficient to enroll me into a kind of complicity with the physicians' professional secrets.

COMPLICITIES: PLACEBO THERAPY

Anton Denisovich was a third-generation physician and a second-generation psychiatrist whom I met early in my work at the Addiction

Hospital. Though overworked (lacking a secretary or a computer, he spent much of his time filling out charts and forms) and underpaid (earning less than he could in private practice, though more than physicians in most other specialties), he was also thoughtful and self-confident—too young and too successful to feel burned-out or unhopeful. Described by hospital administrators as a rising star, he had been appointed the head of a ward only four years after completing his medical degree. Happy to speak to me as a colleague of sorts, he talked about the intellectual pleasure he had taken in working on the big clinical problems of psychiatry, such as schizophrenia. His decision to enter narcology was, like that of most other physicians, financially motivated.

When I asked him about the forms of longer-term treatment offered to patients upon their departure from the hospital, Anton Denisovich explained, "Mainly it is *khimzashchita*—placebo therapy—or we orient them toward rehabilitation programs." By this point in my fieldwork, I knew that *khimzashchita*, which literally translates as a contraction of "chemical protection," referred to a treatment for alcoholism employing disulfiram, a drug that induces a heightened sensitivity to alcohol. I had also read in an English-language medical journal that Russian narcologists sometimes used "placebo therapy" in their practice, but none of the physicians I had spoken to had mentioned it, and I was surprised at Anton Denisovich's depiction of disulfiram therapy in this way. "Can you explain *khimzashchita*?" I asked. "How should I explain it to you? As if you were a patient?" asked Anton Denisovich and then began without waiting for an answer:

> We inject the medication disulfiram. It comes in different forms: intravenous, capsule form, or subdermal implantation. All of these forms are long-acting. If the medication is taken intravenously or orally, it dissolves in the stomach and ends up in the bloodstream and then enters the body's tissues, combines with proteins in the liver . . . and for a certain period of time this medicine remains in the bloodstream. This medication cannot be taken with alcohol, as it blocks the enzymes that break down alcohol. If a patient on this medication drinks and alcohol enters his bloodstream, the possible side effects are dangerous to his health or life-threatening. It can be anything from a flushing or reddening of the face to serious or crippling consequences or even death. . . . This is told to the patient and

he signs a paper explaining that he understands the procedure. And then
the procedure takes place.

I was confused. "Then why is it 'placebo therapy'?" There was an awkward moment when Anton Denisovich hesitated, perhaps realizing that
he was about to reveal a minor professional secret. "Well," he resumed,
"because it is. . . . Because as you understand all patients cannot take
these substances, in part because some of them won't wait out the entire
period, and this would just be dangerous for them. So it's better to give
him a placebo and give him the gift of several months of sober life, than
to inject the real medication." He added that he treated some patients for
as long as three years with this method, giving them yearly doses.[12]

This moment of doubt—when physicians assessed whether I already
knew about placebo therapy, or what I knew—was reprised in many of
my interviews. There were awkward pauses and pained glances; one
narcologist insisted that the difference between using chemically active
disulfiram and a neutral substance was merely a "professional nuance."
Yet despite their hesitations, the narcologists did reveal to me their use of
placebos, and their consequent deception of patients. Of course they also
justified their use of placebos, arguing—not without reason—that certain
(noncompliant) patients could be harmed or killed by active disulfiram.
I also learned that most medical reviews of disulfiram therapy empha-
sized that when effective, it changed patients' behavior not by neuro-
chemical means but through a psychological mechanism: "the threat or
experience of an unpleasant reaction" (Brewer, Meyers, and Johnsen
2000: 329). Though certainly deceptive by North American standards of
patient autonomy, giving patients such placebos was a way of harness-
ing the treatment's potential effectiveness while minimizing the risk of
harm from the drug.

And yet, as I later listened to patients' accounts of the therapy, I felt
uneasy about my knowledge. Their ideas about the potency of disulfiram covered a wide range. This is how Gleb, a middle-aged working-
class man, described the risks of khimzashchita: "Before you take it you
sign a paper saying that if you drink, the doctors are not responsible for
what happens to you. . . . It's fine if it kills you: better that than it para-

lyzing you or something. *We don't know with these drugs. . . .* So each person needs to use his brain" (emphasis added). Yet for every account by a patient that seemed to reinforce the idea that *khimzashchita* was chemically potent, there was another that attested to its *ineffectiveness.* Some patients recounted their own experiences surviving a drinking bout during their course of treatment as evidence for the chemical's lack of potency. Others swapped techniques for counteracting disulfiram's effects. Dmitri, a 12-step counselor, pointed to scars under his shoulder blades where the capsules had been implanted, and explained that during his hospitalizations other patients would tell him: "'Forget it, just drink a little lemon juice.' There were all of these means to counteract it that they'd give out right away, even while you were still in the ward, getting ready for the operation."

While patients heard and circulated conflicting accounts about the chemical potency of *khimzashchita,* narcologists in the hospital worked to bolster its representation as a pharmacological treatment. When I asked Anton Denisovich whether he sometimes administered the actual chemical disulfiram, he responded, "You understand that we can't give every single person the placebo, because we'll discredit the method that way." Not only did his rejoinder indicate a widespread anxiety among narcologists that placebo therapy could easily lose its effectiveness by "becoming discredited," but his statement was itself a speech act aimed at maintaining the legitimacy of the therapy. Whether "the real medication" was ever used or not, it was important to tell this ethnographer that it was used at least sometimes, lest I depict the entire therapy as a sham, as others had done.

INSTITUTIONS: THE HOUSE

To get to the House of Recovery, a center in the St. Petersburg area providing free-of-charge rehabilitation for alcoholism, you have to travel half an hour by suburban train to a village on the city's outskirts. I first visited on a Sunday in January, and a crowd of downhill skiers disembarked at the station; a slope had recently been opened nearby, attracting more visitors to the once sleepy station. From there the House is another forty-five minutes by foot (or longer in ankle-deep snow), past farm fields, traditionally styled Russian village houses, newer dachas, and several half-built mini-mansions. While the House's geographic location on the city's margins mirrors its position in the field of addiction medicine—compared with the Addiction Hospital's centrality—the material condition of its building reflects its relative youth and modest prosperity: an unremarkable red-brick structure, newly constructed and well-kept.

I had heard about the House of Recovery during an early visit to St. Petersburg, but it was in the United States that a colleague put me in touch with Ilya Vladimirovich, a Russian American psychiatrist who has played a key role in the House's foundation and operation. Prior to his emigration to the United States, Ilya Vladimirovich had worked for nearly a decade at the Bekhterev Psychoneurological Institute, one of the most respected centers for psychiatric research in the Soviet Union. In the early 1990s, he had been hired to manage the Russia-focused philanthropic efforts of a former tobacco executive and supporter of Alcoholics Anonymous (AA).[13] Early efforts had focused on bringing physicians and psychiatrists, clergymen and members of the cultural intelligentsia to the United States to tour rehabilitation centers (and in many cases to undergo treatment), with the aim of bolstering the stature and legitimacy of 12-step methods in Russia. By the mid-1990s, Ilya Vladimirovich and his American employer had developed a new strategy. Drawing on the Minnesota Model, a widely used 12-step-based protocol for inpatient substance abuse rehabilitation, they founded the House of Recovery (Spicer 1993).

When I expressed interest in conducting research at the House of Recovery and made it clear that I was willing to make myself useful, Ilya Vladimirovich's response was enthusiastic. Since the money funding both the House and its clinical technologies flowed from the United States, there was a great deal of translation to be done in the management of the center, and I was soon working on English and Russian texts for reports, letters, brochures, and Web postings. At the same time I began regularly taking part in daily activities at the House. Unlike at the Addiction Hospital, there were no bureaucratic hurdles, no forms to fill out, no research contracts, no review of my project. In exchange for my work translating texts, the doors of the House were open: I was allowed to interview patients, join them for their lectures and conversations, and sit in on meetings with the counseling staff. The only restriction was that I was not allowed to sit in on group therapy or closed 12-step group meetings.[14] In fact, here the limits to productive encounters were shaped not so much by bureaucratic exigencies as by my self-identification. While at the Addiction Hospital I had no choice but to temper my obvious association with the staff, at the House of Recovery I found that I was always a potential fellow in recovery or an addict in denial.

The practices of AA and other 12-step programs require specific kinds of self-identification from participants. One longtime substance abuse counselor in St. Petersburg told me that for him, self-identification as an addict was more than a prerequisite to rehabilitation: it was central to the entire process of the 12 steps. Not only does AA function as a technology of self-transformation, in which participants gradually learn to narrate their life histories in a way that enables them to self-identify as alcoholics or addicts, but it also encourages another sort of identification: that of individual members *with* one another through their common experiences (Rudy 1986: 18–42; Denzin 1987: 74; Cain 1991). These two types of identification are linked: telling one's story at an AA meeting is at once a means for the speaker to narrate his or her experience and receive support and also an opportunity for listeners—particularly new members—to reflect on their own common experiences.[15]

Like the American rehab centers on which it was modeled, the House of Recovery offered a program run primarily by recovering alcoholics and addicts. Some of the trained psychologists identified not as alcoholic but as codependent (*sozavisimost'*), a category that has entered Russia with the arrival of 12-step therapy. Originally a term from the 12-step movement that designated as an illness in its own right behavior by family members (typically wives) that supported or, in the language of the program, "enabled" others' alcoholism, codependency has entered the discourse of North American popular psychology as—in its more extreme forms—a pathologization of almost any social relationships that abrogate individual autonomy or rights (Haaken 1993; Borovoy 2001:

98). At the House codependency was a key category, ratifying the inclusion of a number of non-alcoholics into the therapeutic community. For instance, several members of the support staff, who at first had no particular affinity for the program, had gradually learned the language and culture of the 12 steps and had begun to think of themselves as codependent in the broad sense of the term (they did not have family members who abused alcohol). One had gone on to receive training as a substance abuse counselor. The category of codependency thus allowed members of the House community to constitute themselves as parts of a household or family unit linked by experiences of dependence and recovery.

Because mutual-help groups such as AA are—for the most part—restricted to people suffering from addiction (or at least those who believe that they "have a problem with alcohol"; Wilcox 1998: 48) and because their definition of those individuals is based largely on self-identification and self-ascription, they present a particular challenge for ethnographic research. Whereas several social positions are available for ethnographers to occupy in most clinical institutions, the legitimate options in groups such as AA are at once more limited and more flexible.[16] Moreover, the structure of AA meetings makes it very difficult for a visitor not to declare his or her relationship to the program, and thus almost impossible not to get "caught up in it," as Jeanne Favret-Saada writes of her fieldwork on witchcraft in rural France (1990: 191). Indeed, on my very first visit to the House I attended an open AA meeting, during which a visiting speaker presented his story of decline and recovery to the group. As we each introduced ourselves to the group, using the familiar formula—"Hello, I'm X and I'm an alcoholic"—I found I was the only person in the room to simply say, "Hello, I'm Eugene." Telling myself that a disingenuous identification would be patronizing to the House's patients and staff, I continued to introduce myself this way for a few months.

However, several members of the House community persistently refused to accept my disavowal of alcoholism. Eduard was particularly insistent. A burly man with a wide and friendly face, Eduard had spent a decade of his life drinking heavily and barely holding down a series of short-term jobs. When he had finally been persuaded by relatives to go through treatment at the House of Recovery, Eduard was so taken with the program that he eventually became a substance abuse counselor. He presented himself as a simple guy and enjoyed gently poking fun at the House's supporters among "intellectuals and bohemians." On several occasions when we rode the train together, Eduard asked me why I had decided to study alcoholism. I explained as best I could, but found myself relying on what sounded like tired clichés (alcoholism represented such a profound public health crisis in Russia, etc.), especially when compared to his firsthand experiences.

As I spoke, I realized that I had never been asked this question at the Addiction Hospital. To be sure, the physicians there took for granted the importance of alcoholism as a "problem" in contemporary Russia, as did Eduard. What was strikingly different in these two fieldsites was how my interlocutors thought about the connections between personal experience and research interests. At the hospital, the physicians treated me as a kind of colleague, an emissary of "international science." If researchers agreed that alcoholism was an important topic for study, there was no further reason to question my choice; whatever other motivations I might have had, they were extraneous and irrelevant to many of the narcologists. Eduard, in contrast, was asking (indirectly at first) whether my (conscious or unconscious) motivation for choosing to research alcoholism treatment was my own (presumably unacknowledged) addiction. I thought I recognized Eduard's intention because I had already been asked this question, in the same way—not in Russia but in the United States—before my fieldwork began.

When I had told fellow anthropologists about my project, many initially asked whether I had experienced alcoholism in my family. At the time, I had assumed that the impetus for these questions was specific to anthropology (and its neighboring disciplines). For anyone socialized into the assumptions of contemporary academic anthropology, the notion that our research interests are shaped by biographical particularities has become something of a platitude. I was already, like many colleagues of my generation, carrying out my first project in a place where I had familial ties, so it was perhaps easy to extrapolate a similar personal connection to my thematic focus. In the field, as I attempted to answer

Eduard's questions, my colleagues' questions took on a slightly different meaning. It was not only the anthropological creed of reflexivity that made a link between one's life's work and one's personal experiences seem self-evident: the same presupposition was woven through the amalgam of self-help techniques and pop psychology that makes up much of the American therapeutic culture (Rieff 1987). More specifically, this idea testified to the influence that the 12-step movement has had on North American assumptions, as illustrated by the familiar figure of the recovering addict turned substance abuse counselor. However, Eduard's questions were forcing me to encounter this idea in unfamiliar territory.

I was not mistaken about Eduard's intentions. After I collected his life story—over the course of several afternoons in his apartment—he confronted me directly: "Tell me, Eugene. Are you sure you don't have a problem?" There were many addictions, he explained; the dependence to which I was failing to own up wasn't necessarily on alcohol. I told him that no, everything was fine, he needn't be concerned; but I was irritated at his insistence. Over the following weeks, I increasingly felt that my behavior was being observed by people at the House and I found myself (in a reaction similar to the countertransference described by Leo Coleman in chapter 5 of this volume) disavowing an addict identification more deliberately and vehemently than I had done before. At a dinner for the House of Recovery's American donors, I joined one other person at the table in ordering a glass of wine.

Late in the spring I accompanied Eduard and several other counselors to a celebration for a nearby 12-step group. At the registration for the event, everyone was asked their "status"—the appropriate response being one's illness identity (alcoholic, drug addict) and one's period of sobriety (e.g., sober for two years). As I pondered an appropriate answer, Eduard stepped in to explain, "He's codependent." I had never thought of introducing myself this way, but by this point considering myself codependent was beginning to have a certain logic. Could not my field-work relationships with Eduard and others at the House of Recovery be understood in this way? I was, after all, getting pulled into relationships with my informants in ways I had not expected and I was reacting to their demands in ways that I judged (from the standpoint of an imagined ideal ethnographer) to be at best withdrawn and at worst dismissive. More importantly, the notion of identifying me as codependent meant something to Eduard and other members of the House community: it placed me in a legitimate and understandable category and relationship to them. (Somewhat more troubling was the implication that my interest in the House of Recovery, and my research itself, was pathological—that I was addicted to studying addicts and needed help.) Nevertheless, at the next open meeting I attended, I introduced myself as codependent.

As I later learned, my ability to inhabit this category had its own very palpable limits. The major event of the summer was the House's anniversary celebration—an event complete with guest speakers and performances by a folk music band and a clown-mime troupe. The anniversary drew hundreds of the House's alumni from all over Russia and several other post-Soviet states. It was also attended by the program's American sponsor, and I was given the job of translating conversations for him. Toward the end of the day my wife, Iris, who does not speak Russian, gestured for me to come near. She was being addressed by a small woman who was speaking very quickly in a mix of Russian and English. I should add that being American had a very particular meaning at the House of Recovery, where the United States was seen by many as the "motherland [*rodina*] of AA," as one counselor put it.

The woman was explaining that her father had died recently and that she had subsequently learned that most of the men in her family had been alcoholics. She had become convinced, she explained, that the same would be true of any man she married; she felt she was somehow cursed. As I translated I slowly understood what was happening: the woman, assuming that my wife considered herself codependent, was asking for advice. What should she do? she asked. What would be the right thing to do in her situation? We made several very unhelpful attempts at advising her, sheepishly suggesting that she speak to some of the others present at the celebration. The woman persisted, asking my wife again: What did she think of this problem?

It was then that I blurted out that neither of us were alcoholics—that I was a researcher working with the center, and my wife had simply accompanied me for my day of fieldwork. As I spoke, the woman slowly backed away, in mortified shock, saying, "But I thought everyone here was an alcoholic." We mumbled our embarrassed apologies, staring at our feet.

ANONYMITIES: PRIVACY COMMODIFIED

The space of safety and mutual understanding, which my wife and I had inadvertently punctured for this woman, was underpinned by two principles key to both AA and the House of Recovery. The first, as I have already discussed, was the self-identification of members as alcoholics or codependents and their identification with one another through common experiences. The second principle was that of anonymity: specifically, AA's practices of partial internal anonymity and full external anonymity. During the first years of the AA movement (in the 1930s and '40s), external anonymity was primarily a means of attracting members to the program by protecting their identities; as the movement grew it played an additional role in guiding members' dealings with people outside of the program (Mäkelä et al. 1995: 48–50). In addition to helping maintain an egalitarian ethos within the organization and reducing possibilities for self-promotion, anonymity has also been important as a way of symbolically subordinating individuals to the group—or, in the language of the 12th Tradition, "plac[ing] principles before personalities" (Alcoholics Anonymous 1953: 184; see also Bateson 1971; Fainzang 1994: 342). Moreover, anonymity has a particular relationship to identification in the program, in that it is a condition of possibility for the confessional accounts that are central to the ritual of the AA meeting.[17]

At the House of Recovery, the regime of anonymity mediated a particular set of power relations between patients and the counseling staff, which was somewhat different from the dynamic taking place in freestanding AA groups in the city. Whereas patients knew one another only by their first names and initials (unless they chose to disclose more), counselors knew patients' last names and would often mention them in staff meetings. However, although nearly all of the counselors were themselves recovering alcoholics—who would identify themselves only by the first name when they attended a regular AA meeting in St. Petersburg—at the House they were known to patients by their first names and patronymics (e.g., Pavel Ivanovich). This style of address signifies formality and respect; when used by only one participant in a conversation, it is typically a sign of his or her deference in an asymmetrical power relationship (such as servant to master, student to teacher, or child to parent). These relationships were made material in the name badges that everyone—patients and staff alike—wore at the House. Thus while these practices provided for a level of anonymity that some patients—particularly employed professionals, policemen, and members of the federal security services—saw as important, they also contributed to many patients' conviction that they were being infantalized by counselors.

Anonymity of a somewhat different variety had a place at the Addiction Hospital, in the form of what was called "anonymous treatment." This practice had its basis in the narcological register, a Soviet-era institution that was essentially a list, kept by each district-level clinic and hospital, of patients diagnosed with a particular addiction. The register was a key element linking Soviet addiction treatment both to a residentially based system of urban governance and to the state's systems for medical surveillance and control.[18] Patients on the register were prohibited from receiving a gun permit or a driver's license, from working in a number of occupations, and from traveling abroad. Once placed on the register, a name remained there for three years. In short, the register was meant to keep addicts away from potentially dangerous situations; at the same time, the threat of appearing on it was intended to deter potential alcoholics (Tkachevskii 1974; Gilinskii and Zobnev 1998).

During the post-Soviet period, state and municipal clinics treating addiction began to offer patients the possibility of treatment without being placed on the register, for a price (Galkin 1996). This became the legally sanctioned practice of every clinic in the municipal network in St. Petersburg. Part of its justification was that similar "anonymous" services were already available in commercial clinics. Since the laws barring those on the register from owning guns or receiving driver's licenses remained unchanged, the result was the creation of a two-tier system, with very different degrees of state surveillance. Treatment was nominally free of charge for those who would accept having their names on the register, while others, who paid, could escape the penalties and restrictions. From the point of view of some physicians and public health reformers, this system served to further penalize the socially marginalized and poor. Others pointed out that the practices of "anonymity" made it more difficult to hold physicians legally accountable for their actions.

Even those physicians who defended the practice did so in a guilty tone, insisting that "anonymous treatment" simply capitalized on a (now-unjustified) suspicion that some patients had of the state service. For instance, the administrator Grigorii Mikhailovich assured me that the confidentiality of patients' records and doctor-patient privilege was guaranteed by the sixty-first article of the 1993 General Law on Health Care of the Russian Federation (Tsyboulsky 2001: 259; see also Tichtchenko and Yudin 2000: 230). Nevertheless, he explained, "The fear that someone will tell someone or get the information—this still lives." Thus the Addiction Hospital provided the service of anonymous treatment, which was "easier for [the patients], and easier for us, because we get extra money," he added laughing. Yet in the same breath Grigorii Mikhailovich recounted recent attempts by police to access the register, undercutting his argument that confidentiality is secured by a new post-Soviet legal regime: "Just before the three hundredth anniversary [of St. Petersburg], I was sending away policemen. . . . One of them wrote to me saying, 'Give us the lists of the people who have been treated here.' And I replied . . . 'You won't get any lists.'"

Deliberately or not, Grigorii Mikhailovich's account laid bare the institutional incentives for narcologists to stoke fears of such unscrupulous policemen, thereby bolstering the "need" for anonymous treatment. Grigorii Mikhailovich acknowledged that the current demand for anonymous treatment grew partly out of the punitive character of the Soviet system; in his view, "This is what the anonymous treatment is connected to: the fact that there was this punitive system." Yet it was in the interest of physicians like Grigorii Mikhailovich to perpetuate the notion that the confidentiality of patients' records was still not secure. In other words, in order for narcologists to create a demand for anonymous service, patients had to be continually reminded that their information might fall into the wrong hands and led to fear that legal protections of confidentiality and doctor-patient privilege were weak.[19] Given the lack of institutional protections for privacy during the Soviet period and the continued vulnerability of personal information to theft or sale during post-Soviet years, it was not difficult to convince patients of the need for anonymous service.[20]

Though the prices that the narcologists I spoke to named for this service were relatively modest, there was clearly significant money to be made. In fact, revenue from the anonymous treatment of drug addicts had played a part in inciting the conflict that resulted in the murder of the hospital administrator.[21]

·   ·   ·   ·   ·

I found the murder difficult to write about. Despite my efforts to squeeze it into footnotes, it dominated my narratives of fieldwork, threatening to overwhelm everything else. In the simplest terms, it was, like the common practices involving the deception of patients and anonymous treatment, an index of unsteady ethical regimes, uneven state regulation, and a highly commercialized medical sphere. However, it also raised the question of what it had meant to conduct fieldwork in such an institutional site. As I wrote my accounts of fieldwork, this tragedy made painfully clear the necessity of taking my own measures to ensure the anonymity of my informants.

But what about my research topic? Had a year of fieldwork been necessary to learn something about addiction and its treatment in Russia? I have suggested that as institutional spaces that I experienced through my encounters with physicians, patients, counselors, and administrators, the Municipal Addiction Hospital and the House of Recovery were instantiations of strikingly different ideas about illness and addiction. Not only were these ideas inscribed into clinical techniques and material spaces, they were, at least to some degree, implicit in the ways I and my motivations were identified by my interlocutors and in the ways these identifications circumscribed the possibilities for encounters in the field.

For instance, while his persistent questions bothered me, Eduard had every reason to consider the possibility of my being an addict in denial.

The logic of his assumption became particularly clear as I shuttled between the two fieldsites. To put it in overly simplified terms, at the Addiction Hospital, the identification of alcoholism was an act of diagnosis carried out by physicians. At the House of Recovery, it was an act of self-identification carried out by participants. For physicians at the hospital, alcoholism was a disease epistemologically accessible through particular symptoms—some self-reported, some visible to the physician. One narcologist at the hospital explained to me that she could typically see the ravages of long-term alcohol use on the bodies of patients. "You, for instance," she added. "It is clear that you are not an alcoholic." This reliance on visual cues and physical markers of illness has a basis in a neurophysiological style of reasoning long dominant in Russian psychiatry, and in an overwhelmingly biological understanding of alcoholism. It was also a simple reading of my middle-class American habitus: it was clear that I wasn't an alcoholic, because I didn't look like one. At the House, the experience of fellow suffering was valued over professional expertise; anyone could and might be an addict.[22] The notion of codependence expanded this field of possible identifications even further, although it was a category with certain limits and one that I found myself unable to successfully inhabit, despite my own attempts and the efforts of my acquaintances.

Learning something about these starkly contrasting conceptions of alcoholism was not simply a matter of interpreting texts and statements made by my interlocutors, although these certainly were necessary sources. Equally important were what Jeanne Favret-Saada has called "situations of involuntary and unintentional communication," which "although they are commonplace and recurrent [during fieldwork], are never taken into consideration for what they are: the 'information' they have brought to the ethnographer appears in the text, but without any reference to the affective intensity which went with it in reality" (1991: 195). That such situations are just as "commonplace and recurrent" in clinics, laboratories, and offices, where fieldwork is increasingly carried out, as they are elsewhere is a point that would be too self-evident to belabor, were it not for the perception that these spaces, so redolent of modernity and ostensibly so homogeneous, threaten the productive ambiguity and uncertainty central to the production of ethnographic knowledge. Part of the methodological challenge of working in such settings is not only maintaining a sense of unfamiliarity but also remaining open to learning something from the (sometimes profound) failures of identification.

NOTES

This chapter has benefited greatly from the readings and suggestions of John Borneman, Leo Coleman, Daniel Alexandrov, Kelly McKinney, Alessandra Miklavcic, Roger Schoenman, Iris Bernblum, and three anonymous reviewers. Earlier versions of some of the chapter's contents were also shaped by the insights of Joao Biehl, Carol Greenhouse, and Stephen Kotkin. The fieldwork described in this chapter was generously funded by a Fulbright-Hays Doctoral Dissertation Research Abroad Fellowship.

1. On August 26, 2004, the deputy director of the Municipal Addiction Hospital, Larisa Artyukhovskaia, was killed by a bomb that had been left at the doorway to her apartment. The discovery of a similar remote-controlled device near Sergei Tikhomirov's apartment led the procurator's office to initiate a broad investigation into the conflicts over control over the narcology business in the city; Tikhomirov's arrest followed in early October. Reports differed on whether Artyukhovskaia, who was in charge of the hospital's finances, had refused to participate in Tikhomirov's business or had simply refused to share in the profits she herself stole from the hospital (see Andreev 2004; Bezrukova 2006). Notably, this was not an isolated incident of deadly violence in the St. Petersburg narcological sphere. Tikhomirov's predecessor as head narcologist for the Northwest Federal District had resigned after being attacked on the street and severely beaten several times, and a candidate for a deputy post had been attacked by an acid-wielding assailant before she could assume her position (Tumakova 2004). In October 2006, some two years after Tikhomirov's arrest, St. Petersburg's chief children's narcologist, Vyacheslav Revzin, died after being beaten by a gang of unknown assailants. Several days later, Ivan Shvets, the director of a outpatient municipal narcological dispensary, was found dead in an apparent suicide (Stolyarova 2006).

2. In a set of observations that can be generalized to other clinical settings, Van der Geest and Finkler (2004: 1995) note the widespread

perception of hospitals as spaces where the practices of contemporary biomedicine are conducted and reproduced in a relatively uniform manner, regardless of local context. However, as work conducted on the anthropology of biomedicine over the past twenty-five years has shown, this perception of uniformity and relative homogeneity is better understood as the ideology of biomedicine.

3. *OED Online*, s.v. "identification," http://dictionary.oed.com/cgi/entry/50111211 (accessed February 18, 2008).

4. All translations from the Russian (unless otherwise indicated) are mine. Cyrillic letters have been Romanized using the Library of Congress transliteration table, with the exception of proper nouns with commonly accepted English spellings (e.g., Vasilievsky Island).

5. On the Soviet social hygiene movement, see Susan Solomon (1989). On the development of the narcological system, see Babayan and Gonopolsky (1985); Gilinskii and Zobnev (1998: 117–23); see also the accounts in Connor (1972); Peter Solomon (1978: 83–88).

6. Most of the names used in this essay are pseudonyms. In order to simply demarcate the roles of different informants, I use first names (such as Vyacheslav or Pavel) to indicate patients and 12-step counselors and first names along with patronymics (Anton Denisovich, Alexander Sergeevich) to mark most physicians. Because the first name/patronymic combination is a relatively formal type of address, typically used to mark respect or social distance in Russian, its use runs the risk of essentializing the distinction between physicians and patients; but this naming system also gives a sense of the interpersonal hierarchy at play in most St. Petersburg clinics. I have used the actual names of those few figures who have already been written about in the media; they are identified by their first and last names (e.g., Sergei Tikhomirov).

7. Interestingly, early 1990s efforts at problematizing the category of "native anthropologist" paid little attention to the role of language—specifically, fluency and accent—as an important factor shaping ethnographers' positionality in fieldwork encounters (Abu-Lughod 1991; Narayan 1993).

8. In describing his experiences conducting research in a Bangladeshi hospital, Zaman (2008: 147) points to the trade-offs of being a physician-anthropologist: the relative ease of gaining the trust of fellow doctors and some patients versus the occasional difficulty of asking "naive" questions. Unlike Didier Fassin, Paul Farmer, Arthur Kleinman, Laurence Kirmayer, and other physician-anthropologists who have written about their clinical work, Zaman explains that he was not

a practicing physician in the hospital where he carried out his field-work, and thus presented a somewhat ambiguous figure to patients.

9. Interestingly, other patients *did* question the veracity of the pseudo-patients' diagnoses, some even suspecting them to be journalists or researchers (Rosenhan 1973: 252). For a critique of the experiment in "pseudopatient diagnosis," see Spitzer (1975); see Slater (2004) and Spitzer, Lilienfeld, and Miller (2005) for a recent resurrection of this debate. Thanks to Allan Young for bringing my attention to these studies.

10. Of course, such concerns are hardly exclusive to ethnographers work-ing in post-socialist settings. See Lederman (2006) and the other arti-cles that appeared in the special issue of *American Ethnologist* devoted to institutional review boards and ethnography.

11. Given physicians' generally high level of authority in the hospital, in relation to patients, this selection of interviewees led me to question patients' capacity to give consent under such conditions. See Vieda Skultans's discussion of a similar quandary during her fieldwork with psychiatrists and their patients in Latvia (2005: 496).

12. Disulfiram is used throughout the world as an adjunct therapy for alcoholism. As Anton Denisovich noted, it prevents the body from fully processing alcohol: by blocking the action of a key enzyme in the metabolic pathway of ethanol, the drug causes a buildup of the toxic by-product acetaldehyde, with extremely unpleasant consequences for patients. Rather than experience the pleasure and elation of alcohol intoxication, people with active disulfiram in their bodies become flushed and nauseated upon drinking. Disulfiram began to be used by Soviet physicians soon after its introduction, and by the 1980s it was one of the most popular therapies among patients and their relatives. The replacement of disulfiram with neutral substances also became widespread during this time (see Fleming et al. 1994; Mann 2004).

13. Because the organizational autonomy of individual groups is one of the central principles of AA, there is no single narrative of the program's foundation in the former Soviet Union. Nevertheless, though groups formed in different cities under somewhat different circumstances, cer-tain broad conditions allowed for the introduction and development of AA. The earliest groups, which formed during the mid-perestroika period, were facilitated not only by the increasing tolerance shown by the state toward nongovernmental organizations but by the Soviet anti-alcohol campaign that was then under way (White 1996). For instance, a series of joint Soviet-U.S. conferences on alcoholism that began in 1987 brought experts on addiction from the United States to the Soviet Union. Among them were officials representing the General Service Office of

AA in New York and the Reverend J. W. Canty, an Episcopal priest who worked to promote AA in the Soviet Union. These meetings led to the establishment of early groups such as the "New Beginners" in Moscow in 1987 and "Almaz" in Leningrad soon after (Burke 1990). Starting in the late 1980s and continuing through the 1990s, a steady stream of U.S.-based AA missionaries visited the Soviet Union and, later, Russia.

No surveys of AA in Russia have been conducted (and the informal nature of the organizations make this a difficult proposition), but by the time of my research there were at least 10 AA groups in St. Petersburg with more than 150 members, at least 30 groups in Moscow, and, according to some estimates, as many as 300 groups throughout the Russian Federation (Critchlow 2000a, 2000b). Large cities such as Nizhni Novgorod and Kazan had multiple groups, and AA members were active as well in small cities in European Russia such as Kostroma and Ivanovo. Other 12-step-based mutual-help groups, such as Narcotics Anonymous, Gamblers Anonymous, and groups for codependent family members such as Al-Anon, were also becoming increasingly popular in larger cities.

14.   Although anyone is allowed to attend AA meetings designated "open," "closed" meetings are restricted to those who are already members or believe they "have a problem with alcohol" (Wilcox 1998: 48).

15.   There are of course many varying interpretations of the processes central to healing and self-transformation in AA and other 12-step programs. For the purposes of this argument, it is worth noting that many participants—unlike the counselor mentioned above—may not view identification as an important element in the program, focusing instead on the values of humility or surrender or the modest techniques for living, such as "one day at a time" (Valverde 1998: 135–37; Wilcox 1998: 83–107). Indeed, Mariana Valverde argues that AA includes two distinct forms of self-governance, which are continually in tension with one another: a "*theory* of alcoholism as a disease [, which] fits the familiar Foucaultian pattern of identity-based governance," and a set of pragmatic techniques for maintaining sobriety, which "constitute a cobbled-together, low-theory, unsystematic system for habit reform" (1998: 140). Others have interpreted the transformative aspects of AA in much less gradualistic terms as a "spiritual awakening" modeled on Protestant theology (Antze 1987: 173), or as a radical epistemological shift away from a pathological Cartesian dualism (Bateson 1971).

16.   Many researchers—myself included—have dealt with this issue by attending open meetings and conducting in-depth conversations or

interviews with group members outside of the group setting (Mäkelä et al. 1996; Valverde 1998). David Rudy represented himself to the members of AA groups he attended for sixteen months not as an alcoholic but as a "sociologist interested in finding out about AA," and gradually progressed from being viewed as "a tolerated intruder, an outsider, to a near-member" (1986: 2, 3). Members of the AA group that Stanley Brandes studied in Mexico City allowed him to participate in meetings although he did not identify as an alcoholic, categorizing him as an "Admirer of Alcoholics Anonymous" (AAA) (2002: xv). On the other hand, Danny Wilcox was drawn to conduct an ethnography of AA only after a period of having experienced it as a recovering alcoholic (1998: 20–29). See also O'Halloran (2003).

17. For an interesting contrasting case, see Sylvie Fainzang's account (1994) of the French sobriety movement Vie Libre, which rejects anonymity, seeing it as a sign of a moral—rather than a medical—understanding of alcoholism. Arguing that anonymity often signifies the liminal stage in rituals of identity, Fainzang notes that while Vie Libre associates membership into the group with the assumption of a new identity as an *exalcoholic*, AA members stay at this liminal phase, remaining anonymous just as they remain alcoholics, even when in recovery (1994: 344).

18. Like other medical services, treatments for addiction were provided by local dispensaries as determined by an individual's *propiska*, a document that combined the functions of a residence permit with those of an internal passport. The *propiska* system—originally a Tsarist technology of internal passports, revived in 1933—was, and continues to be, a means by which the state attempted to control urban in-migration (Popov 1995; Höjdestrand 2004). (Of course, this system gave rise to a brisk market in permits, as well as to fictitious marriages arranged to obtain them, well before the post-Soviet period.) The link between the register and this residency system, by means of the local dispensaries, provided a grid through which state actors attempted to manage the health of populations.

19. The lack of protection of privacy was linked to a number of concrete factors, including the conduct of medical consultations. Vieda Skultans writes that in Soviet Latvia, psychiatric consultations "lacked the privacy with which they are associated in the West. Access to consulting rooms is seldom restricted to a doctor and her patient. Besides the prescribing nurse who shares the consulting room, other staff and, indeed, patients frequently interrupt an ongoing consultation. . . . Patients were, until recently, in charge of their own notes. In such contexts, problems are publicly shared" (2005: 498).

20. Many thanks to Daniel Alexandrov for suggesting this interpretation of anonymous treatment and the register.

21. At the time of the murder, Tikhomirov concurrently occupied two posts: in addition to being the Addiction Hospital's director, he had, since mid-2003, been head narcologist for the Northwest Federal District (*okrug*). According to news reports of the police investigation, Tikhomirov had developed a particularly lucrative business on the basis of his position as the Northwest District's head narcologist. One of his duties in this position was the licensing of commercial narcology clinics (for the treatment of alcoholism), a service for which he apparently charged approximately $2,000 (Andreev 2004).

22. The tensions between these ideas about alcoholism were played out in disputes over the appropriateness of AA for Russia. With its requirement that physicians participate on par with other members, if at all, AA struck some narcologists as a threat to their professional status, and some leading narcologists argued against it precisely in these terms. For instance, a prominent narcologist dismissed AA in a newspaper interview as "anonymous brotherhoods, where there are no doctors, as 'only a drug addict will help another drug addict.'" "In that case," he asked, in an aside that infuriated many local AA members, should we say that only "a schizophrenia patient will help another schizophrenia patient?" (Dyleva 2004: 11).

REFERENCES

Abu-Lughod, Lila. 1991. "Writing against Culture." In *Recapturing Anthropology: Working in the Present,* ed. Richard G. Fox. Santa Fe, NM: School of American Research Press; dist. by University of Washington Press.

Alcoholics Anonymous. 1953. *Twelve Steps and Twelve Traditions.* New York: Alcoholics Anonymous World Services.

Andreev, Sergei. 2004. "Glavnyi narkolog ubival kolleg?" [Did the head narcologist kill his colleagues?]. *Smena,* October 7; http://smena.ru/criminal/332/ (accessed on April 4, 2006).

Antze, Paul. 1987. "Symbolic Action in Alcoholics Anonymous." In *Constructive Drinking: Perspectives on Drink from Anthropology,* ed. Mary Douglas. Cambridge: Cambridge University Press; Paris: Editions de la Maison des sciences de l'homme.

Babayan, Eduard A., and M. H. Gonopolsky. 1985. *Textbook on Alcoholism and Drug Abuse in the Soviet Union.* Trans. V. Bobrov. New York: International Universities Press.

Balabanova, Dina, Jane Falkingham, and Martin McKee. 2003. "Winners and Losers: Expansion of Insurance Coverage in Russia in the 1990s." *American Journal of Public Health* 93(12): 2124–30.

Bateson, Gregory. 1971. "The Cybernetics of 'Self': A Theory of Alcoholism." *Psychiatry* 34: 1–18.

Beliaev, V. P., and L. N. Lezhepetsova. 1977. "Opyt organizatsii narkologicheskoi sluzhby v Leningrade" [The experience of organizing the narcological service in Leningrad]. In *Lechenie i reabilitatsiia bol'nykh alkogolizma* [Treatment and rehabilitation for alcoholism patients], ed. I. V. Bokii and R. A. Zachepitskogo. Leningrad: Bekhterev Institute.

Bezrukova, Lyudmilla. 2006. "Narcolog-Ubiitsa" [Narcologist killer]. *Trud* 48 (March 21); http://info.trud.ru/trud.php?Id=200603210480502 (accessed April 4, 2006).

Bloch, Sidney, and Paul Chodoff, eds. 1991. *Psychiatric Ethics.* 2nd ed. Oxford: Oxford University Press.

Borovoy, Amy. 2001. "Recovering from Codependence in Japan." *American Ethnologist* 28(1): 94–118.

Brandes, Stanley H. 2002. *Staying Sober in Mexico City.* Austin: University of Texas Press.

Brewer, Colin, Robert J. Meyers, and Jon Johnsen. 2000. "Does Disulfiram Help to Prevent Relapse in Alcohol Abuse?" *CNS Drugs* 14(5): 329–41.

Burke, Justin. 1990. "AA Marks Third Year in Soviet Union." *Christian Science Monitor,* November 20, p. 15.

Cain, Carole. 1991. "Personal Stories: Identity Acquisition and Self-Understanding in Alcoholics Anonymous." *Ethos* 19(2): 210–53.

Connor, Walter D. 1972. *Deviance in Soviet Society: Crime, Delinquency, and Alcoholism.* New York: Columbia University Press.

Critchlow, Patricia. 2000a. "First Steps: AA and Alcoholism in Russia." *Current History* 99: 345–49.

———. 2000b. "The Impact of Sociopolitical Change Since 1991 on Alcohol Treatment in Russia." Master's in Liberal Arts thesis, Harvard University.

Denzin, Norman K. 1987. *The Alcoholic Self.* Sage Publications.

Dyleva, Evgeniia. 2004. "Vodka s semenami konopli pressuet molodezhnuiu subkul'turu" [Vodka with cannabis seeds puts pressure on youth subculture]. *Peterburskii Chas Pik* 26(336) (July 23–29): 11.

Entin, G. M., A. G. Gofman, A. V. Grazhenskii, E. N. Krylov, A. Yu. Magalif, I. A. Nosatovskii, and I. V. Yashkina. 1997. "O sovremennom sostaianii narkologicheskoi pomoshchi v Rossii" [On the contemporary state of narcological help in Russia]. *Voprosy Narkologii* 1: 68–76.

Estroff, Sue E. 1981. *Making It Crazy: An Ethnography of Psychiatric Clients in an American Community.* Berkeley: University of California Press.

Fainzang, Sylvie. 1994. "When Alcoholics Are Not Anonymous." *Medical Anthropology Quarterly* 8: 336–45.

Favret-Saada, Jeanne. 1990. "About Participation." *Culture, Medicine and Psychiatry* 14(2): 189–99.

Field, Mark. 1991. "The Hybrid Profession: Soviet Medicine." In *Professions and the State: Expertise and Autonomy in the Soviet Union and Eastern Europe*, ed. Anthony Jones. Philadelphia: Temple University Press.

Fleming, Philip, A. Meyroyan, and I. Klimova. 1994. "Alcohol Treatment Services in Russia: A Worsening Crisis." *Alcohol and Alcoholism* 29(4): 357–62.

Galkin, V. A. 1996. "Sovremenye zadachi narkologicheskoi sluzhby" [Contemporary objectives of the narcological service]. *Voprosy Narkologii* 1: 71–75.

Gilinskii, Yakov, and Vladimir Zobnev. 1998. "The Drug Treatment System in Russia: Past and Present, Problems and Prospects." In *Drug Treatment Systems in an International Perspective: Drugs, Demons, and Delinquents*, ed. Harald Klingemann and Geoffrey Hunt. Thousand Oaks, CA: Sage.

Goffman, Erving. 1962. *Asylums: Essays on the Social Situation of Mental Patients and Other Inmates*. Chicago: Aldine.

Goldman, A. R., R. H. Bohr, and T. A. Steinberg. 1970. "On Posing as Mental Patients: Reminiscences and Recommendations." *Professional Psychology* 1: 427–34.

Haaken, Janice. 1993. "From Al-Anon to ACOA: Codependence and the Reconstruction of Caregiving." *Signs* 18(2): 321–45.

Höjdestrand, Tova. 2003. "The Soviet-Russian Production of Homelessness: *Propiska*, Housing, Privatization." *Anthrobase*; www.anthrobase.com/Txt/H/HoejdestrandT01.htm (accessed April 2, 2006).

Kozlov, Andrei, Alla Shaboltas, Olga Toussova, Sergei Verevochkin, Benoit Masse, Tom Perdue, Geetha Beauchamp, Wayne Sheldon, William Miller, Robert Heimer, Robert Ryder, and Irving Hoffman. 2006. "HIV Incidence and Factors Associated with HIV Acquisition among Injection Drug Users in St. Petersburg, Russia." *AIDS* 20(6): 901–6.

Lederman, Rena. 2006. "The Perils of Working at Home: IRB 'Mission Creep' as Context and Content for an Ethnography of Disciplinary Knowledges." *American Ethnologist* 33(4): 482–91.

Lincoln, W. Bruce. 2001. *Sunlight at Midnight: St. Petersburg and the Rise of Modern Russia*. New York: Basic Books.

Mäkelä, Klaus, et al. 1996. *Alcoholics Anonymous as a Mutual-Help Movement: A Study in Eight Societies*. Madison: University of Wisconsin Press.

Mann, Karl. 2004. "Pharmacotherapy of Alcohol Dependence: A Review of the Clinical Data." *CNS Drugs* 18(8): 485–504.

Narayan, Kirin. 1993. "How Native Is a 'Native' Anthropologist?" *American Anthropologist* 95(3): 671–86.

O'Halloran, Sean. 2003. "Participant Observation of Alcoholics Anonymous: Contrasting Roles of the Ethnographer and Ethnomethodologist." *Qualitative Report* 8: 81–99.

Popov, V. P. 1995. "Pasportnaia sistema v SSSR (1932–1976)." [The passport system in the USSR]. *Sotsiologicheskie Issledovania* 8: 3–14.

Rhodes, Lorna A. 1991. *Emptying Beds: The Work of an Emergency Psychiatric Unit.* Berkeley: University of California Press.

Rieff, Philip. 1987. *The Triumph of the Therapeutic: Uses of Faith after Freud.* New ed. Chicago: University of Chicago Press.

Rivkin-Fish, Michele R. 2005. *Women's Health in Post-Soviet Russia: The Politics of Intervention.* Bloomington: Indiana University Press.

Rosenhan, David L. 1973. "On Being Sane in Insane Places." *Science* 179: 250–58.

Rudy, David. 1986. *Becoming Alcoholic: Alcoholics Anonymous and the Reality of Alcoholism.* Carbondale: Southern Illinois University Press.

Segal, Boris M. 1990. *The Drunken Society: Alcohol Abuse and Alcoholism in the Soviet Union: A Comparative Study.* New York: Hippocrene Books.

Skultans, Vieda. 2005. "Varieties of Deception and Distrust: Moral Dilemmas in the Ethnography of Psychiatry." *Health* 9: 491.

Slater, Lauren. 2004. *Opening Skinner's Box: Great Psychological Experiments of the Twentieth Century.* New York: Norton.

Solomon, Peter. 1978. *Soviet Criminologists and Criminal Policy: Specialists in Policy-making.* London: Macmillan.

Solomon, Susan Gross. 1989. "David and Goliath in Soviet Public Health: The Rivalry of Social Hygienists and Psychiatrists for Authority over the *Bytovoi* Alcoholic." *Soviet Studies* 41(2): 254–75.

Spicer, Jerry. 1993. *The Minnesota Model: The Evolution of the Multidisciplinary Approach to Addiction Recovery.* Center City, MN: Hazelden Educational Materials.

Spitzer, Robert L. 1975. "On Pseudoscience in Science, Logic in Remission, and Psychiatric Diagnosis: A Critique of Rosenhan." *Journal of Abnormal Psychology* 84(5): 442–52.

Spitzer, Robert L., Scott O. Lilienfeld, and Michael B. Miller. 2005. "Rosenhan Revisited: The Scientific Credibility of Lauren Slater's Pseudopatient Diagnosis Study." *Journal of Nervous and Mental Disease* 193: 734–39.

Stolyarova, Galina. 2006. "Second Drugs Expert Dies within a Week." *St. Petersburg Times,* October 24; www.sptimes/ru/index.php?action_id=2&story_id=19248 (accessed June 25, 2008).

Tichtchenko, Pavel D., and Boris G. Yudin. 2000. "Toward a Bioethics in Post-Communist Russia." In *Cross-Cultural Perspectives in Medical Ethics*, ed. Robert M. Veatch. Sudbury, MA: Jones and Bartlett.

Tkachevskii, IU. 1974. *Pravovye mery bor'by s p'ianstvom* [Legal measures in the battle with drunkenness]. Moscow: Izd-vo Moskovskogo universiteta.

Tsyboulsky, Vadim B. 2001. "Patient's Rights in Russia." *European Journal of Health Law* 8(3): 257–63.

Twigg, Judyth L. 1998. "Balancing the State and the Market: Russia's Adoption of Obligatory Medical Insurance." *Europe-Asia Studies* 50(4): 583–602.

Valverde, Mariana. 1998. *Diseases of the Will: Alcohol and the Dilemmas of Freedom.* Cambridge: Cambridge University Press.

Van der Geest, Sjaak, and Kaja Finkler. 2004. "Hospital Ethnography: Introduction." *Social Science & Medicine* 59(10): 1995–2001.

Van der Geest, Sjaak, and Samuel Sarkodie. 1998. "The Fake Patient: A Research Experiment in a Ghanaian Hospital." *Social Science & Medicine* 47(9): 1373–81.

White, Stephen. 1996. *Russia Goes Dry: Alcohol, State and Society.* Cambridge: Cambridge University Press.

Wilcox, Danny M. 1998. *Alcoholic Thinking: Language, Culture, and Belief in Alcoholics Anonymous.* Westport, CT: Praeger/Greenwood.

Zaman, Shahaduz. 2008. "Native among the Natives: Physician Anthropologist Doing Hospital Ethnography at Home." *Journal of Contemporary Ethnography* 37: 135–54.

NINE

Fieldwork Experience, Collaboration, and Interlocution

THE "METAPHYSICS OF PRESENCE" IN
ENCOUNTERS WITH THE SYRIAN MUKHABARAT

John Borneman

PRESENCE, COLLABORATION, AND DIALECTICAL OBJECTIFICATION

This essay examines the relation of presence in fieldwork to interlocution. Within anthropology in the past several decades, two kinds of criticisms of the fieldwork encounter have had particular resonance: that fieldwork experience and presence do not generate any unique knowledge and that the power/dominance of the (Western) ethnographer ethically taints the knowledge derived from encounters. The questioning of the ethnographer's presence has frequently led to text-based reading being substituted for fieldwork experience, with a corresponding focus on textual representation; the questioning of the ethnographer's power has led to demands for collaboration and dialogue, which in turn often

237

emphasize righteous behavior over a more dialectical understanding of knowledge produced through the manifold conflictual forms of interaction and domination in fieldwork.

Important for the questioning of presence has been a critique of the "metaphysics of presence," most powerfully formulated by Jacques Derrida, as implying that the co-presence of speaker and listener has no distinct epistemological status separate from the nonsimultaneous relationship of the reader to writing. I explore the relevance of this critique to fieldwork and to the notion of "interlocution" in detail in the second part of this essay. Important for the notion of collaboration has been a move away from depicting the aim of fieldwork relations as "rapport" with "informants"—viewed as overdetermined by the power of the ethnographer—to relations in which the ethnographer is an advocate for the other, and knowledge is directed to critiques of the West that undermine the ethnographer's own claims to truth.

One aim of this essay is to complicate our notion of collaboration, usually construed as a kind of dialogue, a working together, to include a second referent: cooperating traitorously with the enemy.[1] The fact is that our interlocutors—literally, those we converse with in the field—frequently fear our betrayal, our working with and passing information on to the other side, as much or more than they look forward to working together with us. Our presence often provokes suspicion of espionage, a deeply unsettling and contaminating discovery—especially for anthropologists, such as myself, who have worked in authoritarian political systems. In both the former East Germany and contemporary Syria and Lebanon, where I have conducted extensive fieldwork, people suspected me of a triple collaboration: both with my own state (the United States) and with theirs, as well as with antisocial or dissident forms of sociality.

A second is to explore presence in the field, when the arousal of suspicion of collaboration in fieldwork encounters causes an "assumption of subjectivity." The assumption of subjectivity leads not to the revelation of passive interior states but to a mode of ethical engagement wherein we are arrested together with our interlocutors in a series of acts of perception and misperception. The upshot of this arrest, at its best an attempt at mutual intelligibility, is a productive doubt about the meaning of interlocution, an indeterminacy that is also an opening to knowledge. Such an opening may lead to an uneasy dialectical objectification that, while limited in scope and perhaps brief, nonetheless provides knowledge of political significance and creates the possibility of elaborating shared knowledge with the people we work with. There are many points of such arrests and consequent objectifications in the course of fieldwork experience. Here, I take up this arrest in interlocution through encounters with the Syrian Mukhabarat (secret service) and the circulation of rumors about me among Syrians.[2]

SUSPICIONS OF SPYING BY ANTHROPOLOGISTS

My own pursuit of knowledge about divided societies (moities) after wars took me initially to the former East Germany, and most recently to Lebanon and Syria, where I was frequently the object of suspicions of spying. What more plausible motive and purpose could I have, in the eyes of my interlocutors—especially those in positions of authority—than to uncover and betray the secrets of social and political order? There are, of course, substantial continuities between my own experiences in establishing trust and overcoming hostility and those of many twentieth-century fieldworkers, including Sally Falk Moore's in Africa (see chapter 6). For instance, working under colonial administrations, Malinowski in the Trobriands and Evans-Pritchard among the Nuer experienced a great deal of suspicion. Several decades later, collaboration and suspicion took slightly different forms under self-styled authoritarian regimes: Clifford and Hildred Geertz found themselves swept up in a police raid at a cockfight in Bali, leading to a sense of mutual complicity; and Julian Pitt-Rivers was awash in gossip in Franco's Spain, where a sense of suspicion permeated relations of the Spanish people with each other as well as with himself.

As the examples of Malinowski and Evans-Pritchard demonstrate, suspicion of anthropologists and fear of their collaboration with authority constituted part of a power differential and a colonial situation that predated the expansion of the national security state in the twentieth century. During the cold war, relations of anthropologists to their informants drew increased and more explicit suspicion, as extraterritorial agencies of the U.S. government and local secret services proliferated and expanded in most of the world's states. Despite substantive differences in motivation and in forms of knowledge retrieval and dissemination, their "intelligence-gathering operations" are quite similar to our "fieldwork," leading to a frequent confusion about who—what subject—people are actually encountering: Are they providing information to an agent of the state or to an ethnographer?

Anthropologists respond to the ubiquitous suspicion of complicity with these agencies in various ways, which often depend on the concrete situations in which they find themselves. One response is to withdraw altogether from investigating domains that might make them persona non grata with the governments that issue or deny research permits; they continue to do fieldwork but steer clear of politically contentious issues. Another is to retreat to mining archives and historical scholarship about a putatively more accessible past (and one that implicates present actors in less compromised ways, at least from an official governmental perspective), so as to avoid being shadowed or even completely barred from doing research. Today's global "war on terror" accentuates both of these trends, while creating new suspicions that will likely shape fieldwork interactions in pernicious ways.

In this essay, I sketch my own response, which has enabled me to sustain a fieldwork presence that poses questions of political significance in everyday life, even though I am dogged by suspicions of complicity. This response should clearly not be understood as a normative standard for relations of all ethnographers with their interlocutors in other places. In this volume alone, many other locations and approaches are described and analyzed: long-term cooperation (Moore), sharing a lifeworld (Stevenson), countertransference (Coleman), taking a stance simultaneously internal and external to a religious experience (Hammoudi), conflictual intimacy (Ghassem-Fachandi), acting alternately as scientist and patient (Raikhel), and sharing the absence of a mother tongue (Senders). Moreover, as presence and interlocution are contingent acts, I do not take for granted my own access to research in Syria in the future.

Something of a disappointment to me in both of my fieldwork sites has been the failure of any secret service—the American Central Intelligence Agency, the East German Staatssicherheit, the Lebanese secret service, or the Syrian Mukhabarat—ever to contact me personally to ask what I knew. Aren't I, an anthropologist, supposed to know informal things, secrets of significance and interest to security services? I have known scholars in other disciplines—history, German studies, Near Eastern studies, politics, education, and economics—who have been contacted by one or several of these agencies, both American and foreign, and a few who were even actively recruited. (None of them, to my knowledge, ever agreed to cooperate.) Other anthropologists in other places have had extremely hostile, direct contacts with security agents, and some have suffered the most dire consequences, such as Myrna Mack, stabbed to death in Guatemala in 1990, and Beatriz Manz, kidnapped and held by the Guatemalan military with CIA help. In the summer of 1986, Steve Sampson was held overnight with his two children in the Bucharest airport transit lounge for reasons the agents said he already knew; later, after their own interrogations by the security service, his Romanian friends revealed to him that authorities suspected him of being a Hungarian spy. I, by contrast, have never had any direct exchanges of this sort of which I am aware, though I certainly have been spied on, followed as an object of interest.[3]

ENCOUNTERS WITH THE SYRIAN MUKHABARAT, INITIAL FIELDWORK

During the academic year 2004–05, I served as Fulbright Professor in Aleppo, Syria.[4] I was free to move about the country without interference, and only after my first extended stay (my first visit was in 1999, and I have returned several times since 2005) did agents of the Mukhabarat contact most of the people whom I saw regularly. While I was living in the ancient and grand souk al-Medina, a market of mostly Sunni merchants now largely abandoned as a living space, agents did follow me at times. In addition to these in-person encounters, rumors were also part of my social presence, and preceded my physical arrival. Only some of these rumors originated with security agents, but all were useful to them and to the Ba'ath Party in circulating suspicion, as well as in ultimately contributing to the particular subjectivity I was able to assume.

Three weeks into my stay, an old, tired-looking, and slow-moving man approached a merchant whom I had visited and asked, "What is John's last name?"

"I don't know," the merchant replied, insouciantly. "You should find these things out before they come into this country, not after." The person who told me this story reassured me that I should not let it concern me.

About eight weeks later, another friend outside the souk told me that a man had followed me to his office near a meat market in another part of city, and asked for a copy of an interview about human rights and universal jurisdiction that I had given before entering Syria to the independent Arabic language newspaper *An-Nahar*, published in Beirut. Syrian authorities forbid the sale of *An-Nahar* because of its critical coverage of Syria (specifically, at the time, of Syrian's presence in Lebanon). I had given this friend a copy of the interview, but his reply to the agent's query was "I read it on the Internet—as do most intellectuals in Aleppo. You have to download it yourself."

About two months later, the Mukhabarat sought out the owner of my apartment (and her son at the Belgian consulate) to inquire not about me but about an American woman who was living in Damascus but visiting me. Their response: he is a free man, and we know nothing about who visits him.

ENCOUNTERS WITH THE SYRIAN
MUKHABARAT, REVISIT

On a return visit to Aleppo about six months after my initial research, my encounters increased in frequency. Security agents seemed to shadow all of my Syrian acquaintances, often interviewing them within minutes of any conversation we had in public. If I left a café or restaurant or my hotel, someone was waiting there outside, not for me but for the person with whom I had talked. Here, too, I have a plausible explanation for how this started: one student's mother had called the security services, against the advice of her husband, to tell them I was arriving in Aleppo. Ziyad, who had during my initial stay been asked to write reports of our conversations, told his mother he planned to meet with me.[5] In my absence, the Mukhabarat had visited the family, asked about me, and requested that they call should I return.

His mother's worry, Ziyad told me, was that he himself might be under suspicion because in the past his maternal relatives had been active in the Muslim Brotherhood; his mother did not want his acquaintance with me to get her son into trouble. I had spent considerable time with Ziyad, a pious Sunni Muslim, and he had come to think of me, at times, as a father substitute, despite the ways in which my own secular orientation continually challenged his respect for me. My advice to him, and to others, was always that he should write accurate reports for the security forces. We in fact discussed little of controversy, and I amused myself in fantasizing about security agents reading about psychoanalysis and the desire of Syrian mothers for their sons, the declining authority of fathers over their sons, divorce and changing family structure in the United States.

Notwithstanding his own double complicity, Ziyad also had his suspicions of me, and he confronted me with them frequently: Did I work for the American government? Did they interview me when I returned? Was the Syrian government interested in my research? Was I Jewish? Somehow Ziyad put these suspicions aside. But he retained a particular distrust for other acquaintances of mine—especially Jihad, a tour guide who came to my lectures and movie screenings at the university, where I was employed, and who accompanied us and a group of students to a hammam one evening. On that occasion, Jihad took the opportunity to tell the students that I was homosexual, even though I had never shared any information about my sex life or orientation with him. My unmarried status alone, which aroused incessant curiosity, continually brought to the fore an apprehension about dissidence and deviation of one kind or another. Wasn't I violating the promise to marry a woman, the most natural and social of promises? And, in the eyes of young men, wasn't I therefore shirking my responsibility to other young men—to care for their sisters? And given my refusal, wouldn't they have to assume that burden? Isn't this promise to marry an obligation that all men, even godless men like myself, are supposed to fulfill? In any case, Ziyad suspected Jihad of working with the Mukhabarat (probably a correct assumption), which in turn framed all of Jihad's motivations as untrustworthy.

My own potential perfidy was not sufficient to persuade Ziyad to terminate our friendship and stop engaging with me, however. Security agents visited him at his home several times during subsequent visits, once to ask him to identify a young man with whom I was talking in a photo—apparently taken with a cellphone camera—of the three of us.

His fear of collaboration eventually resulted in a countertransferential reaction on my part: I began involving him less in my fieldwork—introducing him to fewer people, for example—for fear that contact with me would endanger him. Nonetheless, a measure of trust grew between us, and he began to share with me traumatic events of family history as well as disappointments in his present life (including a suicide attempt), along with his dreams and expectations for the future. In this developing friendship, between an anthropologist and one of his interlocutors, we increasingly spoke to each other not in the voices of stereotypes from elsewhere (as professor, student, Syrian, American, Muslim, agnostic) but each from an "I" appreciative of an indeterminate present. In the exchange of information we tried to make ourselves intelligible to one another.

My interest here is not primarily in why I am identified as a spy or collaborator—it makes sense, my profile is perfect for such projections—but in the effects of this identification on the perception and assumption of subjectivity in fieldwork experience and knowledge production. Eventually I partook in the fears of Ziyad, and even in the fears of his mother: and I began to act on them, assuming the subjectivity they were investing in me (e.g., being more careful about introducing him to third parties, about implicating him in scenes that might endanger him, and occasionally assuming the role of giving fatherly advice about careers or existential paths). Through these encounters I came to share a number of understandings with Ziyad about forms of quiescence, the foreclosure of action as an accommodation of the citizenry with the authoritarian Syrian regime, the possibilities of circumventing forms of surveillance, and the expectations and limits of the authority of fathers over their sons.

I met few individuals who found ways of evading this fear or were able to directly challenge the Syrian Mukhabarat, but it is important not to neglect them. One spirited young woman named Huzama had attended all of my lectures and film screenings at the university, and several times I joined her and a friend in the large university cafeteria. Our sitting together was conspicuous, as I was usually the only professor present, and I usually sat with a group of young men, not with two women. A month before I returned for my second stay in Aleppo, her father, a Communist whom she worshipped, had died in a traffic accident, and she was particularly troubled that the accident claimed only her father; the driver and passenger seated behind him escaped unscathed. Referring to an e-mail I had sent offering condolences, she said she was moved that I understood what she had lost. "Now I am just going through the motions," she said. "I am completing my studies just for him. I have no motivation."

Shortly after we first met, Huzama had told me of a marriage offer received from a Syrian medical student studying in France. Now, she confided in me she had refused the offer. "He didn't want to grant me freedom," she said. That must not have been easy, I replied, knowing that her father was alive at the time of the offer and knew the family of the potential husband well. "I will wait," she said. In earlier conversations, I had encouraged her to be selective. She was both very bright and beautiful. You will have many opportunities, I said; you can do better and need not choose now.

I asked if the Mukhabarat had contacted her the previous spring, as they had other students I taught at the university. No, she said, her last contact was when she was 14. Then, the Ba'ath Party chapter in her school had asked her to join. "I said vehemently in front of the whole class that I would not. Two agents came to my home. My father let them in, was polite, served them coffee. They asked to talk to me. He called me in, but I refused to talk to them. He told them, 'That's her opinion, she has a mind of her own, I cannot force her.' Since then, they have left me alone."

I saw Huzama a few days later, and the first thing she said was "They followed me from the café the last time we met, and wanted to talk to me. I said, 'No, I will not talk to you in public, and not on the street. I am a Syrian citizen, you are a Syrian citizen, we have the same rights. I know Mr. John will not hurt me and I will not hurt him. I have nothing to say to you about him. You can call me, I told them, and I gave them my telephone number, and they later called.'"

I told her she was welcome to write the reports of our conversations that they requested of her, but she refused to cooperate with them in any way.

A RUMOR OF MY PRESENCE IN ALEPPO

Perhaps the largest shadow cast over my research at the university was the interview I gave, mentioned above, on human rights and universal jurisdiction, published in the Beiruti newspaper *An-Nahar* on September 19, 2004, shortly after I had entered Syria. This interview stated that I would be teaching in Syria. For my first seven months in the country, that interview followed me around in distorted form, initially in a rumor about where I was and my possible CIA connection. This rumor was also instrumental in delaying for three months my appointment to teach at the University of Aleppo, despite the approval of the president and vice president of the university, with whom I had become friends. At one point, the heads of most of the departments in the Faculty of Arts and Sciences even wrote a letter claiming that my services were not needed, as I was unqualified to teach a course in any of their departments. (The university president, to my good fortune, did not acknowledge its receipt.) Eventually I resolved this matter by proposing to give a series of open lectures rather than teach a course.

The day before my official university appointment ended, a friend at the university offered a convincing explanation for this rumor and its effects. "Remember the member of parliament, the MP, who called to find you in early September?" he asks.

"Oh yes," I say. "We since have become friends and he also used my work in his teaching."

"Nobody knew where you were back then, but the MP asked that we find you because he had read you were teaching here at Aleppo University. That started a rumor: if nobody knows where or who he is, and a member of parliament wants to know, then we better be careful about letting him teach."

"But the MP told the law school, where he is a guest professor, that they should invite me to teach there," I reply. "He is very enthusiastic about the directions of my research."

"That doesn't matter. Nobody cares much about what you taught or are teaching. And people in the humanities faculty do not talk to the people in the law faculty, so they do not know what the MP said later. They only know, and the dean is very cautious, that there was a call from parliament asking about you. That's enough. But add to that resistance to having you teach, then you have an explanation for why the entire faculty, deans and department heads, decided to decline your services."

"The odd thing," I say, "is that I came here hoping to study rumors in the souk. Souks are notorious for gossip. But I did not record a single rumor that seems significant to me, at least not yet. Yet it was a rumor about me, a false rumor, that framed my entire experience at the university. And I do not find this out until the night before I depart."

A RUMOR OF AIDS

In February 2006, I was back in Princeton and got a call from an American I had met in Syria in 2004. She said she had received an alarming e-mail from a mutual acquaintance in Latakia, a city on the coast. He is a man I had introduced her to: a well-known poet, seductive, irreverent, warm, very funny. He charmed her into an affair—a rocky affair, as these things go—with problems in translation and many misunderstandings. She forwarded me an e-mail exchange of theirs, dated early January (in other words, written about seven months after I had left Syria after my university appointment, but while I was revisiting). It seems as if the poet was unaware of when I exited and reentered the country.

Thank you . . . tender J.

hope to see you too . . . BUT PLEASE I hope you can help me in this . . . without any anger . . . please I'm these days very worry about something . . . was there any chance to get HIV from contacting you !!! because a doctor from Aleppo called Samir Nissaaneh said that john have it and a friend of him from usa!!?? how does he know . . . I think he lies!!?

Sorry J. . . . but truly I'm really very worry. please laugh and say you are not. . . .

The poet apparently thought that J.'s contact with me had contaminated her, which made him anxious that sexual contact with her might have infected him. J.'s tart response to him:

This doctor sounds like an absurd anti-gay, anti-westerner extremist. Neither John nor myself have any STDs . . . anyway HIV cannot be contracted by talking, eating and listening to music together.

J.

I sent e-mails to several people in Aleppo to ask if they had heard this rumor, and whether they knew who this doctor "Samir Nissaaneh" was. Had I indeed met him without learning his name? Such rumors, I wrote, have a life of their own and might effectively make people fear me, spelling the death of any future fieldwork. Two friends wrote back, unable to identify the doctor, and they reassured me that I should ignore the rumor and in any event return soon.

Merely by chance, during the following week I heard the poet being interviewed on National Public Radio. He is a brave man and did not equivocate in discussing Syrian censorship and policing. I decided to contact him by e-mail. After discussing the issue with Arab friends in the States, they advised me to use the Arab literary convention of coding the information or rumor as a dream:

Dear . . . ,

I don't know if you remember me, but I introduced you to J. I hope this finds you doing well, writing more poems, happy, and enjoying life. I am back at Princeton, teaching full time. I recently had a dream, and you were in it, and somebody told you that I had AIDS. Of course, on dreaming this I woke up. I hope you have not had the same dream!

All the best,

John

The poet never replied to my e-mail, but his initial response to the rumor deserves more attention. "I think he lies!!?" is an ambiguous statement. The poet follows what is in fact an assertion with two exclamation points and a question mark, suggesting that he truly wants to dispel the rumor (!!) but nonetheless is unsure (?); hence he must immediately question his own statement. One could rewrite this sentence as a thought sequence: I think he lies! I think he lies! But does he lie? The poet's anxiety is founded in the possible truth that is concealed behind what appears to be a lie.

His response—an inquiry into the source and veracity of a rumor that I might have AIDS—is a tempting way to deal with the rumor, most likely spread by the Mukhabarat (though I have no evidence for my suspicion), but it could never effectively put the rumor to rest. On the surface, the poet turns to the technique of verification employed by Arabs to authenticate Hadith, the prophetic dictums or utterances of the Prophet Muhammad passed on in an oral tradition for a century before being written in the Abassid period, one hundred years after the Prophet's death. Verification of a Hadith required a chain of witnesses whose credibility was subject to strict scrutiny: they had to cite their sources and furnish proof of their own integrity. Such acts as urinating in the street or eating in the marketplace, for example, might in themselves impugn the dignity of a witness and result in the disqualification of an entire collection of orally transmitted Hadith. A single flaw in the chain of transmission was sufficient ground to cast doubt on the moral integrity of the transmitter's reputation.[6]

No comparable procedure exists to verify the authenticity of rumors. The moral integrity of the transmitter's reputation is irrelevant. The sources, in fact, tend to remain hidden. Rumors spread by means of another logic—one resembling Freud's explanation in *Beyond the Pleasure Principle* of *fort-da*, the game of peek-a-boo (1961: 8–10). In this game, the meaning of a presence is assumed through deferral; the object comes into relief only by the alternation of appearance and disappearance. This intermittent presence initiates a process of cognitive augmentation and completion that, in turn, modifies perception, forming a cognitive feedback loop that resonates in the form of a reality effect.[7] This same process characterizes the movement from secrecy to revelation and back to

secrecy again, as well as the relation of anthropologists with their interlocutors in long-term intermittent fieldwork visits.

Members of the Mukhabarat itself deployed the power of *fort-da* by
playing this game with me, deferring any physical engagement with me
in conversation but at the same time inserting themselves into my
encounters with other Syrians through intermittent presence and absence
with them. They first encountered me as a disembodied presence (via
visa application); only later was presence augmented with rumor, which
university employees then appropriated and spread. They disseminated
plausible insinuations (lies?) about my presence in ever-wider circles,
and those stories ultimately gained a momentum and a facticity independent of any process of verification. Over time, the dissemination
required less and less effort by the original agent, who in fact became
secret—for the time being. In such cases, direct refutation or denial is
useless, as the efficacy of rumor depends not on its truth or the credibility of its transmitter but merely on its periodic repetition.[8]

When the source is secret or unlocatable, the repetition occurs more
freely. An absence of source thus itself becomes a cause of potency,
enabling a dispersion of interpretations. Conversely, silence on my part
could not successfully defuse a rumor, as it would allow the rumor to
register in the minds of those listening, without its content being negated
or contested. Any effective strategy must therefore begin with interlocution, speaking and listening. In other words, in order to negate a rumor
one must first repeat it; but that telling, at least initially, guarantees the
rumor's efficacy by keeping its information circulating.

Yet absence also affects the circulation of rumor, and in a way
dependent on sequence and timing. In a subsequent visit to Syria one
year after this rumor began circulating, I heard no mention of it, and
the Mukhabarat, while shadowing me consistently, did not keep
me from meeting people (that I know of), nor did it curtail my movements, except insofar I made decisions in anticipation of what it might
do. Conscious of the presence of security agents and the possibility that
they might accuse people I knew of collaboration, I limited my stay to
less than ten days and was quite cautious in meeting more vulnerable
individuals.

THE METAPHYSICS OF PRESENCE/THE PRESENCE
OF THE MUKHABARAT

This entire sequence of fieldwork experiences in Syria appears tailor-made for a deconstructive reading. My encounters may be said to constitute a text, which can be read as a deferral of meaning. I am inscribed in the Aleppian scene before I arrive physically. My inscription, initially in my visa application, then in a text (a published interview), precedes the rumor of me, which precedes my actual presence in face-to-face encounters. There is a constant deferral of the meaning of my presence. The context is open, unstable, and the subjects of the text are at the same time incessantly disseminating and losing meaning. But is Derrida's critique of "metaphysics of presence" helpful for understanding my own presence and the specific meaning it assumes in the modes of person, text, and rumor? And what is its relevance to the knowledge produced through fieldwork experience under the suspicion of collaboration with the enemy—in Syria?

Derrida's famous criticism of metaphysics does not pass judgment on "experience" per se, and nowhere, to my knowledge, does he address fieldwork.[9] In his early and perhaps most famous engagement with anthropology, he considers a theoretical assertion by Lévi-Strauss about the origin of language (or, more specifically, the purpose of writing) in "archaic societies," a necessarily speculative claim (as this origin or purpose can never be known or proved) that he refutes on philosophical grounds. He questions the assertion that speech has a fixed or stable presence prior to its play with inscription (écriture).

Lévi-Strauss, following Rousseau and de Saussure, had argued that speech precedes writing, and therefore language necessarily originated in speech. Derrida critically displaces this claim, in developing a generalized theory of "writing," by insisting that alphabetic writing is only one form of inscription; he further argued that even sound can be inscription, as can silence, both of which leave traces in the spoken. Writing, therefore, does not restore the presence of speech but stands in a relation of play to it (Derrida 1976: 110). This broad and encompassing definition of writing elides Lévi-Strauss's concern, which is the more literal meaning of writing for the Nambikwara, as it does the significance of the sequence of forms of inscriptions—sound, silence, alphabetic writing—in any particular speech situation, in a specific place and time.

My own encounters with the Mukhabarat should suggest, however, that this generalized theory also has limits when applied to experience and interlocution in time in a specific place: it leaves unexamined an array of important questions regarding the temporal sequencing of presence and the possibilities for speech and understanding that do not approximate the activity of reading. In other words, the fieldwork encounter calls into question the parallel posited by Derrida between reading and listening, between the competency of a reader of texts and that of a fieldworker who must learn something of the grammar of a particular place. If all listening can be subsumed into reading, then why insist on any specific epistemological insight from the art of listening? One result of this subsumption, in the practical world, is that ethnographic skills are understood to be those of "qualitative research" (the reading of utterances in texts for patterns and meanings), as opposed to the skills required for "quantitative research" (performing operations on numbers, statistical modeling). The practice of anthropology without the experiential component of Being There, exposure to the simultaneity of speaker and listener, is therefore frequently reduced to the coding and analysis of interviews.[10]

Following Heidegger's critique of metaphysics, Derrida seeks to refute the idea that speech is a kind of presence (because the speaker and listener are simultaneously present for each other), while writing is a kind of absence (because the writer is not simultaneously present for the reader). To undo this comparison, and the understanding that writing is a substitute for speech, Derrida endeavors to completely remove the criterion of presence from the discussion. For the examination of texts, this argument has much merit philosophically, but it is not adequate—even analogically—to explain the relation of writing/reading texts to speaking/listening in fieldwork experience. Strictly speaking, to follow Derrida's logic here would mean only an insistence on the play and instability of these two forms of knowledge production and not on their relative priority or meaning in specific social science pursuits.

In accounting for the experience of fieldwork, analysis should start—not end—with the understanding of instability and play. Instability is the key to the dissemination of meanings in texts, and to some degree it characterizes all social and cultural phenomena. But it is only one component of the fieldwork encounter. Also integral are elements of temporality unimportant to a Derridean analysis, such as sequence, priority, and moments when time and being are arrested. For some Syrians, my presence as fieldworker was already inscribed in discourse about me before I arrived physically in Aleppo (revealed in requests for the written interview about human rights, rumors of my teaching as Fulbright Professor, a rumor of connections with CIA, e-mail about AIDS). But the subjectivity invoked for me in each of these inscriptions was of indeterminate meaning, part of a particular sequence of encounters with Syrians that were punctuated by moments of arrest and interlocution: that is, by copresence in speaking and listening. My presence, by arresting the perceptions of my interlocutors in very specific ways, disturbed their routines of behavior and explanation, as it did those of members of the Mukhabarat. These arrests opened up the possibility of changing the sequence of experiences and meanings available both to me and to those whom I met.

Another theorization is needed to account for collaboration—for the actual sequence and content of the suspicions of my complicity, as well as for the various mechanisms of their circulation and relative significance. Also requiring explanation is how, despite the instability of my interactions and identities, the suspicions of collaboration I aroused did not always deter my interlocutors from assuming a subjectivity that resists cooperating in the surveillance of foreigners. For example, the published interview with and about me was in fact used by some faculty at the university (though not all) as a substitute for speech, a refusal to engage with me in person. Refusing interlocution, these people granted the interview a status, much as Rousseau had written (and Derrida critiqued), of a "dangerous supplement" to speech. This written text kept threatening to preclude and subvert my own encounters in Aleppo, although at times in specific settings (homes, cafés, the souk, walking on the street) I was able to circumvent its inscription—in large part because of the possibility of interlocution, the simultaneity of the experience of speaker and listener, which offered another, more indeterminate perspective from which to interpret my intention. One professor, in contrast to the majority, deliberately shared the article with his students.

The conditions of my past fieldwork experience are unlikely to replicate themselves. Hence my next visit may be relatively unmarked by these events or, alternatively, so dogged by rumors and the omnipresent security apparatus as to forestall any meaningful exchanges. The fear of being accused of collaboration with me, of "cooperating traitorously with the enemy," constitutes a serious threat to Syrians living under pervasive surveillance in an authoritarian political system. Since my last visit, the article initially published in *An-Nahar* that preceded my actual encounters now appears on two websites of the Syrian opposition. Another collection of my articles on political crimes and social peace has been published in Arabic by a Moroccan press (Borneman 2007a). My book on fathers and sons and political authority, *Syrian Episodes,* has been published, and part of the first chapter is available on the press's Internet site. Several friends from Aleppo have e-mailed me about it (one titled his message "I'm not happy," because my description of the city did not convey sufficient appreciation of its beauty). An Arabic translation is in the works, and I have already been told by a potential translator that the analysis of the Syrian president's relation with his father in the first chapter would have to be omitted for the book to appear in Syria.

My presence is also framed by the American government's identification of Syria as a rogue state in the "war on terror." The timing of presence in the field—during a slight lull in international hostilities or at points of high tension—predisposes many fieldwork encounters to success or failure. In my own fieldwork, a small aspect of which I elaborated above, to the extent I was able to share in some of the fears of Syrians in ongoing encounters without fully succumbing to these fears, I was granted an insight into how subjectivity is assumed or evaded in the context of this particular political form.

In sum, an analysis of my experience with the Mukhabarat in terms of a "metaphysics of presence," an originary point in speech from which "truth" could be made present, cannot do it justice. Being There and not being there (entering, staying, and leaving the field) is the activity, the condition of possibility, that brought into play textual knowledge as well as other knowledge to challenge it. Without this presence, ethnographers are reduced to the lay Orientalists whom Edward Said initially took to task—scholars who mistake what they read for the Other's presence. To take into account this presence, to consider what actually goes on, is not to fetishize a distinction between fieldwork experience and textual knowledge but to acknowledge that partaking in the production of insights produces a unique kind of knowledge, which consists of mutually intelligible objectifications from and through the sequence of our encounters.

TOWARD AN EPISTEMOLOGY FOR ENCOUNTER-BASED ETHNOGRAPHIC FIELDWORK

What might we conclude about an epistemology for encounter-based ethnographic fieldwork? I have distanced myself from currently popular modes of inquiry that do not require the presence of the fieldworker. Approaches such as Foucault-inspired genealogies and Derrida-inspired deconstructions claim to track the historical or logical preconditions of social forms, to trace the effects of "truth" in different power relationships, or to draw attention to the logical instability and ambiguities in textual knowledge.[11] When taken up by anthropologists for the purposes of fieldwork, both finding and interpreting lines of descent and arriving at instability and the deferral of meaning tend to denigrate the importance of experience in the present and reduce all truth to effects of rhetoric and power relations.

My dispute here is not with the utility of these approaches for analysis, as they clearly raise important questions and are useful in generating certain kinds of insights. Rather, my analysis is more narrowly focused on addressing some of the adverse effects they have had on epistemology within anthropology—specifically, on obscuring the significance of experience in fieldwork. These effects have included a threefold elision: an elision of the present as a location, an elision of the location of analysts in complex collaborative relationships of knowledge production with their interlocutors, and an elision of experience as a mode of generating socially significant understandings about an indeterminate future.

I have addressed these elisions in part by situating my analysis in the experience of being there in which imagined future relations and their negations are dialectically objectified. Fieldwork experience located in the intersubjective present, then, is not oriented primarily to a mapping of place or personhood in terms of multiple, prior beginnings, a tracking enabled by the perspicacity of the anthropologist as genealogist or reader and arrived at unburdened by what is happening to the people with whom the anthropologist works in their social context. It is also not synonymous with the history of the present or archival work; it is not primarily a demonstration of the contingency of the past, or a determination of the trajectory of the past.

Fieldwork experience, I am arguing, is an engagement with presence and absence in episodic encounters wherein perceptions are arrested and subjectivities both put at risk and assumed. From this perspective, fieldwork is the registering of sensory impressions, and fieldwork encounters are the beginning of a process of mutual subject discovery and change. Along the way, these encounters may result in dialectical objectifications that make the other—or, more precisely, communicative possibilities with the other—present in written accounts.[12]

NOTES

This essay owes much to critical comments by Abdellah Hammoudi, Parvis Ghassem-Fachandi, and Stefan Senders, as well as the two readers for University of California Press, Jonathan Spencer and Stefania Pandolofo. I thank them.

1. On the shift from "rapport" to "collaboration" as dialogism and complicity, see Marcus (1998: 105–31).
2. All except the final of the specific episodes in this essay are drawn from my book *Syrian Episodes* (Borneman 2007b).
3. In 1996, I applied for access to my files from the Stasi Archives in East Berlin, and was sent the official card from the former secret service documenting that a file had indeed been compiled, but the file itself,

alas, had been lost. In March 2008, an American historian contacted me that she had found a Stasi file from 1987 which contained a plan to send a scholar to refute a paper I was giving at a conference in the Netherlands. To my knowledge, that plan was never executed.

4.   Syria is a secular republic ruled by the Arab Socialist Renaissance (Ba'ath) Party; its president, Bashar el-Assad, inherited his authority in March 2000 upon the death of his father, Hafez el-Assad. In 1963, under the slogan "Unity, Liberty, Socialism," the Ba'ath Party seized power and retains it to this day. In my own limited observations, the party seems to have a more pernicious influence on social life—blocking institutional and personal initiatives, promoting mediocrity—than does the Mukhabarat. With the passing of power to Bashar, the use of fear to control public expression in everyday life lessened considerably, though fear—now manifest in more subtle ways—is still everywhere, largely because the Mukhabarat is still everywhere and has, most likely, sources of power and interests independent of other branches of government. I was told by several acquaintances that up to half of all my encounters with adults will be with security agents, and when I asked others if this was true, they uniformly said yes. This perception, and not the empirical reality, is the key to understanding the reasons for the general acquiescence to authority and general paranoia suffusing public life (see Wedeen 1999).

5.   Throughout this essay, names have been changed.

6.   See the delightful essays on this topic by Abdelfattah Kilito (2001).

7.   I thank Stefan Senders for this formulation.

8.   I owe this insight to Parvis Ghassem-Fachandi, who developed this line of inquiry in accounting for the use of rumors about abducted women in the Gujarati pogrom of 2002. His research confirms exactly this process by which rumors acquire power through being told and heard.

9.   In his use of prescriptive and programmatic texts that describe how people ought to behave or society ought to be constructed, not actual occurrences, Foucault, like Derrida, distinctly contrasted his approach with the attempt ("an admirable one in itself") "of grasping a 'whole society' in its 'living reality'"—in other words, with any experiential-based fieldwork method (Foucault 1991: 82). I thank Jonathan Spencer for this tip and citation.

10. I thank Stefan Senders for suggesting this line of argument.

11. Much of this work remains tied to a notion to a distinction between *der Ursprung* (origin) and *der Anfang* (beginning), initially made by Nietzsche and later explicated by Foucault, that posits the past (*die Vergangenheit*) as the location for multiple beginnings. It is as if the

replacement of origin with beginning cleansed the researcher of the grave sin of essentialism, and instead located the position of the analyst in the genealogist. That genealogist no longer confuses the knowledge produced with truth but, by paying attention to moments of discovery, exposes a multiplicity of beginnings. Such analysts, who now have the sole power over their creations, are freed from the responsibility of having to prove a Weberian social significance; they can merely suggest that they are discovering one of many beginnings and, in a generous gesture, open the field of inquiry for other researchers to discover other genealogies of other events and prior forms.

12.   Johannes Fabian makes the important argument that the problem with representation is "not of a difference between reality and its image but . . . a tension between re-presentation and presence" (1991: 208). I have extended his insight here, arguing that it is necessary to focus anthropological inquiry not merely on making the other present, as he puts it, but also on making present the communicative possibilities with the other.

REFERENCES

Borneman, John. 2007a. *Al-jinayah al-siyasiyyah wal-silm al-ijtimaei* [Political crime and social peace]. Rabat: Dar Tubkal lil-Nashar.

———. 2007b. *Syrian Episodes: Sons, Fathers, and an Anthropologist in Aleppo.* Princeton: Princeton University Press.

Derrida, Jacques. 1976. *Of Grammatology.* Trans. Gayatri Spivak. Baltimore: Johns Hopkins University Press.

Fabian, Johannes. 1991. *Time and the Work of Anthropology: Critical Essays, 1971–1991.* Studies in Anthropology and History, vol. 3. Chur, Switzerland: Harwood Academic.

Foucault, Michel. 1991. "Questions of Method." In *The Foucault Effect: Studies in Governmentality,* ed. Graham Burchell, Colin Gordon, and Peter Miller. Chicago: University of Chicago Press.

Freud, Sigmund. 1961. *Beyond the Pleasure Principle.* Trans. and ed. James Strachey. Intro. by Gregory Zilboorg. New York: Norton.

Kilito, Abdelfattah. 2001. *The Author and His Doubles: Essays on Classical Arabic Culture.* Trans. Michael Cooperson. Syracuse, NY: Syracuse University Press.

Marcus, George E. 1998. *Ethnography through Thick and Thin.* Princeton: Princeton University Press.

Wedeen, Lisa. 1999. *Ambiguities of Domination: Politics, Rhetoric, and Symbols in Contemporary Syria.* Chicago: University of Chicago Press.

TEN

Afterthoughts

THE EXPERIENCE AND AGONY OF FIELDWORK

Abdellah Hammoudi and John Borneman

I

As we reflect back on the essays assembled in this volume, it appears that each deals with a particular defining moment of thinking about and practicing anthropology. They do not aim to define a subdiscipline in anthropology or formulate an encompassing theoretical orientation regarding substantive issues. As a group, the authors differ in ethnicity, gender, and nationality, and in their respective stages of professional development. Though they all live near and work in U.S. and Canadian universities, their research spans societies that vary widely in geographical location, language, and sociopolitical situation: Canadian Inuit, European, Arab, African, Indian, and Russian societies.

Differences aside, these essays are profoundly connected in several ways:

1. From diverse and converging angles, they make the case for a fresh look at fieldwork encounters as a set of experiences. The two complementary notions of encounter and experience are pursued through reflection on the practice of research and writing about serious and protracted involvement with human collectives and key interlocutors. They are also pursued through in-depth explications of particular topics that arose in the field, with a keen interest in how the concrete lives of persons met there resonate—in their convergences, divergences, and conflicts—with the life and projects of the anthropologist.

2. The essays depart from some of the more traditional, nonreflective practices of ethnography, as well as from the current and pervasive practices in the discipline (often heralded as part of an "experimental moment") based on variants of what we characterize as "textualism." In this double break, they also move toward a critical ethnography that makes the *agony of fieldwork* integral to knowledge production. To be sure, critical ethnography is what most anthropologists today claim to write, but the term is used so broadly that it has come to include anything written by people self-identified with anthropology. Such sterilizing inclusiveness has marginalized ethnography as a set of distinctive practices with a transformative character. We have no intention of positing another prescriptive model—a model of the *agonizing* ethnographer. Still, the essays in this volume share an understanding of knowledge derived not from an "ethnographic sensibility" in the close reading of texts but instead from interlocution: intense listening cultivated in conversations. Such listening does not exclude reading practices, but the ethnographer's reading is not her primary activity, literally or by analogy. These odd spaces of interlocution often threaten to overwhelm or consume the ethnographer and thereby situate her in intense and unintended struggles not of her own choosing.

3. Finally, they do not subsume the fieldwork encounter under theory or into its sociopolitical context, but examine its articulation with theory and context. Characteristically and in contradistinction to much current and previous critical practice, encounters are not reduced to grand macronarratives (e.g., nationalism, the cold war, empire, globalization, the clinical gaze), and anthropological

research is not redeemed by assuming a heroic posture. In all theoretical modesty, and in appreciation of the fundamental uncertainty of encounters, these essays nonetheless insist on the veracity of ethnographic accounts that grow out of the ongoing situations in which the anthropologist finds himself engaged. Forsaking any moral high ground, they highlight moments of surprise and ambiguity, and conversations in which anthropologists are brought into ambivalent and indeterminate relations with the people whose human condition they study.

I I

The most long-term account here is Sally Falk Moore's essay on fieldwork in Tanzania that she began in her 40s and then continued for nearly four decades. As she returns to her encounters there, we feel her uncertainties in the very writing of her text. What she has done, heard, seen, and felt is expressed in a style of her own: restrained emotions, a light ironic touch, an appreciation of incompleteness, writing in strokes that coalesce without freezing fieldwork situations. An American, a white woman from the *West* in a former British colony, a lawyer turned anthropologist, she is well aware of the power exerted by the United States on a third world country trying to build a socialist future, of the search for local autonomy vis-à-vis colonial metropoles, and of an emerging *third world* bloc in the context of the cold war. But what she brings most powerfully to these contexts is the ethnographic details of episodic encounters with specific individuals who are entangled in their own struggles for and against power.

Initially, not knowing exactly how to proceed (although she has read the "literature" and received advice from teachers and mentors), her reflexivity takes a surprising form: precedented/unprecedented. Moore tells us that she wanted to collect information that would be confirmed by others—or, at least, that others may be able to confirm, criticize, or dispute what she writes.

Though she is faced with suspicions of the foreigner and bureaucratic hurdles, she collaborates with people from the tribal group she chose to work with. She engages her informants in intensive labor (some eventually become research partners), which enables her to write knowledgeably from a depth of experience. Her processual approach entailed long and sustained relations with younger generations of Tanzanians as well (in particular, from the tribal group studied). The result is multifaceted research that continually corrects many of her assumptions, and carries her well beyond her initial inquiries, with descriptions of lineages and groups, cartographies of property, and changes in the irrigation system and in political form and authority. So much of this account resists pure and simple literary construction. Or, more important: construction resists deconstruction by the simple fact that Moore has to attend to other reconstructions on the ground *and* in the archive.

Moore's account makes no pretense about doing science or theory. She instead steadfastly elaborates an objectivity-in-progress, capturing something of a specific mode of change in diagnostic events, forms of opposition, conflict, and negotiation. She perseveres in writing against the postulates of a universal modernity or a uniform postcolonial subject. Working under the aegis of a "socialist state" intent on prescribing the form the future will take and intent on fabricating *grassroots* opinion in support of its projects, she shares and conveys the skepticism of its citizens. This story is not, Moore asserts, supposed to be about her. She only narrates the predicament of the people as she, the anthropologist, has come to work with and know them. The moment and status of reflexivity are precedented/unprecedented. Reflexive writing, in this case, comes after the fact, but it is predicated on previous moments of careful consideration of her project and position before and during the research process itself. While the current preoccupation with reflexivity is hardly new for anthropologists, some of the forms it takes (auto-ethnography, for instance) and the high expectations about what it can do or reveal may be the result of contemporary apprehensions about any encounter with alterity. At any rate, the anthropologist, as she appears here, understanding that she cannot anticipate the form of encounters she will have in the field, embraces the surprise of the serendipitous event and proceeds to theorize the conditions of uncertainty in fieldwork and indeterminacy in culture.

Whereas Moore elaborates knowledge arrived at through long-term fieldwork in one place (Tanzania), Abdellah Hammoudi takes up recent fieldwork at a new site (the hajj in Mecca) but in an area in which he has long worked. John Borneman also writes about recent fieldwork in a new site (Syria), undertaken (in contrast to the research of the two other senior anthropologists) after long-term fieldwork in another geographical area, Europe (and specifically Germany). Hammoudi's long-term investment in an area (the Arab world and Islam) enables him to engage the pilgrimage as both longtime insider and new arrival. Borneman's prior fieldwork encounters with East Germany's Stasi provide a comparison from which he can learn about the specificity of similar kinds of encounters with secret police in Syria. In both cases, although fieldwork encounters are singular, fieldwork experience is accumulative. This accumulative effect is less the result of personal movement and multiplicity of sites than of in-depth engagement with people in each place.

By comparison, the other contributors—Lisa Stevenson, Parvis Ghassem-Fachandi, Leo Coleman, Eugene Raikhel, Stefan Senders—all write about initial fieldwork of varying durations. Differences in experience conducting fieldwork and in length of fieldwork in one place are undertheorized within anthropology. The kind of encounters, levels of insight, and degree of theorization possible are not the same for a scholar like Moore as for those whose careers are just beginning, and the expectations for intellectual work should be adjusted accordingly. This does not mean, however, that first fieldwork encounters are less productive of experience or less capable of yielding theory. On the contrary, first encounters by relatively inexperienced ethnographers are often more vivid and, though lacking temporal depth, often more filled with surprise and hence capable of generating discordant or unsettling reflections.

In work on addiction treatment in two clinical settings in Russia, Eugene Raikhel is consistently unsettled as what he seeks to investigate is disturbed by apparently tangential events—institutional claims on his time, conflicts within the hierarchies of personnel, a murder. The radical ambiguity of the fieldwork situation results in dilemmas that force him to improvise, above all, in implementing his research project. That encounter-based fieldwork takes shape in a way at odds with the initial plan is hardly a surprising development. More important in this case is that doctors and other local figures of authority with institutional bases of power in the medical profession intervene to redirect his project in ways for which he is unprepared. For Raikhel, these problems are not predetermined by questions posed within biomedical discourse or ethical prescriptions but grow out of an indeterminate ethnographic encounter with two distinct clinical situations in Russia.

Yet Raikhel—unlike a psychologist, for example—must balance a self-identification that will allow for productive experiential encounters with adherence to the ethical and deontological rule of nondeception. From the start, this balancing act proves difficult, although each of Raikhel's two institutional settings present different challenges. While in the state-run hospital he is identified as a "scientist"—with divergent consequences for his encounters with physicians and patients—in the rehabilitation center he encounters a different, and much stronger, demand for self-identification with a legitimate category: either addict or codependent. Even his acquiescence to one of these identities leads to a scene of misunderstanding.

Moreover, how does he avoid deception when one of the institutions in which he works appears to be involved in suspiciously corrupt practices about which he is to remain silent, and employs a form of deception as one of its basic practices: the injection of a placebo in the treatment of alcohol addicts? A mysterious plot develops in which he inevitably becomes complicitous. Raikhel is presented with the stark choice of either quitting or working through unfolding ethical quandaries. As he manages the ambiguity of the situation, fieldwork encounters morph into episodes of a thriller—shortly after his departure, a hospital administrator is mysteriously murdered. Much like Moore, who tries to remain focused on questions of land tenure in Tanzania despite bureaucratic obstacles, Raikhel tries to remain focused on the clinical situation of alcohol treatment as it evolved through the demands of the patients. But the murder—apparently unconnected, at least functionally, to his research problem—interrupts his story, and seems too much a part of the reality he encounters to leave totally aside. Yet inclusion of the episode makes writing about the fieldwork situation more difficult, as it introduces a discordant element into a rather coherent set of questions and answers about the treatment of alcoholism.

The fieldwork encounter thus goes beyond recording responses to questions, or answers to problems, to open up productive uncertainties about the flows of information and disinformation, and about the construction of truth. This complex process of fieldwork involves the exchange of food and shelter at minimum, but usually also gifts, material objects, names and adoptive kinship, insecurities, and friendship, as well as the occasional exchange of hostilities, violence, war, and, at its most extreme, the gift of death. From Malinowski to Mauss and Lévi-Strauss, the insistence on ambiguities and asymmetries in the structures of exchange, along with acknowledgment of the emotional ambivalence intrinsic to circulation and reciprocity, has been at the center of theorizing in anthropology about society and culture.

Leo Coleman, in his essay, finds himself in some of these asymmetrical exchanges in two encounters with religious proselytization outside the parameters of his formal ethnographic research in India. Initially unaware of what he is being given and why he accepts the offer of one interlocutor but rejects the other, he seeks an explanation via an understanding of how his own countertransference in fieldwork encounters parallels certain features of gift exchange. He begins with Mauss's basic insight that that gift exchange is a multipart, multipartnered process that includes several obligations, including the obligation to receive. Then, following Jonathan Parry's brilliant explication of how Hindu charity washes off sin and impurity through total alienation of religious gifts, enjoining recipients not to reciprocate, Coleman analyzes his own withdrawal from some exchanges and his own countertransferential feelings of "hate" in terms of a theory of generalized nonreciprocation in fieldwork. Because the obligation to receive is not equal to the obligation to reciprocate, nonreciprocation in fieldwork should be seen not in the simplistic trope of extraction and domination but rather in terms of an ambivalent love/hate relationship that must be managed. He draws from the psychoanalyst D. W. Winnicott to understand his ambivalent love/hate relationship to his interlocutors, and grasp how psychoanalytic theory might propose to manage the ethnographer's "justified" hatred.

Following Coleman's logic, the opposite of such ambivalence is not hate but indifference—surely the condition that most exemplifies failure to establish an ethical basis for long-term fieldwork among others. Yet ambivalence and nonreciprocity, which are fundamental elements of all encounters, do not orient the ethnographer toward particular kinds of relationships. At its most ethical, what the encounter demands is recognition.

The first condition for recognition is the acknowledgment of a relationship. Hating someone may in fact be such an acknowledgment. So may forms of criticism, which at best go beyond the critique of the dominant anthropologist and her own society to include the interlocutor and his society. Under these conditions of acknowledgment, a new situation of a double-edged critique becomes possible. Contesting, taking issue with our interlocutors—as Parvis Ghassem-Fachandi does with his vegetarian friend in the midst of a pogrom in India, Hammoudi with his fellow pilgrims in the hajj on the subject of religiosity, and Borneman with Syrian friends who seek to spread rumors about him—creates a space of argumentation, in which the partners treat each other as equal. They not only affirm but also contest each other's assumptions. Needless to say, such mutual questioning does not shield the ethnographer from the dynamics of asymmetrical power in the exchange.

Recognition, however, can insist on much more than mere interlocution. Lisa Stevenson, in research among Inuit youth in Canada during a suicide epidemic, explicates demands for recognition that go far beyond knowing. They also require of her an understanding of how the wound in the other implicates her in a "mutual project of discovering the world." Stevenson is arrested by the uncertainty in the lives of Inuit youth and thrown into radical doubt about the value of "preserving life." She is drawn into their world, in which they doubt the assumption that life is worth living, and into a "care apparatus" that tries to resolve their radical uncertainties and prevent this epidemic.

Engaging with the difficult wound, Stevenson comes to recognize, and to some degree understand, the pain of the other without really knowing it, as death is unknowable and the understanding of "tomorrow" among the people with whom she has been talking has been transvalued into a radical uncertainty about life and death. Under these conditions, life is no longer opposed to death but "improvised around" it. This improvisation unfolds alongside efforts of organizations that try to prevent suicide, as well as Stevenson's own interventions, and all acquire significance through the dynamics of recognition within specific encounters.

In the spirit of Wittgenstein, Stevenson powerfully demonstrates that recognition opens up a space of co-inquiry. There is nothing unilateral about her reflections, her doubt is not one-sided, her criticism is not single-edged. Her rich exchange as she shares a loss that so dramatically affects the people she is working with does not blur the distinctiveness of the identities of the ethnographer and the people she tries to understand. Nor does their recognition demand she go native; those she works with also seem to recognize their lives as only one possibility for themselves. Moreover, the wound and ever-present possibility of suicide are not the only dimension of their lives, their everydayness. But as a condition of communication and understanding, Stevenson's recognition of her partners' assumptions about life, including the taking of life, entails acknowledging these as a possible way of living for her too.

To be sure, reaching a deeper level of understanding of how others live, of their traditions and why they practice them, is possible through reading. But the continuity and coherence that a concept like "tradition"—qualified as cultural, discursive, or in any other way—invokes are complicated once one enters into the unstable moments of its instantiation in concrete encounters. Moreover, in a certain social space the frameworks around which closeness and distance are structured, thanks to cultural categories repositioned in moments of instantiation, always morph into unique situations to which encounters provide access. Among the disciplinary approaches to knowledge, only fieldwork presence poses understanding as a matter of recognition between oneself and the *singular* subjects encountered. The difference and distance between oneself and one's subjects in the field often create an identificatory process that parallels that between members of the group one is studying.

Parvis Ghassem-Fachandi explicates this identificatory process and its tense relation to recognition in his detailed ethnographic description of the many levels of reality that inform Muslim-Hindu relations in India.

In the midst of a pogrom in the city of Ahmedabad, in which Hindu nationalists killed and burned several thousand Muslims, he shares an apartment with a young Hindu student of *lower* class/rank who seeks social mobility through education. Most Gujaratis tend to identify Ghassem-Fachandi as Parsi or Muslim (because he eats meat) as well as high-class (read European/American). The young student with whom he had developed a friendship over several years is torn between an identification with the anthropologist's class position and a disidentification with what he insists is the researcher's Islamic origin. Only toward the end of the pogrom did he reveal that he had been active in one of the organizations responsible for the killing spree.

The differences between the anthropologist and his friend become the source of a mutual curiosity and create a space of unusual coexistence, dependent on negotiating the difference between one's taste for meat and secular politics and the other's vegetarianism and religious purity, and between the cosmopolitanism of the one and the village orientation of the other, who is trying to win entry into the urban world. Furthermore, his friend on the one hand at times falls into a visceral disgust for meat, which seems to reflect a general attitude toward Muslims, and therefore maintains a certain distance from the anthropologist; on the other, the young Hindu exempts Ghassem-Fachandi from his radical anti-Muslim views and even seeks to protect him from the violence to whose logic he acquiesces and in which he becomes complicit. Both scenarios reveal the need to identify "the Muslim" in the foreign friend, that which the student then can either oppose or generously accept. Ghassem-Fachandi infers from this relationship that what is to be eliminated by the subject is internal to him—the displacement of humiliations derived from a history of caste identification that now must be disavowed, marketed politically as "Hindu vulnerability"; this wound is being worked through both in the pogrom and in the relationship with the anthropologist.

At any rate, it is clear that these radical differences produce an effect of mirror imaging, which, given their proximity in age and the friend's projection of *Islamic* ethnicity onto the anthropologist (even though he is of mixed German and Iranian parentage), resonates with a *mirror stage*. This dynamics of identification leads both the anthropologist and his interlocutor to explain to one another the meanings of their actions; their conversation becomes a constant and dangerous rearticulation of the self in the interplay of conscious and unconscious wishes. Their peaceful rearticulation of attraction/rejection parallels the violent rearticulation among "intimate" enemies—Hindu and Muslim groups—that is then under way.

A final aspect of closeness and distance illuminated in these essays is the relation between identity and power. In the past quarter century, no concept has been more popular than "power"—used most often as a weapon to hurl at prior generations of anthropologists, who have been criticized not for ignoring relations of authority among the people they studied but for inattention to the power dynamics between themselves and "native" peoples in fieldwork settings. More often than not, the many subsequent attempts to address this issue appear somewhat self-justifying. They make a virtue out of necessity, all the while overlooking the serendipity of most fieldwork situations. In any case, the power of the anthropologist may often be illusory, especially over the agony of fieldwork. Anthropologists can be avoided, ostracized, denied information, and made to feel extremely weak and unwelcome, irrespective of the advantages they might bring with them to the field in terms of economic or cultural capital. To get people interested in the anthropologist's project and the type of knowledge she seeks is a very difficult enterprise, and after a point it always proceeds helter-skelter. Whatever the status of this critique of power, nowadays anthropologists are in fact generally quite sensitive to and explicit about the power dynamics in their relationships. The actual depictions of power in the field cannot be subsumed under any general theory; power takes many forms, and each essay in this volume attests to a specific configuration.

One of the questions posed by Stefan Senders, in his essay on the experience of Germans repatriated from Russia, involves the conditions of knowing when the vulnerability of both the subjects studied and the ethnographer positions them as symbolically castrated. "Ethnic Germans" are being asked to acquire a mother tongue they are already assumed to possess. On the occasions when language mastery is not assumed, the ability to tell a narrative of the repression of German language and culture while they lived in the Soviet Union—that is, a story that negates their most affirming experiences—may substitute as the sign of authentic German identity. The ethnographer's location, as listener, reproduces their lack by asking them to communicate their stories in a language over which they have little control. Senders analyzes how speaking, as a very sensuous and expressive act of translation, is experienced in two different domains: in bureaucratic settings where the mother tongue is proof of membership in a people, as well as the means by which one acquires legal security, and in intimate domestic spaces with the ethnographer. In both these situations, he comes to understand his own interactions in terms not of performance but of risk and submission. He argues that here, through submission rather than domination, ethnographic knowledge becomes transformative rather than extractive.

III

Given the diversity of predicaments in fieldwork, the notion of encounter may offer a useful conceptual angle for analysis. For one thing, by definition fieldwork implies a planned encounter with people. At the same time, many encounters are unintentional and accidental. Both planned and accidental encounters unfold under unpredictable conditions that nonetheless can result in fortunate outcomes. That is to say, anthropologists engaged in fieldwork encounters hope to find themselves in ongoing relationships that intensify and multiply over time, resulting in knowledge that develops incrementally with the uneven accumulation of insights—a process that entails constant revision of what one has learned. To set this dynamic in motion, the anthropologist's presence is the only precondition. Encounters may take other forms, such as reading what is written or screening what is filmed about people, including what they write or film about themselves, but these are of an essentially different nature.

An encounter is connected to the episodic. Episodes can either be initiated by the anthropologist or can serendipitously happen to him. They can be of variable duration; they are processual, with beginnings and ends; they can be unique events, with no precedents, or repetitive or cyclical ones; they can have multiple ramifications beyond the initial set of experiences. It is impossible to predict the knowledge they may produce, but to experience and live through many episodes introduces complexity within description and interpretation. Therefore, episodes never merely confirm interpretations; they also usher in situations that give rise to doubt and further questions. While previous situations may make certain structures visible, new situations may dissolve these insights. Moreover, episodes engulf the anthropologist in occasions and practices outside her control, forcing her into a deeper and more quixotic relation to knowledge.

Encounter-based fieldwork opens to a level of experiential depth that eludes other approaches. Encounters that embrace a notion of depth are quite different from those approaches that favor surface mapping. They necessitate an appreciation of duration—a working through, partly through repetition, of experiences that progressively teach the anthropologist what might be important and vital to her interlocutors. In that process, many things are likely to remain outside of view unless presented to the anthropologist in an encounter, and many interpretations resist modification unless challenged by new meanings that other episodes bring.

Finally, what is the relation of depth to the location of the anthropologist? This question is often framed in terms of the difference between indigenous and foreign locations, or between cultural closeness and distance. But it is not obvious that the native, or the "halfie," has any decisive epistemological advantage with regard to depth. To be sure, at an initial stage of fieldwork, the indigenous person may have an advantage in language and doxic knowledge, a society's taken-for-granted, deep-seated ideas and beliefs. But to engage in encounter-based fieldwork, he must also unlearn his assumptions and create distance in order to reconsider almost everything familiar. This unlearning and distancing seem to be the sine qua non of achieving deep description and interpretation. The process of unlearning can be contrasted with the efforts of the non-native anthropologist, inversely, to learn more in order to overcome distance. From both locations, it seems that openness to the encountered and episodic enriches understanding through an process of unsettling.

In one, the indigenous person must shake off what has already been learned; in the other, the foreigner must acquire some of the knowledge acquired by others through their formal socialization. In both cases, depth comes at a price, and success depends more on engaging in a difficult process than on any initial advantages conferred by one's specific location.

Beyond everything else, episodes of fieldwork encounters situate the anthropologist in vulnerability. Such placement carries risks but also makes the anthropologist alert to a kind of critical questioning in real time that is indispensable for those seeking to appreciate the dynamics of contexts in which meanings unfold.

Biographical Notes

JOHN BORNEMAN teaches anthropology at Princeton University. He has conducted fieldwork in Germany, central Europe, Syria, and Lebanon, and has published widely on issues of kinship, sexuality, nationality, justice, and political form. His most recent ethnographic study is *Syrian Episodes: Sons, Fathers, and an Anthropologist in Aleppo* (2007). His current work is on incest and child abuse in Berlin.

LEO COLEMAN is an assistant professor in the Department of Comparative Studies at The Ohio State University. His dissertation (completed in 2008 at Princeton University) is on the history and politics of electrification in Delhi, India, from colonial installations to present-day privatization. He has conducted historical and ethnographic research in both Britain and India.

PARVIS GHASSEM-FACHANDI is an assistant professor in the Department of Anthropology at Rutgers University. He received his Ph.D. from Cornell University in 2006, and also completed a Magister in Ethnologie at the Freie Universität Berlin in 1998. He taught at Princeton in 2006, and held a postdoctoral fellowship at the Center for Religion and Media at New York University in 2006–07. Born in the divided former West Berlin, he grew up in Germany, France, and Canada. His field research has focused on ethnicity, religion, and violence in Gibraltar, the

United States, and India. He is currently completing a book on the 2002 anti-Muslim pogrom in Gujarat, India.

ABDELLAH HAMMOUDI teaches anthropology at Princeton University. Educated in Morocco and France, he has also taught in both countries and in Spain. Early in his career, he conducted fieldwork on the development of tourism in eastern France as well as on development projects in North Africa, and since then he has done research in Morocco, Libya, and Saudi Arabia. He has published extensively in English, French, and Arabic on forms of religious authority, ritual and religion, colonial anthropology, and culture and authoritarianism in Arab societies. Most recently he has written on phenomenology, theories of practice, and ethnography. His most recent book, *A Season in Mecca: Narrative of a Pilgrimage* (2006), was initially published in French (2005). He is currently completing a book on canonical rituals of Islam.

SALLY FALK MOORE is the Victor S. Thomas Research Professor of Anthropology at Harvard University. She held professorships at the University of Southern California and the University of California at Los Angeles, and was a visiting professor at Yale before coming to Harvard in 1986. Among her many honors, in 1999 she was named the Huxley Memorial Medalist and Lecturer by the Royal Anthropological Institute in London, and in 2005 she received the Law and Society Association Harry J. Kalven, Jr. Prize. She has devoted nearly half a century to foundational issues in law and society, African studies, and anthropology more generally. Her publications include *Power and Property in Inca Peru* (1958), *Law as Process* (1978), *Social Facts and Fabrications* (1986), and *Anthropology and Africa: Changing Perspectives on a Changing Scene* (1995). She is currently working on a memoir and a collection of papers. Together they make the point that anthropological fieldwork is in many respects like a picaresque novel taking place against the background of a carefully defined topic of exploration.

EUGENE RAIKHEL is a postdoctoral fellow in the Division of Social and Transcultural Psychiatry at McGill University. His dissertation (completed in 2006 at Princeton University) examines the knowledge and treatment of addiction in late and post-Soviet Russia. His interests include post-socialist transformations and the anthropology of psychiatry and bioscience.

STEFAN SENDERS is a senior instructor in psychiatry at the University of Rochester, and a visiting scholar in the Cornell University Peace Studies Program. He has conducted fieldwork in Ghana, West Africa, and Berlin, Germany. His current work concerns post-traumatic stress disorder among veterans of the wars in Iraq and Afghanistan. Recent publications include *Money: Ethnographic Encounters* (2007), edited with Allison Truitt, and "Academic Plagiarism and the Limits of Theft: A Case Study" (2007).

LISA STEVENSON is an assistant professor in the department of anthropology at McGill University. She received her Ph.D. in 2005 from the University of California, Berkeley, and completed a postdoctoral fellowship in the Department of Social Medicine at Harvard. She has conducted fieldwork in Guatemala and Nunavut, one of Canada's northern territories. Currently she is working on a book manuscript documenting her work with Inuit youth in Nunavut.

Index

Abedi, Mehdi, 26, 32–44, 48, 50–51
Abu-Lughod, Lila, 41
affect, 8, 58, 77, 98, 104. *See also* disgust
African socialism, 153–58, 162, 165–66, 171, 173–75, 177–80
agony of fieldwork, 260
ahimsa (nonviolence), 80–81, 83, 85, 103, 105
Alcoholics Anonymous: ethnographic study of, 218, 230n16; methods of, 217, 230n16, 231n17; in Russia, 216–22, 229n13, 232n22
Anderson, Benedict, 97
Appadurai, Arjun, 4
Arendt, Hannah, 66
Asad, Talal, 8, 26–32, 49–50, 53n3
assemblages, 5, 11, 16
authority. *See* bureaucracy; ethnographic authority; power
auto-ethnography, 4, 179, 262

Ba'ath Party (Syria), 257n4
Bakhtin, Mikhail, 18
Barthes, Roland, 26, 33
Bataille, Georges, 17
Benveniste, Emile, 51
Bhabha, Homi, 17

Boas, Franz, 3, 8
Borneman, John, 14, 198, 203, 263
Bourdieu, Pierre, 13, 31, 52n2, 53n3
bureaucracy: bureaucratic authority, 6, 60–65, 68, 185, 190–91, 210; ethnographers' encounters with, 57, 65, 68, 152, 166, 178, 202, 216–17, 261, 264, 270
Butler, Judith, 17

caste, 10, 84–86, 88, 93, 97–98, 99–103, 105, 107n11, 108nn17,20, 268. *See also* culinary practices
castration, 6, 192, 193–95
Central Intelligence Agency (CIA). *See* secret services
Chagga (Tanzania): and African socialism, 154–55, 162–63, 166, 171–75; and education, 154, 157; ethnography of, 161–62; and land tenure, 153, 167–68, 169–75; modernity, 155
Christianity, 27–30, 36, 38, 51, 66, 95, 131, 190–91, 230n15; in Africa, 155–56, 162, 180; American Evangelical, 139–41; Word of Faith, 123–24, 146nn10–11
Clifford, James, 1–2, 4

Text: 10/14 Palatino
Display: Univers Condensed Light 47, Bauer Bodoni
Compositor: BookComp, Inc.
Printer and Binder: Sheridan Books, Inc.